FINDING MYSELF IN A NIGHTMARE

A MOTHER'S HEALING JOURNEY THROUGH HER DAUGHTER'S ADDICTION

BY JUDI TURKHEIMER

Published by the Unapologetic Voice House
www.theunapologeticvoicehouse.com
Scottsdale, AZ.

Identifiers:
Paperback ISBN: 978-1-955090-05-6
E-book ISBN: 978-1-955090-00-1

Library of Congress Control Number: 2021913405

Cover designer: Meredith Hancock
(https://mhancockmedia.com/)

Edited by: N. Amma Twum-Baah with Amma Edits LLC.

Dedicated, with so much love, to my daughter.
She is the bravest person I know.
And to her siblings,
whose love and support have never wavered.

CONTENTS

INTRODUCTION

Life didn't stop because my heart was breaking. Like a cruel prank, sometimes the insults accelerated. There came a moment, however, when I knew if I could just move beyond the ache, I would be okay.

Born from the realization that my daughter was addicted to drugs; my body, mind, and spirit suffered the most intense, deep, debilitating, searing pain I had ever experienced. I was no stranger to pain. As a teen I had endured self-loathing, profound loneliness, and suicidal thoughts and action. At age 40 my difficult, sixteen-year marriage imploded, resulting in a devastating divorce. As a single parent, I raised my three children as best I could, simultaneously struggling to reinvent myself in the workplace. I mourned the intermittent deaths of dearly loved friends and family members. Nothing compared to the emotional challenges I endured as a result of Kayla's drug addiction.

My grief seemed to have no bounds. Elizabeth Kübler-Ross defined the five stages of grief: denial, anger, bargaining, depression, and acceptance. Stages didn't each arrive once and depart after a specific period of time or in a predictable order. They repeatedly cycled with varying intensity, sometimes shifting moment-to-moment.

In the beginning, denial was my constant companion; then depression set in. Anger exposed victim thinking, "Why me?" I didn't consciously express my sense of victimization, but subconsciously I roiled in it. I bargained regularly, begging unknown powers for relief, for change, for healing, and for my daughter's return to health.

Acceptance was the most obscure stage. Eventually my spiritual foundation grew sturdy enough to support levels of acceptance. That helped but did not cure the pain. Fear was my constant bedfellow. I didn't want to face the very real possibility of losing my daughter.

With gradual acceptance came the recognition that Kayla's drug use was not intended to hurt me. Her actions really had nothing to do with me. She was broken in her own right, and heroin was the vehicle she chose to relieve her pain. Her own lessons were embedded in her process. I prayed she would learn them and not die. She had to take responsibility for her health and well-being; I could not do it for her.

But Kayla's addiction WAS about me. Intuitively, I knew the Universe had been trying to get my attention for a long time. Despite a lifetime of spiritual work, big lessons about self-worth and authentic happiness remained elusive. Though opportunities to learn had been many, I had steadfastly ignored the gentle knocks on my emotional door. The

Universe was done being gentle. This was a hammer to my head. The trick was not to pass out.

Kayla's addiction would serve as a catalyst for me to grow emotionally and spiritually. It had the same potential for Kayla and for others close to us. Whether or not to accept the challenge was a choice.

Over time I learned that loving my daughter unconditionally didn't mean enabling her. I learned my role in her recovery was to recover myself, not from drugs but from self-loathing and self-abuse. I learned unconditional love had to reside in me, be about me, and travel through me.

This is my story of transformation as I made my way through the years of Kayla's addiction and early recovery. In order to tell my story, it was necessary to share much of Kayla's story as well. My perspective is the only perspective represented on the following pages. I've pieced together events and feelings to the best of my ability. Names have been changed, and some identities have been made intentionally vague to protect privacy. While real and accurate, the sequence may be slightly off. In no way does that alter the primary goal or message of this book.

My wish for those reading my story is multi-leveled:

First, I wrote this book to connect with those people who love an addict and are going through a similar nightmare. I want you to know you are not crazy, not abnormal, not wrong, and not bad. It's not your fault. I imagine we all cycle through similar emotions when faced with a crisis of profound magnitude. It's okay. You are not alone.

Second, I wrote this book to share the steps and missteps I took so that perhaps, in your quest to help your loved one, my experiences can give you some sense of direction. There is no guidebook. This is not meant to advise or direct you. Any opinions expressed are my own to be taken or left. Simply, I want to give you an overview of what you might look for and see in your addict, what is possible, and how you might cope and proceed.

Finally, and perhaps most importantly, I wrote this book to encourage you to find your center, your strength, and yourself. As an inspirational life coach, I learned volumes about walking my talk, caring for me, and loving myself unconditionally. Opportunities to examine my shadows - beliefs and patterns that kept me dark - were abundant. Through the pain, I learned to forgive myself. Ultimately, I learned to love myself and consequently emerged a better, more compassionate version of me. My wish for those who read this book is that you, too, can find the path to acceptance, self-love, and wholeness, whatever the outcome for your addict.

Living this nightmare, I was surprised by the inner strength I discovered. Practicing "tough love" was the hardest, most transformative action I've ever taken. Once I understood tough love was about saving my daughter's life, I stayed true to love, and I got tough. I learned to be tough not only with Kayla but with myself as well. There was no giving up.

As I came to believe I could help Kayla best by loving and growing myself, opportunities to heal emerged. As I stopped resisting my lessons, I learned. As an emotionally whole individual, responding to life made a little more sense.

If you love an addict, I hold you. I honor your pain and your fear, your anger and your sorrow. I urge you to continue to love your addict fiercely. Never confuse love with enabling. Never confuse love with accepting abhorrent behaviors. Never confuse love with allowing or levying abuse. Love without condition, and seek information.

I pray for the safe recovery of your loved one!

Namasté. My light reaches out to your light. We are one light.

Heal yourself, heal your children.

CHAPTER ONE:
SIGNS

"Didn't you see the signs?" they asked. In my mind, I saw the pointing fingers of accusation highlighting my failings. Assuredly, there were many. Part of me felt angry and defensive; however, feeling inadequate was an old, familiar story that easily took up residence in the basement of my psyche. Believing myself to be a failure and withdrawing from life were comfortable habits.

I came to understand that people were naturally and innocently curious, and sometimes asked infuriating questions. *If I HAD seen the signs, don't you think I'd have done something to stop her? If I HAD seen the signs, I am the world's worst parent because I didn't stop her. DID I see the signs? WHAT SIGNS?*

I had no idea what I was looking at or for. I never had reason to know the signs of drug abuse/addiction. It was a completely foreign land with a language all its own.

In truth, I wasn't angry with "them," I was angry with myself. I had accepted a full-time job beating myself up for

NOT seeing the signs. Sometimes I fantasized that if I had better understood or had awakened earlier to what was going on, would've-could've-should've, I could have magically, somehow, put an end to my daughter's spiral into drug addiction before it began. Pipe dreams. The plague of guilt and despair kept me stuck.

I learned to forgive the ignorance of those who asked "silly" questions or made comments that, at times, hurt deeply. Each in his own way, they tried to understand my nightmare and help ease my pain. They overcame their natural aversion and joined me, if only for a moment.

I even came to understand those who disparaged our suffering and condemned our struggle, calling it a "choice." That group reasoned that people battling "real" illnesses such as cancer, diabetes, or heart disease had no choice as they fought for their lives, but addicts, well, they did. They contended that addicts willfully entered the drug world, purposefully making themselves sick. They argued it was a decision, not a disease.

Though I didn't fully agree with their logic, I applauded their willingness to engage at all. Venturing into the topic of addiction was both scary and painful, and brought forth strong emotion from everyone.

In the beginning, I was as ignorant as the next guy, maybe more so. The truth was, I really didn't want to understand. I wanted it to go away and if IT wouldn't go away, I wondered, "Could I?"

In the end, I would dramatically transform in the most unforeseeable ways. I would become an unexpected ally to the cause. I would write a book.

CHAPTER TWO:

BACKGROUND

It was 2011. Despite supplementing my work as a substitute teacher with life coaching (or vice versa), and tired of barely making ends meet, I had taken a year off from work to earn my master's degree in teaching. Paying for school with a student loan, a withdrawal from the equity loan against my house, and a generous gift from my parents, it was a leap of faith made in the hopes of improving life for my children and me. I was halfway through the program, working in overdrive. Student teaching, writing lesson plans, attending classes, studying, and writing research papers, I had little energy left at the end of the day. Unbeknownst to me, Kayla's drug abuse simmered.

As a single parent, I was running our household, shopping, cooking, cleaning, and paying bills as best I could. The fibromyalgia from which I suffered was in full flare as I pushed my body through long, stressful days. Shortly after spring semester began, I developed a chronic sinus infection that rendered me beyond exhausted.

Kayla and I often commiserated about the demands of school, comparing homework challenges and quirky professors, and discussing class work and the happenings on campus. We were attending different colleges, but school was school and we were able to appreciate each other's daily grind.

I was excited to be attending school concurrently with my kids. With one in college and one struggling through high school (my oldest had earned his degree and was working full time), I felt good about providing an example not only of good study habits and perseverance, but also of how to reinvent oneself and improve at any age. As a positive role model, I believed my kids would feel, if not see my strength and courage, hard work, and determination. I trusted my efforts would encourage them to grow.

Around mid-April, as the completion of my degree neared, I added job hunting to my "to do" list. I was convinced the year of sacrifice would pay off in a teaching position that would provide a reliable income and benefits. That, I anticipated, would transform our lives.

I blanketed the area with job applications. As exhaustion persisted, my pain and frustration increased.

Despite my efforts, I was not offered a single interview. By autumn I was diagnosed with a grape-sized cyst between my jaw and sinus, the cause of the chronic infections I had suffered through the previous eight months. Surgery to remove it was scheduled and, with the new school year already under way, my resolve to find a job began to falter.

Additionally, the four-year romantic relationship in which I had been involved was coming to an abrupt end. I felt more and more discouraged and downtrodden in my own life.

As the season progressed, the whispers of Kayla's addiction got louder. Did I see the signs of drug addiction? Nope. Not yet. But dis-ease was in my midst.

My intuition began to light up with a knowing that something was terribly wrong. Friends and family commented on Kayla's appearance and behavior, sometimes boldly suggesting that drugs were at cause. I pushed it all away, unwilling to face the truth, unable to metabolize the barrage of painful messages being thrown at me. Pieces of a puzzle were being dropped before me, but I couldn't see the picture they were screaming to form ... I didn't want to.

I was tired, afraid, and overwhelmed. I wanted to run. I wanted to hide. I wanted to avoid. I wanted to sleep. I went to bed.

In addition to increasing worries about Kayla's health, the accumulated stress of the previous year debilitated me. Daily, I pushed myself to do what had to be done. As soon as I was able, I would crawl under the covers and invite sleep. But life didn't let me sleep too long. Life had a way of compelling me forward, like it or not. I had children to feed and bills to pay; I had responsibilities. I ached for relationship, imagining it would provide me a warm respite from my woes.

I resumed substitute teaching and halfheartedly looking for a job.

Years prior, when Kayla was sixteen, she had gotten a cashier job at a local grocery store. Always a hard worker, she quickly earned a customer service position. She enjoyed her work, and was well liked and respected by peers and management.

After graduating high school in 2010, Kayla landed a better paying job with a non-profit organization located at a nearby university. It was difficult for her to leave the work family she had come to adore, but she was excited to move beyond the demands of a retail job. She had friends at the non-profit, it was closer to the community college she was scheduled to attend, and the work was not difficult. I loved that she was working in a more academic, nine-to-five setting.

Kayla seemed to enjoy the new environment and the people with whom she worked. They rapidly embraced her and praised her exemplary performance. That came as no surprise. Kayla's work ethic, in addition to her generous, kind, smart, and witty personality, made her easy to love. She reported that the work was boring; however, knowing her college classes would demand a great deal of time and energy, she concluded boring was okay.

For a year, work and school kept Kayla busy. She met a young man in one of her classes. She and Jason started dating. She seemed happy, healthy, and productive.

As Kayla planned for her second year of college, she felt her hours at the non-profit were insufficient to cover her expenses. Since I was unable to help her pay for school, gas, and supplies, she needed to make more money. She returned, part-time, to the grocery store to supplement her income.

With two jobs and a boyfriend, Kayla was rarely home. Once the semester was under way, I saw her even less. When she wasn't busy with work or in class, Kayla often went to the library to complete homework.

On the rare occasion she spent time at home, Kayla shared detailed accounts of her daily activities. I commended her for her maturity, hard work, and dedication. I was proud of her determination to cultivate success.

In large part, Kayla's absence kept her changing behaviors well hidden from my view. Things were not as they seemed. Unbeknownst to me, Kayla had stopped attending community college. In fact, she never began that second year. She wasn't at the library either. The money she needed had nothing to do with school.

CHAPTER THREE:
RUNNING AWAY

As the whispers demanded, "She's using drugs!" I plugged my ears to stop the echoing words. Like a young child, I subconsciously chanted, "I can't hear you. La la la la la." But of course I heard the words: **she's using drugs**. They cut through me with precision.

Instead of jumping to action, I deflected, avoided, withdrew, and rationalized. Hearing didn't mean comprehending, processing, integrating, or accepting. I had no way to connect with those terrifying, unfamiliar, nightmarish words. I didn't want to. I pushed them away.

The interesting thing about running away was that everywhere I went, there I was. Insidiously, the truth kept finding me and, like a well-choreographed dance, I kept pulling away and hiding. At a young age I had learned to withdraw and shut down for emotional protection. As was true for many patterns developed in childhood, there was no longer a healthy benefit. Shutting down only served to push my pain deeper inside. I knew I would have to wake up, eventually.

My body was a mess. I had come to believe fibromyalgia was largely a result of stress turned inward over time. The rate at which I was stuffing emotional stress was cataclysmic. As the triggers accelerated, the pain intensified. Routinely going directly to bed after work, my body conspired to help me avoid what was right in front of me.

Noticing the disturbing changes in Kayla's mood and behavior, her brothers had been making their case for me to wake up. They pleaded with me to do something. When friends and family offered warnings of suspicion or presented compelling evidence, I denied it all and pushed it away.

Toward the end of October, we were scheduled to attend a Saturday morning wedding. As we got ready for the early affair, I noticed that Kayla had lost a lot of weight, her skin was pale, and her long hair looked greasy and stringy. She had dark circles around her sunken eyes, and the beautiful dress she chose to wear hung shapelessly on her thin frame.

Hearing my concern annoyed Kayla. Defensive and dismissive, she insisted the long hours at work and school left her exhausted. I knew exhaustion well and reluctantly accepted her excuse.

At the wedding, Kayla connected with another guest. I remembered well how awkward family parties could be for youth, and I was delighted by what looked like easy camaraderie. In retrospect it became so clear. That young man, it turned out, was also struggling with drug addiction. Their easy camaraderie was another whisper. I would later learn Kayla had been "high as a kite" that day.

An acquaintance from my past stepped back into my life after more than thirty years. Finding we had much in common, we set about getting reacquainted. Ben was comfortable, kind, and familiar. I didn't know him well, but I trusted him. His attention energized me and I was relieved by the pleasant distraction from my day-to-day woes.

Generous and eager to spend time with me and mine, Ben offered to treat Kayla and Jason to dinner. I was warmed by the gesture and delighted to have Ben get to know my beautiful daughter. At the restaurant, what began as a lovely gathering quickly deteriorated. Conversation was tedious and strained. Ben was unusually reserved, and the burden of facilitating was work I resented.

After Kayla and Jason left, I questioned Ben about his silence. When he told me the kids were "obviously high," I reacted with anger. I dismissed his observation as ridiculous and determined that he had no idea what he was talking about. I was fully aware, however, that he DID know the signs, and the gnawing truth grew louder.

The comfort of Ben's companionship and embrace waned. The allure faded. Though I grew to care for him deeply, I knew he had simply provided a pause in the chaos of my life. It was not time for me to be in relationship with a man.

My disposition toggled between stress and despair. At every turn money was vanishing, jewelry and goods were disappearing, and my mind seemed to be failing. *I was sure I put those earrings away. Where could they be? Did I leave them in a pocket? On a table somewhere in the house? Didn't I have an extra $15 in my wallet? I could swear I had an extra $10 in that drawer. Did I use that "mad money" I stashed under the driver's side mat and just forget? Did Kayla pay me back for (fill in the blank)? She said she did. Where could I have put the money?*

My desire to believe Kayla continued to override my rational thought, and I allowed confusion to take center stage. When I questioned her, she lied masterfully saying things like, "Oh Mom, you know how you're always misplacing things," and "I put it (payment) on your nightstand, I can't imagine what you did with it. Did you lose it again?" and "I didn't take your (fill in the blank), and I can't believe you are blaming me for your own problems." She effortlessly preyed on my insecurities and naiveté.

Kayla's performance was convincing enough to cause me to doubt my own sanity. I seriously wondered if I was losing my mind. In truth, I wanted to believe her, despite growing certainty she was lying. It was easier to turn against myself than to acknowledge her addiction.

On November 1, 2011, I wrote in my journal, "Eighty dollars missing from my purse, maybe a hundred. I'm ninety percent sure Kayla took it. There is zero likelihood that it left my purse without one of my kids' help. Cleaned out— so disturbing. I can't even process. Shit, I meant to lock up my jewelry before I left for work. Hopefully it will still be there when I get home. I'm so upset, I can't even write about it. With no proof, I can't act on it with 100% certainty. She is so passionately denying, of course. Why is she stealing? What does she need the money for? That is the more compelling question."

I was still denying Kayla's drug involvement, still resisting the glaring truth. My life was in chaos. I was unsettled in work, in relationship, and in future. I tried to connect to some vestige of strength. I was doing my spiritual work. More and more I felt I was in touch with my feelings. More and more I thought I was living in the moment and in my own truth. More and more I was grasping for escape.

One mid-November afternoon, Kayla joyfully shared that she had applied for a scholarship to culinary school. She sent me a copy of the essay she wrote in which she expressed her passion to cook and explained how, based on the school's profile, she saw herself as a good fit. She was excited by the possibility of acceptance and enthusiastically envisioned how such an opportunity could positively affect her life.

I was proud of Kayla's ambition and effort. In that moment of "normalcy," it was easy to let myself view her as productive, healthy, and motivated. I eagerly sought such moments to contradict mounting evidence to the contrary. I was willfully fueling my sense of confusion.

On November 28, 2011, I wrote in my journal, "Another $100 gone missing. I'm angry with myself. I knew I needed to put it away, and I got lazy. Very expensive mistake—but more importantly, Kayla—she is a wreck—if she's stealing my money she is using, lying, and hurting me deeply. I know it's not personal, but it is."

I was still willing to endure the excruciating pain of confusion and self-doubt, the significant loss of money and things, the violation of my basic sense of security, and the demise of my own emotional wellbeing, rather than confront the reality of my daughter's drug abuse. I was making it personal instead of recognizing it had nothing to do with me. I was the lightning rod, helplessly absorbing the assault.

Grandma died two weeks after Kayla entered the world. At six months old, Kayla was given Grandma's Hebrew name during a tearful and glorious ceremony. The love I had for my grandmother was amplified through the love I felt for my daughter.

About a year before Kayla's journey into drugs, I had bemoaned not having a piece of my Grandmother's jewelry to wear. Loving her deeply, I yearned for the sense of embrace I anticipated would come from such an item.

Hearing my plea, with love and utmost generosity, my sister gave me a pair of Grandma's gold hoop earrings.

Though I didn't remember seeing Grandma wear them, I felt her loving energy move through them. I wore them often and held tight to feeling she was with me. I cherished the gift.

The startling and devastating realization that Kayla had stolen and subsequently pawned Grandma's earrings crushed me. Their monetary value was minimal, but the sentimental value was immeasurable. I would learn that an addict seeking a fix doesn't care about sentiment.

When I confronted Kayla, her tap dance was eloquent. Though my heart knew the truth, she was just convincing enough to generate doubt in my mind. *Did I actually misplace them? Where could they be? How could I be so careless?*

Once again, the pain of loss was compounded by confusion, self-doubt, and self-deprecation. I wondered if I was truly losing my mind, and in some ways, I was relieved by the possibility. It would mean the nightmare ahead would not involve my daughter's mortality.

The contradictions were inconceivable. I couldn't fathom how Kayla could possibly be doing drugs while holding down two jobs and going to school. I reasoned that she was a typical teenager with a lot on her plate. I continued to deny, dismissing the reality that was right in front of me.

Life continued. Bills needed paying, house needed cleaning, and at age sixteen, my youngest still needed support. I had withdrawn from most other aspects of life; avoiding phone calls, declining invitations, and dismissing interaction of any kind. Still, I yearned for a significant other to join my life. I yearned for human embrace. I sought distraction. I went to bed.

The moments of disconnect were coming more frequently. Kayla's stories didn't make sense. Sometimes the orchestra in my head played its desperate song, "Wake up! There's something terribly, overwhelmingly, most assuredly wrong!" But I chose not to attend, not to listen, not to wake.

Work-sleep-work-sleep, isolate-deny, survive.

I pushed people away and simultaneously wanted companionship and connection. I wanted someone to take my pain away. I felt helpless, hopeless, and alone.

I received word that Kayla was acting strangely and falling asleep at work. In response, I reasoned that her demanding schedule continued to leave her exhausted. Days later, when Kayla's supervisor, Lucy, told me Kayla had been caught "snorting a white powder off her desk," I was horrified. I continued resisting the truth. I remained paralyzed to act.

With increased frequency, warnings filled my growing chasm of fear. I continued to tell myself "it isn't true," "they are mistaken," "they misunderstood." Clearly, however, I knew the truth was, again and again, knocking on my door. I fortified the locks.

Lucy backed off, leaving me to my own delusions. A wise woman, she knew I had to find my strength before I could address the monster. Once I did, she would prove herself invaluable as one of the many angels helping to guide me through the nightmare.

During those first months, isolation was key to my survival. Over time I would come to realize it truly took a community, and community was patiently waiting for me to be ready.

As more money and belongings disappeared, my rationalizations grew more creative. *I thought I had a twenty, I must have spent it. Darn, I misplaced those earrings again. Where on Earth did I leave my camera? I'm getting so forgetful. I'm sure it'll turn up.*

Kayla effortlessly fueled my doubt, insisting my stress was causing me to forget things. Though some days I was easily convinced I was losing my mind, deep inside I knew better. Something stronger than my denial, stronger than my fear, stronger than my insecurities, kept me moving. One foot in front of the other, I crept forward.

Kayla's health was visibly deteriorating. Chronically gaunt and thin, she slept a lot. On quite a few occasions I caught her vomiting, sometimes in the garden by the front door to the house. When confronted, she easily delivered an explanation: She had eaten too much because she was depressed; having her period made her sick; the food she ate was bad. Her excuses were quick, fluid, and plausible.

I had no idea I was looking at classic symptoms of heroin abuse. I listened, trusted, and accepted. I wasn't quite ready to face the truth, but the truth was getting louder. I was beginning to wake up.

In December I caught myself having the startling thought, "My daughter is a drug addict." I pushed it away. I still didn't know what those words meant. They terrified me.

I had only ever heard sentiments of disgust and fierce judgment about drug addiction. In my mind, drug addicts were uneducated, poor, derelict people with awful home lives and abusive parents who failed to nurture or guide them. It had been easy to condemn those faceless nobodies. Because of my egregious beliefs, Kayla's descent into drugs caused me to feel significant shame and tremendous guilt. I stuffed it down.

On December 14, 2011, I wrote in my journal, "Another $25 gone missing from my wallet. It feels so heavy in my heart and chest. She has robbed me of so much more than paper money. I'm so disappointed, sad, and yes, the actual money is an issue. I wanted to go out with Charlotte on Friday. Now I feel like I haven't the ability. No money. Ugh! My own damned fault. I should have hidden the money. Damn it! I work my ass off to support her drug habit??? Not fair, not right, so disheartening."

Nonetheless, I left money and jewelry out, subconsciously hoping beyond hope that Kayla wouldn't take it. I wanted to prove the nightmare wasn't happening. By then I knew what was right in front of me, but I didn't want to engage. I tried to pretend it out of existence by ignoring it. It kept pulling onto my driveway, ringing my doorbell, and pounding on my door.

Feeling the financial sting was also helping to wake me up. Monies I needed for daily subsistence were disappearing. I had to pay my bills. The fear was overwhelming, and the truth was sinking in.

I was cranky and vocal with Kayla. I was constantly demanding that she explain, justify, and reform. I thought it could be that easy; more discipline, more structure, more consequence. She placated me with her brilliant lies.

I turned to yoga for moments of peace and took solace in my belief that the Universe would guide me. I didn't know what else to do. I worked to reduce my stress. Breathe, trust, be in the moment... keep from going insane. Survive.

For years we had celebrated Christmas with special family friends. They had seen us through our biggest challenges and continued to love us, warts and all. Though Christmas wasn't our holiday, the kids and I always looked forward to the celebration, sharing the warmth, joy, and great food.

Losing a loved one to overdose many years prior, our friends had tragically experienced the pain of addiction up close and personal. They knew the signs all too well. On Christmas 2011, as the evening with family and friends progressed, the warning came, "Kayla looks high."

Our friends loved Kayla almost as much as I did. I wondered how they could be so harsh. In that moment, toward friends who had seen me at and through my worst, I felt resentment. It was my defense.

My excuses came easily: "No, she's been working hard," "She's just tired," "She doesn't feel well." But the internal nagging was relentless. Addiction didn't get better, it got worse. The messages and signs didn't let up; they got louder, bolder, and more colorful. The danger didn't dissipate; it grew more imminent. My "safe hiding place" was no longer safe. I began acknowledging that the signs were real. I had to wake up and help my child. I didn't know where to start.

In those early days, it would have been helpful to gather information. My perception of drug abuse was dangerously ill informed and mostly incorrect.

Could I have changed the trajectory of our experience had I known the signs sooner? Perhaps, but when I stumbled upon information, I ran away fast. I simply wasn't ready, or able, to face it.

Forgiving myself would come. I did the best I could in the moment. In that six-month moment, I couldn't look at what was plainly before me. If I could have, I would have.

CHAPTER FOUR:

NEW YEAR, NEW HOPE

As was often my practice at the entry to a new year, I reflected on my life. Determined to improve my outlook, on the morning of January 1, 2012, I wrote in my journal, "Thinking about me. What's in store? How do I maintain optimism? How do I move forward? Find energy? Be who I'm meant to be?"

By the end of the day, I was back to feeling nervous, insecure, and ungrounded. I prayed to the Universe for guidance and my next step. Sometimes it was all I knew to do.

I yearned to find my center and release the chronic grip of the nightmare. Though I finally acknowledged my daughter had a problem, I continued to pretend to the outside world. I wasn't ready to invite others in.

Keeping myself isolated, I tried my best to manage Kayla's deviant behaviors. No part of caring for an addict made sense. An alien called addiction inhabited the vessel I thought of as my child. The drug called the shots. Over time,

I came to understand I had been witnessing the ravages and voice of heroin. My daughter had disappeared.

It took time to fully accept what I knew to be true. As I struggled to address Kayla's addiction, I couldn't help but see my beautiful, smart daughter before me. Her act, the alien's act, was convincing. That was the trick. The drug wanted me to believe I was interacting with Kayla, and my desperate desire for normalcy made me the drug's unsuspecting sidekick.

Kayla constantly agitated any sense of peace that settled, even momentarily, on our household. The harder I pushed, the harder she pushed back. Routinely abusive to her brother and me, she turned every communication into an attack. The audacity of her accusations was unparalleled.

An exquisite liar, Kayla had a knack for causing me to doubt even the words I said with confidence. When I pointed out her abnormal behaviors, she demanded she was fine. She insisted any problem I cited lay solely with me. She blamed me for every confrontation and demanded she needed space from me. She threatened to move out.

All too comfortable with my guilt, anguish, and self-loathing, my logic was turned upside down. How to manage my child remained elusive. Thinking professional input would help, I made an appointment with a well-credentialed, local psychologist. Since she was already familiar with my family, I felt we could make quick progress, foregoing parts of the get-to-know she already knew. When I called for an appointment, I conveyed my concern about Kayla's drug use. I explained that I was seeking confirmation and guidance.

Days later, in Dr. Ashol's office, Kayla complained venomously about how badly I treated her. In turn, I complained about Kayla's behavior and changing moods. After thirty-five of our forty-five allotted minutes, Kayla abruptly rose from the couch, stated that she'd had enough, and left the office to smoke a cigarette.

Alone with the therapist, I asked what she thought I should do about Kayla's drug usage. She responded, "We have to establish trust between you first. Then we can address the drug issue."

I couldn't believe what I heard! A trained psychologist was telling me I had to earn my drug addict daughter's trust before I could address her addict behaviors! That was like being asked to pet a hungry tiger until it feels comfortable, then it will cuddle with you and purr. Really? IT'S GOING TO EAT YOU!

I was outraged, disgusted, and sorely disappointed. And I paid for that ineptitude! Despite my awareness of Dr. Ashol's gross incompetence, her lack of urgency tacitly gave me permission to step back into denial. "Surely," I reasoned, "if a qualified psychologist doesn't feel Kayla's drug use is an urgent matter, I don't have to either."

Kayla felt the shrink was a waste of time. I had to agree.

Rewriting the story once again, I told myself Kayla was a responsible teen going to school and holding down two jobs. Her life dispensed plenty of pressure so maybe what I was seeing was, in fact, typical teenage tribulations.

Nonetheless, Kayla and I were arguing all the time. Each confrontation yielded the same threat. She wanted to move out.

Kayla's threats triggered my money fears. As long as she lived at home and attended school, I received child support. If she left, I worried the money would also go. "How then," I wondered, "would I pay the bills?"

Worry served no purpose. Another non-productive habit, it robbed me of what little energy I had and solved nothing. "Breathe and let go," I told myself. It was a momentary fix, a physical break from the stress. While taking a deep belly breath, it was physiologically impossible to feel stress. No matter how brief the relief, it helped.

I also found relief through a variety of tools I had cultivated, including affirmations, mantras, meditation, yoga, exercise, journaling, and art. As I engaged with each tool, I was able to release negative thoughts and lose myself in the moment.

Affirmations helped me reinforce positive thoughts and feelings. It was a mental game in which winning was a matter of believing. Sometimes I wondered if I was fooling myself. Sometimes I felt better. I had nothing to lose except the pain of self-sabotage and misery.

At the end of each journal entry I affirmed, "All is in divine right order. I am guided and protected. My spirit is in charge of my life."

CHAPTER FIVE:

SHARING THE PAIN

For a time, I pushed the nightmare away and tried hard to focus on "other." Despite the difficult breakup with Leo, my boyfriend of four years, followed by an unsuccessful flirtation with Ben, I continued to focus on men, or lack thereof. I viewed the slightest encouragement from a man, real or perceived, as fodder for elaboration. I cycled between fantasy and the impossible.

I tormented myself with a detailed, standby fantasy in which Leo, longing for only me, swept me off my feet, wanting to make everything right in my world. The disappointment was small compared to the real-life challenges I faced.

In an odd way, I had become numb to Kayla's thievery and the sting from objects lost. I told myself "things" didn't matter and spun my feelings into a warm cocoon in which they could lay dormant. I had largely ignored the impact of Kayla's behavior on my youngest child, Avery. He was sixteen and had his own challenges. As he began to experience loss, he pleaded with me to stop her.

One by one, Avery's video games and electronics went missing. Oddly, my response was to defend Kayla. I demanded that Avery must have misplaced his things or admonished him for not taking better care to put them in a safe place. I couldn't see his anger, couldn't hear his frustration, pain, and sense of helplessness. My need to deny was stronger than my need to protect him. It was too much for me to process. I was dealing (or not dealing) with my own challenges full time.

When Avery declared that his laptop went missing, I felt a bullet pierce my heart. Without facility to cope or take action, my response, once again, was to shrug it off and blame him. I was at a complete loss for how to address that newest affront, so I didn't. I ignored the crisis. I ignored the impact on Avery.

Avery was understandably devastated by my inaction. He sought help elsewhere, to no avail. With no means to replace his laptop, he did without. I fed my guilt, and it grew. He withdrew.

It was easy to forget I wasn't the only one affected by the addict living in my home. Avery's sense of safety and well-being had been systematically eroded. He had been violated and betrayed, not only by Kayla, but also by his mother. My pain crippled my ability to help with his.

Another startling blow came with another phone call from the non-profit. Kayla had left her Facebook account open on a desktop at work. A co-worker found it and, as people are prone to do, snooped. What she found was explicit conversation regarding drug acquisition. The discovery was reported to management and once again, I was talking with Lucy.

Surprisingly, Lucy explained that University policy mandated employees with addiction issues be helped, not fired. She assured me they would keep an eye on Kayla, and where opportunities for assistance arose, she would seize them.

I was overcome by a sweeping sense of relief! Someone else would take care of the problem! I was off the hook! I could continue my inaction. *Kayla still had a job, so it couldn't be that bad, right?* I didn't have to DO anything.

Relief was short lived. Enduring daily assaults from my addict prohibited rest. Sitting in my pain, I had a profound revelation. We were each proceeding on our own life's path. If Kayla's journey and the demands of her soul brought her to drug addiction and death, I would have to find acceptance. I had to obey the demands of my soul as well. I had to keep going.

Both startling and liberating, my revelation allowed me to distance myself a bit. It gave me resolve to keep moving forward in my own life and reminded me that I had less control than I might have liked to believe.

My mandate was to discover my authentic self, love myself unconditionally, and survive the nightmare. Whatever happened, I knew I would be all right. I pleaded with the Universe not to make my worst fears come true.

Kayla's addiction had ignited every conceivable negative emotion in me, and I turned each inward. By the end of January, tortured on every front, I began to question my self-sabotaging thoughts, beliefs, and behaviors. Dysfunctional childhood patterns dominated as I struggled for basic survival. The struggle was reaching its apex.

Waking early one morning, a knowing voice decreed, "This is going to change you for the better. You will come out strong and whole." I didn't know how, but I wanted to believe!

On and off, I had been working with a spiritual counselor since my divorce almost ten years prior. Katherine was more than someone I paid for services. Over the years we had grown a deep connection and friendship. She had been helping me identify and shift dysfunctional patterns, as well as self-sabotaging thoughts and behaviors. It was time to seek her counsel again.

Embarrassed, ashamed, and deeply pained, I had spoken to almost no one about Kayla's addiction and its consequent impact on my life. I anticipated that full disclosure to family and friends would result in condemnation, judgment, shock, confusion, and a million questions I was ill prepared to hear, let alone answer. I didn't have the emotional fortitude for the onslaught.

Katherine urged me to open to my inner wisdom. She helped me see the childhood patterns that stopped me from taking action. She explained that by shutting down and denying, I was handing my power over to outside forces. I had made myself a victim. I had rendered myself powerless.

I realized that, subconsciously, I perceived lack of power to be easier. By not taking control of my thoughts and behaviors, I could continue to hide and avoid. Avoidance felt like protection. Katherine helped me recognize the lie. Giving my power away was exhausting and disabling, and complicated the solution. I wasn't really avoiding; I was suffering. There was no relief in hiding.

Inviting me to look at my situation objectively, Katherine encouraged, "Stand outside yourself and look at Kayla. What is best for her? Don't believe what she says and don't allow her to manipulate you. See the reality of what she's doing. She's doing it to herself."

Katherine encouraged me to find support by going to a meeting. She suggested CoDA (Co-Dependents Anonymous), Al Anon, or Nar Anon; each predicated on the Twelve Step program used in Alcoholics Anonymous (AA) and Narcotics Anonymous (NA). Al Anon and Nar Anon were designed to help family and friends of addicts by sharing experiences and stories. They invited members to "take what they like and leave the rest." CoDa focused on eliminating co-dependent behaviors and developing healthy relationships.

I hated the idea of going to a meeting. I was an introvert. I didn't like putting myself in group settings, let alone sharing my innermost pain with strangers. Though I rejected the idea, I trusted Katherine completely. She had planted a seed.

For months, profound loneliness had been my constant companion. The sense of isolation was deafening. With Katherine's help, I came to realize my loneliness wasn't

about being cut off from others; rather, it was about discon-
nection from myself. Though I had been steadily working
to empower myself for years, Kayla's addiction demanded
I take a much deeper look.

Ironically, as anguish and pain increased, the call to grow
me, love me, and connect to my authentic self increased as
well. Failing to value or love myself fully was an old story
I urgently had to rewrite. With Katherine's help, I began to
identify the work I needed to do. The first step was to get
real about Kayla's addiction. At the same time, I needed to
open my heart to what was happening to me. There was no
denying the truth; I was a mother who was terrified! I felt
raw and more vulnerable than ever before.

As I healed my own wounds, energetically I would show
my children how to heal theirs. Perhaps I couldn't change
Kayla's beliefs and behaviors, but I could absolutely change
mine! I was motivated to model healthy behavior that I
hoped would shift us all.

Mom and Dad were no strangers to the complicated struggles of my life. Emotionally and financially, they had assisted
me through plenty. Picking up the pieces after my difficult
divorce, they helped me navigate through single parenting,
returning to the world of work, and the challenges inherent

in living independently. Every day they were there to encourage, guide, and support me.

Despite her unconditional love, my relationship with my mother had been strained and often adversarial. In her company, I routinely felt misunderstood. Within the nightmare, my relationship with Mom would shift, and in many ways, she would become my best friend. There were always silver linings.

For months, my parents had been hearing the gloom in my voice when they called. Worried, they always questioned me and offered their help. I usually made excuses and got off the phone fast, but I had reached a saturation point. I was no longer able to hide the facts. I wanted them to know the truth. I needed them to know the truth. I needed their support. It was time to share the nightmare.

I arrived at Mom and Dad's house drawn and tearful. I was well aware that nothing could prepare them for what I was about to say. Far worse than any of our preceding family crises, Kayla's addiction was a matter of life and death. In person there was no hiding my feelings. Sitting in their family room, trying hard to be strong, the tears trickled through the tiny cracks of the dam holding back my emotion. Without warning the dam split wide open, releasing the raging waters. In that moment, I wondered if they would ever stop.

I spit out the words, "Kayla is addicted to drugs."

New to their ears, foreign to their thoughts, and shocking to their systems, the questions immediately poured forth:

"What do you mean?" "What kind of drugs?" "Where is she?" 'How long?" "How did this happen?" "How do you know?" "What are you doing about it?" "Is this because of that boyfriend?" "Is she using needles?" and finally, "What can we do?"

I answered their questions as best I could, "I think it's heroin." "No, I don't think she's using needles." "I don't know about the boyfriend." "I don't know what to do."

A side note:

Dozens of people asked some variation of the same question, "How did she get caught up in drugs?" or "Who pulled her into that world? Was it the boyfriend?"

Rarely are our loved ones strong-armed to use drugs. Kayla was vulnerable. She attracted people with whom she felt connection. Combined with a genetic predisposition to addiction, having found acceptance, excitement, and/or escape, she alone chose her path.

In an effort to make sense of tragedy, it is easy to lay blame at the foot of "another." While projecting our sense of personal guilt or shame may temporarily help us "feel better," it is really just a trick. Responsibility always resides with the individual. Kayla was driven by her unique needs and responsible for her own choices.

Kayla was raised in a "say no to drugs" home where communication about such issues was open and blunt. Nonetheless, she sought an escape from her demons and found drugs as a vehicle. It's hard to know why people make devastating choices.

Overwhelmed by my parents' questions and magnified fear, I asserted, "I know you are upset. I know you will have more questions and will need to process what I just told you. You have each other and you have friends. Please feel free to talk to whomever you want (you don't have to keep this secret) but I am having enough trouble getting up each morning and doing what I have to do. I can't help you. Please don't seek answers from me right now."

I respected, appreciated, and loved my parents, and wanted to make it all right for them. I simply didn't have the energy or the means. The truth was the truth. I couldn't change the facts no matter how much I wished I could.

For a couple of days following that conversation, my mom called asking questions about Kayla's whereabouts, her behavior, whether I had talked to her, what had changed, and what actions I was taking. Lovingly, she would also ask about me; how I was feeling and what I was doing for myself.

As her calls amplified my stress, I was angered by my mother's failure to respect my wishes. At the same time, I understood she wanted to help and was, herself, hurting deeply. Each time, I did my best to calmly explain that I had no answers. Each time, I reiterated that I needed her not to ask. Each time, I fought back my tears.

Three days after I delivered the devastating news in my parents' family room, I went to a yoga class. An hour during which I could forget my troubles and connect with my body and spirit, yoga was my respite. While I was in class, Mom had called and left a message on my cell phone. She asked that I call her back. Concerned by the tone I heard, I called as soon as I got to my car. She immediately began questioning me about Kayla's whereabouts and whether anything had changed.

I was so raw, so emotionally spent, so tired and overwhelmed, that in that moment, I found the strength to establish non-negotiable boundaries on my own behalf. Once again, I reiterated that I had no new information. I said that when I did, I would let her and my dad know. I also reiterated that I did not have the bandwidth to address her worries or help her work through them. I did not have the bandwidth to talk every day or to face her questions. I did not have the bandwidth to talk about my life or myself. I had just enough energy to get up in the morning and get through my days. I was in survival mode. I then told my mother that if she continued to call in the same manner, I would stop answering the phone.

While my heart ached to have spoken to my mother harshly, I knew I was protecting what little peace I could garner. That was a turning point. I had truly begun the process of learning to love myself. Setting boundaries, it turned out, was an essential step. Identifying and protecting my needs was paramount to healing my spirit and living a happy life. I wished it hadn't taken a crisis, but the Universe had finally awakened me.

My parents learned to respect my wishes. As a result, it became easier to connect with them, and a much healthier relationship evolved.

After confiding in Mom and Dad, I continued, in large part, to keep to myself. Exhaustion necessitated withdrawal, and withdrawal further isolated me. However, staying alone was becoming emotionally untenable. Little by little, I began to share my concerns and fears with a select few.

I tried to work through my pain and confusion, sometimes venting, sometimes ranting, and oftentimes crying. No one really understood what I was going through. *How could they?*

The result was a mixed bag. Sharing the details of my nightmare, in addition to the repeated requirement to explain and field questions; frustrated, aggravated, and further depleted me. Clearly, everyone in whom I confided sincerely wanted to help. Some were happy to offer uninformed advice; others offered strong compassion, perhaps pity; still others stayed quiet, listening, not knowing what to say. Too painful, the subject created discomfort and a sense of vulnerability for everyone. While deliberately or not, there were those who avoided me as well.

I didn't have the energy to demand different. Trying to educate and/or assuage misunderstandings took effort. I needed to use what little energy I had to take care of me and mine. I found myself avoiding contact unless absolutely necessary. It was a vicious cycle.

As if the emotional challenges weren't enough, my body was miserable. My skin hurt, my joints ached, my muscles spasmed. The fibromyalgia was in overdrive, with no respite in sight. But life continued... obligations, family, work. I pushed through.

CHAPTER SIX:
CONFUSION

With Kayla out of the house most of the time, it was difficult to track her comings and goings. Occasionally I was able to confirm she was at work, but most of the time she lied about her whereabouts. I tried not to question. Ignorance was bliss.

When Kayla was home, we clashed terribly. I accused, she denied; I wanted answers, she provided lies; I wanted solutions, she wanted drugs. She spent most of her time behind a closed door, I assumed sleeping.

The discord between us had become unbearable. By early February, Kayla was frequently sleeping at a friend's house. Eventually she would be staying with Eva and her mother, Iris, full time. It was a subtle evolution that took time for me to recognize.

With Kayla spending most of her time at Eva's, life felt less chaotic. Out of sight, out of mind, the immediate challenges quieted some. Knowing she was in a safe place with a friend I adored and her mom whom I trusted, I felt relief.

Still, the tracks of Kayla's drug use didn't disappear (pun intended).

Kayla and I didn't speak much; we emailed or texted occasionally. She was still involved with Jason and swore he was clean. Mid-February she wrote to tell me her boy-friend had been unjustly fired from his job. Furious, she was lodging a written complaint with the Human Resources Department (HR), claiming he had been "unfairly targeted."

Kayla wrote, "He was fired literally for wearing his (company) jacket on a day he was not scheduled to work. Another employee who was new had asked him to help him get the mop out of the closet in the bathroom, that's why he was seen going into the bathroom with another person, but it wasn't like anything fishy. They really were just looking for any excuse to fire him because they don't like him. If you had witnessed the types of things I witnessed in that store while he was working, you'd really be appalled at how much discrimination they have just because he's white. It's sad. But things are looking good so far, HR agrees with us."

Knowing I was a strong writer and editor, Kayla asked me to review the letter she had written on Jason's behalf.

I had been experiencing Kayla's emphatic, passionate, confusing communication for months. The scenario she described seemed particularly unusual and suspect, but I had lived a sheltered life. I doubted my intuition, thinking perhaps she was describing a side of life I just didn't under-stand. (In fact, she was... she described the side of life that abuses drugs.) My thoughts felt fuzzy. I gave her the benefit of the doubt.

For a year, Kayla had been driving an older, used car she had proudly purchased with her own, hard-earned money. Sadly, it not only suffered from a variety of mechanical issues, but it seemed to invite bad luck. Twice, while parked in the grocery store lot, her tires had been slashed. Additionally, quite a few dents mysteriously appeared on the car's body. Believing it was jinxed; Kayla began to express discomfort about driving her car.

Finding the damage suspect, I questioned Kayla about people who may have had a vendetta toward her. It seemed unlikely that her car's plight was random. She denied knowledge of any such cause for the damage. Citing other employees whose cars had been subject to vandalism, she told me the parking lot had become unsafe. The police, she said, had been contacted on several occasions.

When I asked what was being done to secure the parking lot and her safety, Kayla said the police told her there was nothing they could do. Once again, her story seemed suspicious, but I accepted her explanation. *After all, what did I know about such things?*

Meanwhile, after moving to the city, Kayla's older brother no longer needed his five-year-old vehicle. In graduate school and eager to pay back the money he borrowed from my equity loan; Gabriel prepared to sell his car. Claiming her car was no longer road worthy, Kayla begged, badgered, and pleaded to take over Gabriel's payments, thereby making his car her own.

Indeed, her car seemed to be a magnet for trouble, but I was ignorant to Kayla's regular trips to the worst areas of the inner city. I was oblivious to the risks to which she routinely exposed herself. Her desire to score drugs blinded her to danger. Her car revealed clues I could not yet decode.

I blocked my instinct. A people pleaser from a young age, I wanted to be a "good mom." I wanted to help make Kayla's life more comfortable. *Isn't that a parent's job?* Despite the nagging in my gut whispering (maybe shouting) that I was making a mistake, I allowed her to assume the payments on her brother's car.

For a short period, Kayla paid her debt fully and on time. When she stopped making regular payments, Kayla agreed to have the money directly deposited into my bank account. I warned that if she didn't, I would confiscate the car and sell it. She skillfully avoided paying or paid a fraction of the amount we had agreed on. Her excuses and lies kept me off balance.

One evening, I found an envelope and note on my night-stand, "Mom, I can only give you $150 now. I only got paid $220, they did not pay me for last Friday because they did payroll early. Jason and I are going to sell his magic card collection and I'll be able to pay you more.—Kayla"

Unbeknownst to Kayla, the envelope also contained the withdrawal ticket from the bank. It revealed, "Cash paid to customer $357.98."

As missed payments piled up, my resolve for confrontation waned. I reasoned that Kayla needed the car to get to work. Though her "old" car languished on my driveway, it was no longer drivable without substantial repair and expense. I worried that without a car, work and school would be impossible and her condition would worsen.

My logic might have been reasonable for a misbehaving child but not for a child on drugs. I fretted, raged, and worried, all the while beating myself up for my failures. I didn't know what I didn't know.

In my journal I ranted passionately about taking the car away from Kayla, emphasizing the urgency to do so. I imagined the benefits from such an action: she wouldn't be able to see her boyfriend anymore (I blamed him for perpetuating her drug use), she wouldn't be risking her life driving while high (she swore she never drove while high), and she would have to face her demons and me (not run and hide). I fantasized that she would be healed. Additionally, I would be relieved of the financial burden I was carrying.

Still, I did nothing but threaten. I couldn't find the courage to do more. Family members urged me to action, but I continued to stall. Facing Kayla's fury was too much for me to bear.

I well knew the bright, shining light that was the essence of my daughter. I prayed daily that Kayla would connect to her own brilliance. At the same time, I wondered, "How can I expect her to see her brilliance when I can't see my own?" The mirror reflected the very personal work awaiting my attention. Once again, the message was clear: If I was to help Kayla, I had to help myself first or at least concurrently. I was powerless to force her recovery, but I was one hundred percent in charge of my own health. I allowed myself to settle into a place of trust.

My ability to focus on my own growth waxed and waned. At times I had clarity and enthusiasm. "I'm ready and willing to deem myself worthy," I wrote in my journal, "worthy of joy and success, worthy of love and living, worthy of greatness." Self-loathing, shame, guilt, and fear had consumed me most of my life. Finding value in myself, even for a moment, felt good. Though my mood jumped up and down, a little bit of light was breaking through. From where I had been, it felt like a huge leap.

At times when I felt despondent, I would quiet my mind and hear the message, "Keep creating." Letting my creative side express itself was healing and nurturing. I made art, walked in nature, took photographs, journaled, and cooked. When I tapped into my creative, I was able to lose myself in the moment, still my mind, get into what Deepak Chopra called "the gap," the space between thoughts. Creativity allowed me to feel useful, productive, and worthy. Those moments nourished me and helped clear my thinking.

During moments of clarity, I caught glimpses of my gifts and talents, and of my authentic self. Intuition guided me to next right actions. Those direct messages helped me feel peace and built my confidence.

Humility instigated prayer. Though I was not religious, I did believe in the energetic power of prayer. I wrote in my journal, "Please help me to trust. Help me to open to opportunities buried in this challenge. Help me to see the steps needed to find stability—financial and emotional. Help me to be strong and to support Kayla through her struggles."

While denying Kayla's addiction, I couldn't bear to seek information. It felt too much like acceptance. With Kayla staying at Eva's house, it seemed for the foreseeable future, the need became clear. Distance provided space in which to explore the monster. Finally, I mustered the courage to do some research.

There was a plethora of information available. I found websites offering facts and opinions on everything from simple medical beliefs, to the science and purpose of drugs. Multitudes of detox and rehabilitation centers promoted their unique methodologies for kicking the habit. Grim statistics on overdose and recovery loomed. I found online lectures and articles, organizations and support groups. There were books and movies and counselors and commentary.

Drug abuse had its own language. I had to learn a new vocabulary: detox, rehab, recovery, "people, places, and things," using, shooting, reach, and more. There was no step-by-step guide, however, nor guaranteed solution. My courage was growing, but I skillfully avoided anything too deep or detailed.

I learned that the physical nature of heroin addiction made successful, independent withdrawal not only unlikely, but also dangerous. Kayla would need to medically detox at a facility where professionals could monitor and assist her.

I asked Kayla to get help. I begged her to get help. I fought with her to get help. She refused treatment. She said she wasn't "that bad."

CHAPTER SEVEN:

STEPS TOWARD HEALING

Not knowing what else to do, I continued to focus on healing myself. "How," I questioned, "can I be functional, self-loving, and whole, despite the cavernous ache in my heart?"

Once I opened to finding information, it came without effort. Synchronicities abounded. Spiritual teachers I had previously followed were speaking directly to me! The lessons they spoke were my lessons. I listened. I learned.

At some point, the day-to-day, omnipresent, all-encompassing sadness faded. When I noticed I wasn't feeling sad, I felt guilty. Common when grieving loss, I subconsciously felt that holding onto the sadness honored my daughter and proved my love for her. That belief was a fraud.

In the background, a perpetual sense of impending doom droned, but for a time daylight came through the windows. I made a list of things that would help me feel better: selectively socializing, cleaning the house, clearing clutter, finding a new job, extreme self-care, reaching out to the people I love, going to the gym, creating art, time in nature. Fervently, I wanted to find HAPPY.

I set goals that were easy and manageable. I defined small, specific action steps like: "just clear the night stand," "clean one toilet," "do one load of laundry," "drive to the gym," "apply for one job," "take a walk in nature (my happy place) for fifteen minutes," "call Mom and Dad," "weave," "pay one bill." I focused solely on the single task before me.

Accomplishing one small goal felt good, and sometimes I found I could do more. If not, I allowed myself to be satisfied. When my body or mind was not able, I forgave myself.

My prayers continued. I wrote, "Dear Universe, please take my fear from me and give me the strength to support Kayla as she needs. Help me trust; help me open to the opportunities embedded in this challenge. Help me take the steps needed to heal and become emotionally and financially stable."

Every day I asked to be shown how to best access and use my gifts in service to others and to myself. I wrote my intention on the bathroom mirror as a reminder.

Despite my progress, or maybe because of it, I began to feel increased urgency to help Kayla. As I became empowered to help myself, I was able to push through my anxiety and think more clearly. I became willing to do what was necessary to help my child heal.

For years I had been picking up the pieces of the kids' disappointments and pain, with little or no input or assistance. Finally acknowledging the grave potential for Kayla's future, I knew I was in way over my head. I would have to cast aside my pride and seek advice.

After some consideration, I identified someone I'd known long ago. I knew he had experienced his own battle with addiction and, if willing, I anticipated he'd be able to help in a way many others could not. It was an uncomfortable, difficult call to make for many reasons, but I was optimistic that George would offer a perspective I couldn't see on my own. I felt sure he would have invaluable wisdom and be able to help me help Kayla.

Grateful that George answered the phone, I felt awkward and ashamed as I humbly explained the reason for my call. Relaying what I had observed, I told George I thought Kayla was using heroin and shared that she felt her problem was "not that bad." I told him that when asked to go to detox, Kayla had resisted. I answered his questions as best I could.

Not prepared for the harshness of his reply, I felt dizzy as I registered George's response. Almost matter-of-factly, he told me Kayla would have to hit rock bottom, there was nothing to be done. I pleaded for more, but more didn't follow. The conversation ended abruptly.

I was devastated by what I perceived as George's defeatist view and dismissive tone. I berated myself for being foolish enough to reach out to him. With the wind knocked out of me, I renewed my resolve to deal with the situation on my own.

As I struggled to move forward, another challenge blasted me. Opening the mail, I discovered that child support for Kayla had been terminated. Devastated, confusion, anger, shock, and overwhelm swept through me. My body shook and my thoughts spun out of control. *What was I supposed to do?* In addition to living the nightmare that had overtaken my little girl, and consequently me and her brothers, I was hit with the blunt reality: I would no longer receive income I relied on, income I needed to help Kayla! *How could support be terminated when Kayla needed more than ever?*

Slowly, I came to accept reality. Feeling alone was familiar, and I had survived so far. While terror infiltrated most of my thoughts, I was determined to rise above it. I had no idea how to proceed.

CHAPTER EIGHT:
SUPPORTED

In truth, I was far from alone.

Flying in to attend a concert with my oldest son, Gabriel, Sarah came from South Carolina for a brief visit in early March. An honorary family member, Sarah was one of my dearest friends and Gabriel's as well. Over the years, as I muddled through life, she had provided countless hours of love and support. As I navigated the nightmare of Kayla's addiction, she was my rock.

During Sarah's previous visit, Gabriel had still lived at home. When he moved into his own apartment in the city, Kayla took over his slightly larger bedroom. The smaller room she had enjoyed through her teen years became her closet. Both were a disaster. Upon arrival to my home, Sarah expressed understandable concern over what she observed in Kayla's rooms.

In the smaller room, beyond the graffiti covered walls and paint splattered furniture; Kayla's clothing lay knee deep on the floor and trash mingled with valued belongings. I anticipated Kayla would eventually tire of living in such chaos, and someday she would clean. Given the many challenges consuming my days, it was not my primary focus. I generally chose to close the doors rather than instigate a confrontation.

Despite the chaos, I was actually quite fond of the graffiti. Several years prior, with my permission, Kayla had begun using Sharpie markers to write phrases, song lyrics, words, and greetings on her walls. Pictures and symbols added colorful points of interest. Friends wrote messages of endearment and humor, and I even contributed some motherly wisdom to the mix.

I thought the graffiti was both artistic and fun, and a healthy, largely innocent outlet for a teenager. Periodically, Kayla and I would lie across her bed musing over this or that creative offering. Sometimes I would try to guess the origin of a comment or phrase; other times we would giggle over a joke or nonsensical statement. I rarely, if ever, objected to a contribution. And while I didn't love the spattered paint, I saw it, too, as a creative endeavor.

Seeing Sarah's reaction, and knowing her propensity to clean and organize, I urged her to ignore the disarray. Wanting her and Gabriel to enjoy their time together, I implored them to go out and do something fun. Since I had to work, I offered them my car and suggestions for where they might go. Thinking about them spending the day having an adventure of joy did my heart good.

Unbeknownst to me, Sarah and Gabriel already had a plan. Sarah dropped me off at work and drove my car away without a hint of what they were plotting. I was sad I couldn't join them.

At the end of my workday, Sarah retrieved me from school. Getting in the car, I eagerly inquired about her day with Gabriel. She refused to tell me anything. Ignorant to the shock that awaited me, I made pleasant conversation during the brief ride home.

Entering my house through the front door, I was paralyzed by what I saw. With a clear view into Kayla's old bedroom, the glare of clean, white walls blinded me. Primer paint obliterated every one of Kayla's memories. Taking a closer look, I noticed the carpet. Shaking, I demanded, "Where's Kayla's stuff?"

Almost matter-of-factly, Sarah explained that they had filled twenty-three large trash bags with Kayla's clothes. They had taken eighteen to Good Will. Another five awaited my consideration.

I cried and withdrew.

Sarah and Gabriel's overwhelmingly loving and generous gesture left me paralyzed. As the shock wore off, I felt deep loss and sorrow, then rising anger. It felt as though they had erased my daughter.

Fear quickly replaced anger as I considered the likely consequences. *How will I break the news to Kayla? She'll be furious! She will never forgive me. I wouldn't blame her.*

Guilt and dread raced in. My head was pounding and my heart ached. I felt defensive, indignant, and defeated.

What they had done felt wrong. *What if Kayla wanted those things? She wasn't even there to choose!*

In response to my accusations of thoughtless action, Sarah and Gabriel gently assured me they had been very considerate, only purging what was old and unsightly, inappropriate, or unnecessary. Anything Kayla could use, they explained, waited in those five remaining bags.

"And what about the walls?" I pleaded. "Did you at least take pictures? How could you do this without my permission?"

The response was deafening, even at that stage. With pained expression, in her calm and nurturing way, Sarah assured, "Judi, you don't need memories of that stuff. Those walls were alive with drug references. Judi, it had to go, it was bad."

Knowing me well, Sarah took me by the hand and led me to the bedroom Kayla had been sleeping in. She showed me a pile of small waxed papers she had gathered. They looked like saltwater taffy wrappers. I wondered where Kayla had gotten taffy and questioned the intensity of her sweet tooth because the pile was substantial. Once again, my naiveté was showing.

"No," Sarah gently corrected, "these are not taffy wrappers. They are heroin wrappers."

OH MY GOD! How could I be so stupid? How could I not know? How could this be happening? I was looking at dozens, maybe a hundred wrappers. The pain came in relentless, breaking waves, crashing hard on my mind and body. It was plain, in my face, undeniable. My daughter had a big problem! It was "that bad"!

How were Sarah and Gabriel so calmly able to accept the truth? I couldn't focus. I wasn't able to accept the truth. I wasn't close. I was mad. I was mad at them. I was mad at Kayla. But mostly, I was mad at me. *How had I let it happen?* I went numb.

As I calmed, I felt deep gratitude. Sarah and Gabriel had begun the process. Indeed, it was necessary and healthy.

That day, I mourned my daughter's youth. I mourned her departure from my home as it suddenly seemed clear she was not coming back. I mourned my own lost innocence. I mourned for the feelings Sarah and Gabriel must have hidden in order to help me.

I thought I had admitted Kayla's addiction, but I continued to play games in my head about its urgency. I rationalized and made okay what was clearly not okay. No more.

I went to my room to cry, to feel, to rage, and to come to terms. Sarah and Gabriel had done what I was unable to do on my own. They cleaned Kayla's mess so that I could heal someday. I hurt beyond words. At the same time, I felt loved beyond worth.

Both evenings of Sarah's brief visit, Gabriel and I invited Kayla to join us for dinner. It had been years since she had seen our dear friend, and I knew Kayla missed her brother, whom she adored. I was certain she would want time with Gabriel, and I knew Gabriel wanted time with his sister, too.

She didn't respond the first night; the second, she declined.

I reasoned that Kayla was angry because I had forbidden her boyfriend from coming to the house. The last time he had been in my home, Avery's laptop disappeared. Kayla vehemently denied that Jason was using or that he stole the laptop, but if he hadn't stolen it, she did. It was easier to believe it was him.

While cleaning Kayla's bedroom, Sarah had discovered a letter. Written to Jason, the letter confirmed they were using together. It was one more piece of evidence I couldn't refute. Kayla was a mellifluous liar.

Along with the lies, Kayla's belligerent insistence, anger, and defensiveness continued to grow. The sense of loss I felt was real. Hijacking Kayla's kind, generous, playful, and loving character, the drug delivered a conniving, selfish, reactive, single-minded monster.

I writhed with the thought that Kayla was gone. I reminded myself that although the beautiful young woman I knew seemed to be missing, she was somewhere close. As long as she was alive, there was hope.

The roller coaster of emotion: loss/hope, fear/love, disgust/forgiveness, guilt/self-love, pain/healing, kept me feeling exhausted and unstable. There was a hole in my heart.

Kayla and I were on separate paths, intricately woven together. I knew I could not mandate the steps of her journey, nor could she mine. I had to accept that I had no control over her. I believed; however, I could impact her best by my example. Despite my constant companions, pain and fear, I had to ensure my survival. I had to heal. I had to learn self-love.

I coached myself to believe and trust, and to keep taking the next logical step. I was battling on two fronts: urgently seeking solution to save my baby, and working to love and save myself. Deep down I knew I would not only survive, but I would come out of the nightmare whole. I had the tools.

Sarah returned to South Carolina. Gabriel took the train home to his apartment. I had my locks changed.

I requested Kayla get professional help. Since she was a legal adult, I could not force her. I asked her to check into detox or rehab. (I didn't know the difference or the process.) She danced around the topic and avoided action.

Seeking any possible solution, I asked Kayla if she would work with an alternative healer. She didn't refuse.

CHAPTER NINE:
HIRING HELP

A lways asking big questions like, "Why are we here?" and "What is beyond this reality?" my spiritual journey took off dramatically in my early twenties. I found meaning and connection in the lessons of metaphysics, and comfort and wisdom from people I came to consider my gurus; including, Wayne Dyer, Marianne Williamson, Byron Katie, Deepak Chopra, Caroline Myss, Don Miguel Ruiz, Eckhart Tolle, Iyanla Vanzant, Debbie Ford, and others. The more I tuned in, the more I was able to make sense of the challenge called "life."

Eventually I became aware of my "extra sensory" gifts; strong intuition, visions that came to fruition, "knowings" I had no ability to know; and as a life coach, I channeled healing information to my clients with no understanding of from where it came. I had friends and acquaintances with gifts that astounded and excited me. I learned never to say "never."

Always seeking like-minded people, I'd met Margaret some years prior. She wowed me with stories of her vast experiences and "freaky powers." The scope of her credentials, along with professional confirmation of her authenticity, compelled me to believe in her ability to heal others. Additionally, I had come to trust her.

With no manual for the best way to proceed and Kayla resisting medical detox/treatment, I decided to approach Margaret for help. Kayla had opened the door to possibly working with a healer, and I was willing to take the leap to make it happen.

Days after Sarah's visit, I reached out to Margaret. On the phone, I shared my observations of Kayla's behavior. I described what I had endured over the past months. I asked (maybe pleaded) if she had experience healing drug addiction. I asked if she had expertise to treat Kayla. I asked if she would help us. I no doubt sounded, as I was, frantic and desperate.

To my great relief, Margaret confirmed she had experience treating addiction. She agreed to work with Kayla. She would require $2000 up front, and I would have to purchase a substantial supply of supplements.

I never questioned Margaret's fee. She deserved to be paid what she was worth; however, barely making ends meet, it was a lot for me to scrape together. I justified the cost by comparing it to my daughter's life. I rationalized, "What's a little more debt?" further resolving, "If I have to sell my house to get Kayla well, I will. Anything to save her life!"

Despite apprehension about whether Margaret's healing protocol would work and anxiety over the financial burden,

I went in headlong. I stood in trust and hope. Kayla started working with Margaret immediately.

Margaret became the moderator, referee, and director of communications between my child and me. Kayla was no longer living with me. We spoke infrequently on our own.

As promised, Margaret provided a list of homeopathic supplements for me to purchase. As I understood it, the goal was to detox Kayla naturally, safely, and permanently. (Margaret's assistant would later tell me that Margaret was "not detoxing Kayla." Instead, she was "offering a viable system of information and support.")

I questioned my decision to hire Margaret often and ultimately shifted my view on spending money I didn't have. Kayla absolutely required my unconditional love and support, and there were justified expenses I was willing to incur. However, I came to understand the only way for Kayla to recover was through her own commitment, willingness, resolve, and action. Destroying my own health, safety, and welfare on her behalf would take us both down.

Often consumed by my shortcomings, I sought reminders that I had valid needs, real talents, and a right to be happy. Society often frowned on self-care, sending demeaning accusations of selfish behavior rather than messages of support. I wanted confirmation that time spent growing and nurturing me was responsible, respectable, and reasonable. I wanted validation that I was worthy. I had to find the strength and conviction to push past society.

Taking care of myself was closely linked to taking care of Kayla. As such, I had to become what I wanted most for her. I had to detox from beliefs and patterns that kept me stuck in a cycle of self-deprecation and unhappiness. I believed I was in a battle to save my daughter's life, but in many ways, my own survival was also on the line.

CHAPTER TEN:
ATTACKED

Shortly after beginning work with Margaret, seemingly out of nowhere, Kayla sent me a scathing email.

Mother,

> *I cannot put into words how furious and hurt I am because of the way you have been handling this situation and the ways you have been acting... I came to you and told you I wanted to check myself into a 5-day detox program because I felt I had gone a little overboard taking drugs and I needed to go through the process of withdrawal in a controlled and comfortable environment so I could stop. My thought when telling you this was that you would be understanding of my needs and wishes and supportive of me getting clean with the help of professionals. Detox is not rehab. I never felt like I needed REHAB or any long-term professional help, because my situation is not a big deal and could be much, much worse.*

> *I expected you to be upset, but you have blown this WAY out of proportion, gotten people involved who have no need to be involved who I specifically asked you NOT to get involved, you have stretched the truth*

and have disrespected me and my wishes and have made this a living hell for me, instead of the easy and comfortable step I needed to take for ME, that I decided and planned for ME. To be completely honest, to me and everyone who is actually being supportive of me, it looks like the only reason you are acting this way is because you want to feel sorry for yourself and you want others to feel sorry for you. In therapy, I will tell you how I've seen this from you my whole life. But this is not okay and needs to stop, NOW. If you want to feel sorry for yourself, I can't control that. But don't use ME as an excuse to get attention from everyone else. I take full responsibilities for my actions. I may include others in the blame for the problems I have in my life, like (people) not being there (for me) and certain things that you and Avery and the rest of our family do, and I may blame my problems for driving me to recreationally use drugs, but I never will and never have blamed anyone for being the reason I ever used drugs. I know it was my choice, and now it is my choice to get clean. Which also means that it is NOT your choice, and you cannot do it for me. I wanted to do it. I want to do it MY way, and I'm taking full responsibility for that. However, that doesn't mean that I am the "creator" of my problems in life. You and I both know the people we live and grow up with influence our mental self, and I am fully 100% not making myself a "victim" here, but it certainly feels like YOU are making yourself the "victim".

(Someone said) that you told them I am using HEROIN, that I came to you and said that I wanted to check myself into a full in-patient rehab, that you are so worried about me because I'm so skinny and strung out and all these things that are entirely untrue. I imagine you have told these same things to everyone else; I know you told (my grandparents) something that is a far cry from the truth because of the voicemail they left on my phone, and I don't appreciate that at all. You know that our family has always made me feel outcast and unworthy, ... (another family member) has told lies about me doing drugs long before I even touched a drug, and this stunt you pulled is only going to make that worse for me, and now I have to go through hell to gain the respect of my family back for absolutely no reason. The first and foremost thing you should know is that I am NOT using heroin, I never was using heroin, and I never told you that I was. You just assumed. I told you I didn't want to talk about it, because really there was no need to talk about it, because it was never a big deal and I didn't want you to get worked up about it. But apparently you have made some story and lifestyle up for me in your head. I told you I wanted to go

to detox. Detox, again, is NOT rehab. It is a few days where I would go through the process of withdrawal comfortably so that when I get out after A FEW DAYS, my system would be clean of ALL toxins and I would no longer feel physically compelled to take ANY drugs.

I have been speaking to (a friend), and he has been understanding, supportive, and open to helping me in the ways that I know I need help- in short, being the person I thought you could be when I initially came to you. I have also spoken to Lucy, hoping that she could have provided some helpful advice. She did; however, because of the nature of the problem and the fact that she is my boss, she asked me to speak to a professional and have them call her to confirm that I am taking action with this problem. I spoke to Margaret, hoping she could provide that professional confirmation, and to my surprise she has provided much, much more for me. I have been working with her to create a treatment plan that is right for ME and only me, because I am the only one who truly can make myself better, and know what's best for myself. Margaret will speak to you in further depth about how you can be a support, but mostly that will include backing off and letting me handle this on my own. Margaret proposed many solutions, and we found one that spoke to me, and that we are going to follow through with. I don't need your help with this; you have proven to be more of a burden than help.

I would appreciate if you would inform everyone you felt compelled to get involved with this that you made a mistake and that you were wrong, and maybe you could tell them the real story. From this point on, I am not going to let you be involved in this situation, I am going to do it on my own and go where I want for as long as I want, because I know what I need and obviously you can't help me the way I thought you could. I regret telling you more than I regret using any drugs in my whole life, and I will not be telling you anything else that goes on in my life for a long, long time.

I'm sorry for whatever damage my REAL situation has done, and I apologized as soon as I told you, if you recall, and I mean it. But I am not going to apologize for what you have made up in your head. I would have liked to work on family therapy, as I mentioned in the beginning of this, but you need to be open to my needs, and the issues I have with you, instead of just sitting back and feeling sorry for yourself.

I am doing this on my own now. I have a boyfriend who has multiple years clean and sober, who has been supporting me since day one, and shown me nothing but love and care and kindness, and if it weren't for him I probably would not have made it this far. As for me not coming home, I have not felt comfortable being in the same house as you, you blow up and lash out and make my head want to explode, and that is not an environment that I feel safe in. It actually does more harm than good for me. The time I have spent not at work, I have been at Eva's house, and that is where you can assume I am if you don't know. I need to be stress-free right now if I'm going to get through this. I need to feel like I am in a place that no obstacles will get in the way of my health. You have blown this whole thing WAY out of proportion, and it has only chased me away. I can't handle my family members, friends, and loved ones calling me left and right telling me "I need help" and "how could you do this to your mother?" and that "I'm a terrible person." It's not fair to me and is only counterproductive, not to mention they have been completely misinformed by you. Please respect my wishes and listen to Margaret and be the mother I need you to be right now.

    Kayla

It was hard to breathe. I thought we were making progress, but Kayla's assault said otherwise. I was barely able to read her shocking accusations, her denials, and her blatant lies. I sent the letter on to a trusted family member. He responded simply, "Lies, take the car."

Once again, I resolved to repossess the car. Besides wanting relief from the financial burden, I had finally concluded the car was enabling Kayla to support her drug habit. Additionally, fender benders, scrapes, and other unusually dramatic wear were steadily reducing its resale value.

Self-doubt expanded again. "Was I wrong?" I wrote. "Had I blown things out of proportion?"

Kayla's accusations were wildly inaccurate. Those regarding my communications were pure fiction. I had never said most of those things. The line between reality and illusion was blurry. *Was any of it true?*

I responded to Kayla's email:

Kayla,

> *I can't even read this. The lies flow so easily from your lips. You need help. The detox which you promised to check into is still illusive.*
>
> *Come home, get into detox, then we can reestablish a sense of normalcy. If I don't have the car back by the end of today, I will report it stolen. It is my car.*
>
> *I love you deeply and what you are doing to yourself affects all of us. I can't change you or force you, but I can do the best I can to help you realize what you are doing to your life.*
>
> *I love you; I will always love you, Mommy*

A reply email came swiftly:

> *YOU HAVE TO FUCKING READ THIS. CALL MARGARET. I CAN'T FUCKING STAND YOU.*
>
> *You are doing EVERYTHING wrong. I need you to read this and talk to Margaret before I actually do something overboard. You are a drama whore.*

Threatening self-harm was not a new tactic. Kayla well understood the depth of my love, and that my desire to keep her safe and healthy was paramount. She preyed on my insecurities, knowing she could keep me off balance. Skillfully pushing my buttons, she played me like a fiddle.

I had placed my faith and resources in Margaret's healing powers, but at times her demands tested me. Consulting Margaret about the letter, she emphatically requested I not sell the car. She asked me to give Kayla time to work through the herbal detox she had prescribed.

Reluctantly, I agreed to wait.

With the car issue suspended, at least temporarily, Margaret proceeded to lambast me for my reaction to Kayla's email. As I listened to her harsh reprimand, I felt like a five-year-old child. I heard judgment and condemnation. I heard that I was bad and unworthy. I rapidly spiraled downward.

Packed with lies and irrational claims, Kayla's email had triggered me to feel angry and defensive. Contrarily, Margaret believed the email was Kayla's way of reaching out. She viewed the email as positive communication and admonished me for "shutting her right down." She told me Kayla was working hard to heal and that I had to stop interfering with her process.

I felt shut down. I felt unheard. I felt lost. I stumbled forward as best I could.

I wrote in my journal, "In retrospect, there is merit to both sides. I feel what I feel and am entitled to that. In a perfect world I would be able to push my reactions aside and open my arms to this so called 'reaching out'. I need to learn to be non-judgmental and supportive. I need to learn to cast my ego and fear aside.

"Dear God, help me find my own center, help me get out of victim mode, help me love unconditionally—love myself, love myself, love myself—love others with clarity, find joy. Please help me to be patient. Please help me support Kayla through her struggles and not add to her struggles. Thank you for all I am and all I have, which is abundant."

Years later I would learn that Kayla's brutal accusations regarding my words and actions were the direct result of a conversation with someone I trusted.

Judgment was plaguing me. I still held a lot of judgment about drug abuse and abusers. I judged people who judged me (or who I perceived to judge me). I judged myself for what I believed to be my responsibility in causing Kayla's fall. I judged how I felt and how I thought and how I proceeded.

I wrote, "Help me to stop questioning why. Help me to see through a lens of love so that I can be at peace and accept that I have no control, nor am I responsible for others' choices, not even my daughter's. How I wish I had sent her for help when she was fifteen, but I was in denial and unable to see what was happening. Help me to forgive myself."

My harsh judgments conspired to further isolate me. The loneliness pressed hard. I felt empty as I moved through the necessities of my days. In conversation, people focused on Kayla, consistently failing to inquire about my well-being or life. I tried to smile and inquire about theirs. Lack of balance was painful. Answering questions about Kayla was painful. Having no one to confide in was painful. Being unhappy and frightened was painful.

I turned to my fantasies and thoughts of relationship with men. Living in that world, despite its inherent disappointments, was less painful than the real world. I pretended that an intimate relationship would make me better. It was a lie.

Kayla and Margaret met weekly. Alternately, the three of us met together. As became routine, Margaret began each meeting with energy work, "piecing back together energy patterns that were broken," and then we would talk. We discussed the necessity of us each taking responsibility for our own actions and what that meant in the context of Kayla's addiction. Margaret explained how I could best support Kayla as she went through the detox process and how I could best support myself as well.

Not always gentle, Margaret pushed me to the cliffs of emotion. Sometimes I was left feeling belittled, degraded, and ridiculed. Frantically seeking balance and peace, however, I pushed through. I reminded myself that I trusted Margaret professionally and personally. I was fully invested. I encouraged myself to learn and grow through the discomfort.

During one session, Margaret asked me to articulate what I loved about myself. I drew a complete blank. I felt awful. *All those years of inner work and I still couldn't find anything to love about myself? In the face of a debilitating crisis did anyone love herself?* I wondered about that elusive self-love. *If I learned to love myself, would I still feel so debilitated? Would I still hurt so much?*

Margaret also asked if I thought I was a good mom. My initial reaction was, "Really? How could I possibly think of myself as a good mom? I've raised a child who turned to drugs to numb her pain!"

As I thought about it further, however, I realized "when we know better, we do better." I had made plenty of mistakes, but I did the best I could. I loved my children without condition and worked hard to provide them with varied experiences and opportunities. I listened to what they said and didn't say, and guided as seemed appropriate. I tried hard to protect them while also giving them wings. I laughed with them, dreamed with them, and cried with them. I worked to empower them with strength and resolve to move through life's struggles. I supported them in self-discovery and encouraged them to feel their feelings. I respected that they each had a unique path and worked to help them find their way. I recognized I was not the only influence in their lives. I tried to let go of that over which I had no control.

Though I was certainly a work in progress, deep down I knew I WAS a good mom. I also knew I had to find the courage to do for myself what I wanted to do, and did, for my children.

Given my inability to answer in the moment, Margaret suggested I make a list of what I loved about myself at home. I journaled prolifically, seeking strength to complete the assignment. Eventually I found the confidence to begin. My writing ended with the following statement, "My biggest failure is to think I am failing others. The truth is, I am failing me."

As Margaret challenged me to do my own work, I trusted she was pushing Kayla similarly. Though I missed Kayla terribly, not facing the day-to-day assault of attitude and lies was a great relief.

I had been hungry for an expert to tell me how to proceed and desperate to hand my worries to someone else. I wanted to hear things were progressing and to believe we were on the right track. I wanted my daughter back. I wanted to wake from the nightmare. For a while I got what I wanted. I chose to believe Kayla was improving. I worked toward my own healing. I held onto hope.

CHAPTER ELEVEN:

CALM BEFORE THE STORM

After many months, my ex-boyfriend and I were talking again, revisiting the idea of friendship. I appreciated Leo's apparent support. His father had been an alcoholic, and Leo demonstrated an understanding of my struggles that most others could not. I still loved him, or at least maintained a fantasy of love. At the same time, with limited contact, my desire for and frustration with him forced me to look inward for answers.

Leo was often busy with his children; watching their sporting events, taking them on college tours, and going on fantastic vacations. I was jealous of the time he spent with them and not with me. I envied his financial ability to provide for his children what I could not provide for mine.

In many ways, I viewed Leo as a perfect parent. So devoted to his children, he sacrificed his personal pleasure (time with me) to enrich their lives. By believing such thoughts, I accentuated my own guilt. I berated myself, highlighting that while he seemed to do everything for and with his kids, I struggled to get out of bed. Old patterns of self-loathing and guilt snuck up on me.

But things were never quite the way they seemed. Once again, I reminded myself I had done the best I could with what I had. Besides, I was watching Leo's behaviors through rose-colored glasses. I well knew my view was selective and that he had his own issues from which he ran. At least, I reasoned, I was willing to look at my problems and work toward healing.

I urged myself to focus on the next healthy relationship. I pushed myself to see beyond my self-made fantasy to the truth. Once again, the call came to love myself.

Day to day, I struggled with my health. Whether or not I consciously acknowledged the worry and fear, my body felt it and was speaking loudly. I sought the tools that kept me going: affirmations, yoga, meditation, nature, art, journaling. Deep down I knew I would be okay.

Iris, the woman who'd opened her home to Kayla, reached out to discuss "our Kayla."

"I have no problem with her staying with us for a while," Iris wrote, "particularly if it's to allow you guys time to work on your relationship. I know how difficult our girls can be! I just hope my allowing her to do so hasn't caused you any discontent; that's the last thing I want for you."

Kayla had been unofficially living at Iris's house for over a month.

Iris continued, "I hope I'm not being too forward or out of line... I was hoping you could let me know your thoughts on what the problem/issue is between you. I think she's been here long enough now that I should prompt her to begin to solve her problems and work toward healing your relationship. ...I just don't want her staying here to escape her responsibilities and avoid the issue at hand..."

Iris had already spoken with Kayla. Kayla told her our discord had to do with "some drug related issues," but denied any responsibility.

Embarrassed for not reaching out first, I embraced Iris's communication and concern, and offered to chat over coffee. I wasn't sure what Iris understood about Kayla's condition and was terrified that if I confessed, she might ask Kayla to leave.

We met at an outside café. I was prepared to tell Iris everything I knew, without filter, and braced for the worst. To my great surprise and relief, Iris revealed that she already knew Kayla was addicted to heroin. She explained that she had seen it before and said her experiences taught her to have a thick skin.

Iris considered Kayla "like her own." She assured me she would get Kayla back on track. She said she was strong and able, and was "in for the long haul."

I offered to pay Iris for the expense of having Kayla live with her. She vigorously refused. Knowing about my financial struggles, she told me to take care of my home and the child who still lived there. She insisted she was able to manage just fine.

Disclosing that she was quite strict, Iris set forth her expectations. Less emotionally attached or easily manipulated, she would demand that Kayla toe the line with chores, curfew, and more. Iris felt that as a "guest," Kayla would be more respectful and compliant. She intended to hold Kayla one hundred percent accountable for her behavior.

Fully understanding what she was up against (much more clearly than me at that point), Iris assured me she would "see Kayla through this." Relief and gratitude swept over me. I cried. Another angel sat before me. In my naiveté, I found respite and hope.

Over the following weeks, Iris would offer me considerable support. Seeming to know exactly what I needed to hear, she advised, "You can only do so much for everyone on your own before it starts to beat you down. Focus on making yourself well first."

As March concluded, it appeared that Kayla's health was improving. Margaret validated my impression. She was residing in a safe environment, our ability to communicate improved, and her previous rants and irrational demands quieted.

Knowing how much I abhorred her smoking habit and feared for her health, one evening Kayla texted that she decided to quit smoking cigarettes. To that end, she had purchased Nicorette gum but emphasized, "no promises."

Not unlike her mom, Kayla could be "all or none" in her behaviors. I chuckled at her new focus and applauded her effort. I cautioned her not to bite off more than she could chew. Faced with the choice between heroin and nicotine, I had accepted that she would continue smoking.

Nonetheless, I felt hopeful. I reasoned that for Kayla to focus on her smoking habit, she must have her drug habit well under control. I viewed her declaration as a testament to her progress and found gratitude in the possibility.

CHAPTER TWELVE:
HALF CENTURY

After receiving my master's degree in May of the previous year, my parents wanted to throw me a celebratory party. I had consistently objected. On the occasion of my half-century birthday, they redoubled their efforts.

Sadly, I had no energy to surround myself with people or celebrate. My life was in perpetual crisis, and my body was in chronic fibromyalgic flare. Not being one to socialize in groups anyway, I found uneasy comfort in quiet isolation. To my parents' disappointment, I insisted there be no party.

My singular birthday wish was to enjoy dinner with those whom I loved most in the world, my children and parents. With my oldest living in the city, and Kayla living with Eva, it had been a long time since I had my family all together. Mom and Dad graciously agreed to treat us.

Having planned a nurturing day for myself, on April 2, 2012, Avery and I woke early, got in the car by eleven o'clock, and headed to the Edwin B. Forsythe National Wildlife Refuge where salt water met fresh water and all kinds of migrating birds stopped for fuel. A two-hour drive, we took our time, stopping for a lovely lunch on the way. The weather was perfect. I loved watching the birds and breathing in the sea air. It was rejuvenating.

Mid-day, Kayla texted, "Happy Birthday!" Then she texted that she had a gift for me. Upon my return home, I found Kayla's gift waiting on the bench beside my front door. Knowing my love for birds, the canvas she left featured a bright yellow goldfinch she had drawn and painted with acrylics. It was still wet.

Kayla's deeply personal gesture and thoughtful effort warmed me. I felt hopeful. I wondered why she didn't wait to give it to me at dinner.

After cleaning up and changing our clothes, Avery and I headed out to collect Gabriel from his workplace. Mom and Dad were already at the Italian restaurant when we arrived. We waited for Kayla.

Finally arriving more than half an hour late, it was clear Kayla was high. She looked disheveled, and big, black circles accented her tired eyes. When questioned, she made artful excuses.

Wanting to enjoy my fiftieth birthday, I tried not to dwell. I chose to embrace and cherish the time I had with my family. On their best behavior, no one addressed the obvious, but anxiety was palpable. We made neutral conversation and got through the meal.

My heart hurt. I wiped away tears as I drove home.

CHAPTER THIRTEEN:
SELF PRESERVATION

Trouble had been brewing within some of my family relationships for some time. Instead of caring conversation, barking often took center stage as the primary mode of communication. Striving for cordiality at family gatherings, I tried not to create additional friction.

A week after my birthday, at my parents' house for a holiday meal, a pressure cooker blew. Years of pent-up disgruntlements were unleashed, rushing accusations of my wrongdoings toward me. Taken off guard, I silently absorbed the unexpected assault. At its conclusion, with the oxygen sucked out of my lungs, I left my parents' house and sought refuge in my car. Sitting in the driver's seat, I raged, wept, and processed. When my body stopped shaking, I drove home.

I had long before learned "what you defend becomes real." I was not interested in lending validity to the onslaught of complaints. I was not interested in adding fuel to that fire. Ultimately, I concluded the attack was not about me; rather, it was about the attacker. While I would spend time reflecting on my own behavior, I knew, instinctively, in that moment, I had to preserve what little energy I could. I had to step away from toxic behaviors, old patterns, and unrealistic demands. I was trying to survive. I wanted to heal. We all had issues to work through.

Living with the horror of Kayla's addiction while trying to maintain a stable environment for my youngest child and myself, I was in self-preservation mode. I had to set a boundary that asserted, "I will not tolerate being treated this way."

Setting boundaries was empowering but not painless. My resolve and consequent actions didn't solely impact me. My whole family was affected. As I ceased going to family events, their expectations for my participation were shattered. Because I chose not to discuss the accusations levied at me, the family grew more frustrated with me. I was doing what I had to do. I had no control over their judgment. I tried to detach.

I received a letter in which the concluding words were, "I am so done with you." Such a mandate left little room for negotiation or reconciliation. I accepted the impasse.

In truth, I felt done too. I was no longer willing to expose myself to abuse. While I twisted with self-defeating thoughts about being a "bad girl," I also felt relief. Pleasing others took a lot of energy. I was no longer willing to please at my own expense.

Nonetheless, with the best of intentions, family members took turns pointing out my failings and encouraging me to settle things. They inadvertently pushed me further away. I had come too far to turn back. I had to honor my needs.

For over a year, I declined to go to holiday dinners and other gatherings where the potential for confrontation was present. As an unexpected benefit, I was spared the endless and painful questions about Kayla's health. But being demonized by family brought a different pain. I was alone, clinging to a life raft in the middle of an ocean of fear.

Not surprisingly, with the added stress, my fibromyalgia got worse and my emotions began spiraling downward again. I circulated those old, comfortable feelings of failure and self-loathing. My body was rejecting me, my work barely paid the bills, I had no romantic relationship, and obviously I was a failure as a parent. Darkness came swiftly.

Fortunately, I was getting better at moving negative feelings out, replacing dysfunctional thoughts with healthier ones. I had to focus on healing and was determined to succeed. I had to find compassion for myself and for my inner child who wept silently. I affirmed, "I will be strong. I will be happy."

By mid-month, Kayla's honeymoon with Iris was over. Iris texted, "I had it out with Kayla last night over her ignoring repeated requests to clean the landfill which used to be my guest room. She has flat out disrespected me, which I am taking care of in my own way," and, "I wouldn't be surprised if she decides to move home very soon…I didn't want you to be unprepared for the possible onslaught of victim outrage she might be slinging your way today…. sorry."

I feared it was only a matter of time before Iris would be fed up and kick Kayla out. "And then what?" I wondered.

As predicted, Kayla began to text about the great injustices she had to endure living with Iris. Considering my options, I knew having her come home was more than I could handle. At the same time, I wasn't prepared to turn her out on the street. With great dread, I mentally prepared for the possibility of her return home. *A good parent would let her come home, right?* She was my responsibility and I would do what I had to do.

To my great surprise, Iris remained kind and remarkably supportive of my feelings. When I asked how she was doing, she assured me, "I'm fine doll."

Iris's lighthearted response provided me immense relief. She continued to apprise me of Kayla's abhorrent behaviors and whereabouts. She asked only that if Kayla moved home,

I let her know so she didn't worry. I was abundantly grateful for her help.

I relayed Iris's updates to Margaret, who counseled that Kayla was deliberately behaving badly to force Iris to kick her out. She instructed me not to let her move home, commenting, "She can sleep in her car or call her dad."

For many years, the kids and I shared a cell phone plan. As I questioned Kayla's behavior and progress, it occurred to me that I could "eavesdrop" on her phone activity. Viewing phone records, I found a repeated dial to what I learned was a known, local drug dealer. In addition, there were multiple, frequent calls to an inner city where drugs were abundant. My antennae were once again quivering, demanding I pay attention.

I shared my discovery with Margaret. She remained unconcerned; assuring me she was "detangling...peeling off the layers of illusion and delusion for you both..." She felt the work she was doing with Kayla was shifting her on a deep level and that the objectionable daily behaviors would change in time.

Once again, I placed my faith in Margaret's expertise and dismissed the warnings.

Meanwhile, Kayla was texting long tirades complaining about the unfair treatment she was receiving at Iris's house.

She insisted that Iris's demands were crazy and unreasonable, and she began to plead her case to move back home.

"I'm so sad all the time because I'm in an environment that tells me I'm just a waste of space, a liar, and a thief," Kayla texted.

Additional texts followed: "Mommy, I'm so sad. I'm ready to be home. I have come all the way and I'm ready to be home," and, "I'm tired of being here Mom. I'm locked out all the time. I have to let myself in through the back door, which is IMPOSSIBLE to open, and it's just not right anymore. I need to be home. It's time."

Despite Kayla's pleas, I knew it was not time for her to move back home. Such a move would be a detriment to us all. Though she had been visiting more regularly, I always sent her back to Iris's, obeying Margaret's advice and my gut instinct.

One evening, after leaving my house and returning to Iris's, Kayla texted, "I really hate this."

Feeling the ache in her words, my heart sank. I hated it too. It took all of my strength to send her back to Iris's. I yearned for her to be home in my embrace. I yearned for her to be healthy.

Trying to fortify us both, I replied, "Kayla, think of how far you have come. It will only get better. Sad is ok. Feel what you feel. I love you so much."

The battle between what I knew was best for Kayla, and for Avery and me, and the emotional yearning for life to return to "normal," posed a daily challenge. I had to be firm, I had to stay strong, I cried in silence.

As Kayla's petition to come home intensified, sorting through the disparate accounts of "the truth" became mind numbing. Iris told me Kayla was uncooperative, a complete slob, disrespectful, and defiant. Kayla told me Iris was unreasonable, unrelenting, irrational, and that "every time I move or breathe, I'm gonna be in trouble." Margaret reiterated that Kayla was creating chaos in order to come home and that I was absolutely not to let her.

Kayla obsessively flooded texts of sadness and abuse to my phone. She insisted she was clean and ready. I was spinning and aching for real connection with my daughter. There was no peace. Over and over, I returned to trust.

Trusting the Universe was a powerful action. Although in some ways it felt like a copout, I truly believed I would be guided to the next right step. I trusted that things were in perfect order, albeit painful. Again, I focused on healing me, learning from what was happening, feeling for my intuition, and accepting the guidance given by the professional I had hired.

I recognized that wanting to protect my children from pain was a natural parental instinct. As I yearned to help them through their respective challenges, I often had to restrain my inner caretaker. After all, "help" was a subjective verb. Pain often motivated forward movement and personal growth. Certainly, I wouldn't have chosen pain for myself either, but little by little I was growing as a result ... and the pain kept coming.

Unable to sustain the onslaught of Kayla's demands to come home, I told her outright I would not permit her to return. I relayed Margaret's sentiments: she was creating chaos in order to manipulate coming home, and she could leave Iris's house whenever she wanted and live in her car.

Masterful with words, Kayla reacted with fire, "So basically, even if (Iris) kicked me out, you'd make me live on the street? No, I'm not trying to get her to kick me out, but the more she gives me ultimatums and makes me feel like shit, the more I just want her to throw me out."

I urged Kayla to start appreciating Iris for giving her a place to live, food, even clothing. I encouraged her to make peace, and to be gracious and humble. I reminded Kayla, "She was there for you in your time of need. She cares. Be thankful, even if you are angry."

Kayla shot back, "Here's the deal. I'm tired of living under a roof where I am accused of lying and stealing and a whole slew of things that I have changed and I have worked so HARD to not lie and steal. She accuses me of lying if I tell her that my phone died…literally everything, and there is not one thing I have stolen. I have been through hell and back, done everything within reason that is expected of me and sacrificed a LOT to be the better person I am now. Right now there's nothing left for me to change. I am more than willing to admit where I am wrong, but here I am only BEING wronged. I am not going to keep myself in this environment anymore…. I was told two weeks and I'd be home. I will not live here past then. I CAN'T."

Naïve and emotional, and eager to please my daughter and ease her pain, I was ignorant to the billowing lies and manipulation in Kayla's communication. I was unaware that within those texts laid confirmation of continued addiction.

Kayla claimed she was "cured." Clean and sober people understood that addiction remained a part of them forever, never "cured." If actually recovered, she would have referred to herself as "in recovery." She obsessively complained about her struggle and sacrifice, and constantly claimed she was being wronged. If she were in healthy recovery, she would have acknowledged personal responsibility, not only for her life, but also for the damage she had levied as a result of her choices. There was no humility, gratitude, or grace in her attitude.

Kayla's comment, "nothing left for me to change," offered the most damning evidence of continued addiction. That wasn't true for anyone, especially not someone who was recently abusing drugs to numb her pain.

And then there were the threats. The ultimatums. The indignation.

I sought to distance myself from the charge of Kayla's anger. My empathic sensitivity easily absorbed the pain I perceived. There was no question Kayla was hurting, but I didn't need her pain to be my pain.

We battled back and forth. Kayla was relentless about her need/demand to come home. I stayed firm in my opposition, fortified by my expert's advice. Margaret reassured me that Kayla was not in harm's way. She insisted Kayla had to take responsibility for her situation. She felt there were too many "holes in Kayla's stories," rendering the claims about her living conditions improbable.

I trusted Kayla was, in fact, creating her reality, and only Kayla could change it. My heart was locked in an unbearable tug of war with my head.

Kayla's pleas pounded me:

"I feel that my whole self has changed and when I hear Margaret say nothing has changed it makes me feel like all my hard work is for nothing and honestly, I want to give up. I'm not giving up though. I'm frustrated and I'm sad and I feel like the place I'm in is keeping me from moving forward more. I'm just looking to get this moving FASTER. It's almost the end of April. I'm not where I want to be."

"I'm hearing that I should just accept being treated like dirt and I won't be allowed to come home until I don't want to. I know when I'm victimizing myself and I'm really not here. I'm being treated like I'm not human and that's not okay."

"I am humble and grateful, but there is a line and it has been crossed."

"I'm working my ass off to make this right. When can I come home?"

"I want to be home with my mommy."

I tried to meet my daughter's drama and manipulation with compassion and reason. I encouraged her to do what I was doing; take steps to heal, to love herself, to change her experience. I urged her to look deep inside and fix what was damaged. I reminded her that no one could take away the truth.

Nothing made sense when dealing with an addict. Kayla would use any means to wear me down. She preyed on my ignorance, compassion, guilt, and fear.

Over the following days I received pages of texts. Always pushing her agenda to come home, Kayla complained vehemently about living with Iris. She said she felt abused and misunderstood, reviled and alone. She begged me to let her return to her own bedroom and resisted any explanation I offered for why I wouldn't. She made no attempt to be reasonable. Every text became an attack as Kayla twisted my words to her advantage. I often found myself doubting even the things I said with utmost confidence. That wasn't new.

Though I knew, at least in part, Kayla was reacting to Iris's tough love; self-doubt, guilt, and heartbreak held my hand. I didn't realize I was at the precipice of embracing tough love also.

CHAPTER FOURTEEN

THE WALLS CRUMBLE

It had been almost two months since I had hired Margaret to work with Kayla. As April was coming to an end, I discovered a crushing truth. Kayla had stolen my credit card, charging thousands of dollars to unknown vendors. The most recent charge had only been a few days prior.

Shaking, crying, swirling, I felt profound confusion, followed by despair. My heart raced, my face flushed, and my stomach churned as I processed the betrayal inherent in Kayla's act. I couldn't breathe. Panic, rage, sorrow, and fear cycled in a vicious tornado, ripping everything solid from my grip. *She stole my cash, my jewelry, Avery's electronics, and now my credit. How could she stoop so low? How could she do this to me?*

I was in shock.

I reached out to Margaret.

Margaret responded, "Breathe...call the credit card company. Do damage control... I will call you later."

I knew the credit card company would cancel the card and credit the funds, pending investigation. I also knew there were bigger problems with which to contend. Kayla was still stealing my money. That was assuredly not the behavior of someone who was clean.

Perhaps most distressing were the legal implications and the looming question of whether or not to press charges. "Should I report my child?" I wondered. "Should I impel her into legal trouble that will last a lifetime? Should I allow her to face the natural consequences of her behavior?" I was devastated and terrified. *What was the right action? How could I choose?*

Another crushing blow came days later. Kayla had also stolen my checks.

In my head, hard line voices shouted, "She has to hit bottom!" "She's made her own mess and has to be held responsible!" "Don't enable her!" Softer, opposing voices pleaded, "Don't add to her mess," "She shouldn't have a felony on her record," "God forbid she go to jail."

I was tortured. *If I prevent natural consequences, am I enabling her to use again?* It was an impossible Catch-22.

An immediate reaction could have resulted in catastrophe. I took time to reflect and consider the right response. I changed my mind a dozen times.

Ultimately, the thought of my baby in jail was more than I could handle. I was not emotionally prepared to be the impetus for her legal consequences. I wanted to save my daughter, not make her life harder. On the other hand, I wondered if serious legal consequences could shock her into sobriety by proving the drug life was no life. I weighed each side carefully. I called Kayla.

When Kayla didn't answer my phone calls, I texted what I had discovered and demanded a response. Within moments she feverishly texted back:

"Every time I used (your credit card) I wanted to die. I know this is the worst thing in the world, and obviously now I won't be coming home even though it's the only thing in the world I want. I am sorry and I know you're pissed and don't believe me, but now I just don't know what to do with myself or anything. I don't have a reason to live."

"I had every intention of telling you though. And I AM clean."

"I wish I had never done it."

"And I'm gonna pay every cent of it."

"I actually just applied for a second job last night. I'm trying to do the right thing Mom. I really am. I used it when I was on drugs and then I stopped for like a month when I got clean. I started using it because I felt like I had no other choice. I felt so pressured all the time and I'm so depressed and I don't want to lie to you anymore. I just want to come home. I don't care if you lock me in my room for the rest of my life. I want to come home and I want to go to school and I want to be a normal person again. I'm sorry I'm the worst person in the world, but all the work I've done and getting clean, that is real. I don't want to work with Margaret anymore. I just wanna do the right thing and come home. I never wanted to hurt you."

"Can you please just do me a favor and not tell my (siblings or grandparents). Please. I will do whatever you want me to do, just don't tell them."

Flashing, neon, red flags were flying in every direction. I was angry, I was hurt, but mostly, I was terrified. I could not, would not agree to Kayla's conditions. I told her to do the hard work of changing her ways and her thinking.

I questioned Kayla about her sudden disillusionment with Margaret. She told me, "It's taking too long with Margaret, Mom. I'm so depressed that I can't even function and it's because I want to be home. I feel like Margaret doesn't listen to me or what I want. I NEED things to move faster.... I don't understand what the hard work is. I was pretty sure I did all the hard work. I've been depressed for ten years. It's unrealistic to not let me home until I'm 'happy.' I don't know what else to do and I'm getting no direction from Margaret. I need to come home."

As an afterthought Kayla added, "But it's not like I was using it to buy drugs. I don't even think that is possible."

Unsteady and distraught, I met with Margaret to discuss the situation. She mandated that Kayla and I not communicate with each other until further notice. She insisted that I "leave it alone" and that "Kayla was making good progress." In addition, Margaret instructed me "not to tell anyone."

I was awash in confusion. My emotions were raw. Everything seemed blurry. *What, specifically, was I supposed to keep quiet about? The credit card fraud? The work we were doing with Margaret? Her opinions?* I had a lot to process and "not telling anyone" was an unrealistic impediment. I needed support and emotional nourishment.

On top of everything else, I had torn my calf muscle. Hobbling through my days, the additional physical pain and exhaustion imposed a new sense of vulnerability. Overwhelmed again, terror took center stage.

In an effort to help my calf heal, my mom had offered to lend me a shin brace. Needing some tender loving care, as well as wanting to pick up the brace, I left my meeting with Margaret and headed to my parents' house. My dad was home alone.

When I felt most challenged, I could always count on Daddy to hold me gently, validate me, and convince me things would be ok. He took one look at me and knew I was in bad shape. He questioned me with concern, compassion, and urgency. He wanted to help me and I wanted his help.

I tried to stay strong and silent. As my father repeatedly expressed his concern and asked me what was wrong, the emotional pressure mounted. Finally, my main burst. I spilled forth what had happened.

Sharing my burden with my dad provided a moment of relief. I worried about the impact the news would have on him, but reasoned that he and my mom could support each other. Mindful of Margaret's mandate, I implored him to keep the information strictly between him and Mom (I would never ask that a secret be kept from a spouse). I emphasized that the rest of the family was not to know. I went home to weep.

In addition to her mandate not to speak with Kayla and not to tell anyone, Margaret had also asked me to formulate a written list of requirements for Kayla to return home. Later that evening, I responded to her request in an email:

> I am NOT remotely thinking about taking (Kayla) back currently. This betrayal runs deep. I simply don't trust anything coming from her lips. She was so convincingly sober and "honest," and it all came crashing down. This was a deliberate, calculated lie right up until I caught it. She begged me for gas and cigarettes when all the while she was having a field day with my money...or lack thereof. I want to know what she is going to do to make Avery and me whole. I want to know why I should EVER trust a word she says. She is an actress and she has caught me in her drama one too many times. She may want to destroy herself, but I can't let her take Avery and I with her. I'm sickened.
>
> I think the car should be sold. I don't want to pay her way anymore, not the car, or the insurance, or the liability. I've considered letting charges be pressed on her for the credit card theft. Maybe that would shake

*her up enough to heal. Maybe the state would send
her to rehab. She has the ability to work thirty hours a
week She works half of that, maybe, and then STEALS
money. She will have to work those thirty hours consistently and get another job, and a good part of that
money will have to go to me.*

Though I didn't believe there was any likelihood that
Kayla would come home, I made a list. I required proof
that Kayla had changed her ways (was 100% clean), repayment of the stolen money, proof of hours worked, a sense
of safety for Avery and me, no boyfriends in the house, new
productive outlets that didn't include drug friends, a clean
room, and contribution to the upkeep of the house.

As the crisis progressed, I became aware of a recur-
ring, alarming undertone in Margaret's communications.
Despite her ongoing counsel, she seemed to be intentionally
discouraging our continued work together. Though money
was an issue, I had made it clear I was willing to continue
paying. The truth was, I preferred the financial burden to
the emotional. Margaret's employ was the only thing giving
me hope.

CHAPTER FIFTEEN:
CAN IT GET WORSE?

Unexpectedly, Kayla showed up at my house. Hurt and angry, I was willing to abide by Margaret's order not to communicate. Besides, I saw no real benefit to a visit. I simply couldn't listen to Kayla's excuses and demands anymore. Without allowing any conversation, I sent her away.

As Kayla registered my resolve, the blood drained from her already pale face, and her body succumbed to the disappointment. Dejected, she turned and walked slowly down the path, away from the house. Without hope or purpose, she was a lost soul.

I didn't know how to manage the crushing emotions I felt. Ripped from my flesh, my heart lay devastated on the hard earth. *What was I doing? How could I send her away?* There were no good answers. The tears rushed out.

I isolated myself. There was nothing else to do. I knew I had support, but no one was going to fix the mess for me. It was tedious to field uninformed advice or pretend life was fine. As I searched for relief, I wondered if things would be different if I had a man in my life. I felt alone and fragile.

I chose to sit in my pain. There was nowhere to run. I had hoped for Kayla's return home as much as she had. Obsessively replaying the past, I twisted in the easy lies she told me. I recounted the passionate texts she sent, proclaiming her readiness to move home. I cursed the knowledge that all the while she was deceitfully spending my money.

In my journal I wrote, "'Be strong,' that's what they say. 'She has to hit bottom.' 'You can't change her.' I know all this, yet she is my flesh, my breath, my baby. How do you just shut those feelings down? How do you move through life with this gaping hole in your heart? I don't know where to turn anymore. I'm just numb. I spend a lot of time alone, even with people around."

I began receiving calls that Kayla wasn't at work. The illusion of sobriety was rapidly disintegrating.

The chaos intensified. My dad shared his grief with the wrong people. As a result, Kayla was fielding a barrage of texts berating her for what she'd done. The texts seemed deliberately designed to demean and humiliate.

Understandably, Kayla was unnerved by the attacks. She repeatedly reached out to Margaret for guidance. Margaret wasn't responding.

Margaret left me a voicemail conveying the following sentiment: You didn't listen to me, I can't work this way, I wish you and Kayla good luck.

Summarily, Margaret had cut us off.

Stunned and frantic, I called Margaret to clarify what I believed to be a gross misunderstanding. She didn't answer or return my call. Resigned, I called Kayla to deliver the news.

Despite her previous comment about wanting to discontinue work with Margaret, Kayla was predictably distressed. "Mom, I need Margaret, she's my lifeline," she pleaded.

I advised Kayla to contact Margaret herself, assuring her that Margaret would never be so insensitive or unprofessional as to leave her hanging. Kayla immediately sent Margaret a text saying, "Please don't quit, I need you."

Margaret replied, "Don't worry, I'll be in touch."

Kayla never heard from Margaret again.

Kayla and I would navigate the future together. We were both in shock and beyond disappointed by Margaret's choices. I was worried for Kayla's health, and tortured about how we would proceed. With surprising confidence, Kayla assured me, "Now is the time to move forward."

With assaults still coming, Kayla texted, "I understand why (you told my grandfather), but can you please keep this in mind the next time I ask you not to tell the family something? Even if it's something little. I don't anticipate anything this bad happening EVER again, but this is exactly what happened when you found out I was using. I asked you not to tell and then you told one person and suddenly everyone knew, but they really didn't know what they were talking about."

In a bizarre turn, I had become the bad guy, groveling for Kayla's forgiveness. I defended myself, insisting I told my father because I needed support. After all, I was going through a lot too.

It was incomprehensibly ironic. I had a drug-addicted daughter who stole my credit and checks, and was demanding I abide by her rules. *Was I supposed to follow her rules to my own detriment? Why was I following HER rules?* Nothing made sense. I was racked with guilt.

Feeling betrayed and somewhat indignant over his breach of confidence, I confronted my dad. He humbly apologized and told me he should no longer be involved, not to tell him anything, that it would be better if he didn't know so he couldn't make the same mistake again. He said he didn't "want to create any more problems" for me.

I was devastated by my father's response. I understood he was hurt by my confrontation, and I knew he felt badly about his misjudgment. More than anything, however, I needed his counsel and support. I wanted him to be there for me. His declaration left me feeling completely abandoned and more alone than ever. I was struggling to tread water.

Taking the blame for how things were unfolding, I berated myself for telling my dad in the first place. *Why would I put him in that position? What was I thinking?* I convinced myself I was wrong to have said anything. I ridiculed myself for being weak, selfish, and foolish. I agonized over my own bad judgment. While I wanted my parents to understand what was happening in my life and appreciated their support, I should have known better than to share. In that moment, I felt as though I had lost my whole family and that I was the worst human in the world.

I apologized to Kayla and relayed her grandfather's apology as well. I took full responsibility for betraying her and for instigating Margaret's decision to stop working with us. I was apologizing for not keeping her drug induced, bad behaviors secret! I was upside down and turned around.

Feeding on my insecurities, Kayla continued to levy demands. She was good at that. She told me she enjoyed her privacy and if she were ever to trust ME, she would need my assurance that I would keep all information about her confidential. It was all so confusing. I had created a mess.

As insults and accusations escalated publicly on social media and privately via text, Kayla sought my counsel. I wrote to her, "We will have to figure this out together, but I can tell you two things...1) if you are clean there is hope, and 2) trust needs to be earned."

I advised that a fire couldn't be sustained without fuel. I told Kayla to stop engaging, which she did. Though I was still reeling from the credit card theft, I was eager to find a space for healing between us. I was glad she reached out to me for help.

After seeing the public hostility levied at Kayla, Iris lovingly lent her support, addressing the comments she read on social media with wisdom and grace. I was encouraged by her input. "It hasn't been an easy road for (Kayla)," Iris wrote, "and until she's okay with herself, she won't be able to work on relationships with others. Just some food for thought... Sadly, there are casualties in situations like this.

I can feel your hurt and frustration just from the few comments you've made, and I'm sorry for that."

As public and private attacks escalated, I chose to intercede in an effort to create understanding and compassion. I explained that we were dealing with our crisis as best we could and if anyone felt slighted or attacked, it was not intentional. I said that it was a personal crisis and pointed out that everyone deals with crisis differently. I apologized for any hurt feelings.

Additionally, I asked for love and support instead of name-calling, accusation, judgment, and hostility. I suggested that when Kayla and I could share, we would, and I asked that our process be respected. I invited inquiry and said we would answer questions as we were able.

As a final request, I implored, "Please don't be cruel because you disagree with the way we are handling this crisis."

I received responses that confirmed none of what I had attempted to communicate was heard. Despite my best efforts, the beratement continued. Appalled, disappointed, and profoundly hurt and saddened, Kayla and I were strangely united. In some ways it brought us closer than we had been for months, and that felt good.

Expressing her anguish, Kayla texted, "I'm so fucking tired of people in our family thinking it's okay to speak to me like a piece of shit. I deserve an apology and they need to know that when I say it's none of their business, it's really none of their fucking business."

I tried to be compassionate. I tried to be supportive. I tried to shift the focus. I encouraged Kayla to take responsibility for her own actions and move forward for her own sake. Kayla's words, "Family shouldn't do that," echoed in my thoughts.

I wrote in my journal, "Funny thing about family, they say they love you but when you most need their support, they feel threatened and lash out."

I was drowning again, still. I sought reason and respite in what I knew to be true: Change instigated reaction. Our "tribe," those people with whom we were in closest relationship, relied on us to behave in a predictable manner. When we shifted, fear and instability sometimes arose, prompting negative backlash. It wasn't conscious but could be loud and ugly.

I had no idea what the future held, but one thing I knew for sure; Kayla and I were changing every day. Without a doubt our tribe was reacting, and it wasn't pleasant. At a time when we needed the most understanding, we were receiving the least.

For months I had blindly followed Margaret's advice and obeyed her directions. Without Margaret's counsel, I needed to once again determine the best way to navigate my relationship with my daughter. I still didn't know the signs of drug addiction and was eager to believe the words Kayla spoke. Though incongruent with my observations, I clung tightly to the promise that she was clean.

CHAPTER SIXTEEN:
ANOTHER PROFESSIONAL

It was May, another new month. A friend inquired about my health. My reply said it all, "Things here have been mostly a roller coaster of hell, with an occasional pause at the top of the hill when you think it might be turning around.... I am hopeful that Kayla is clean at this point but can't be sure. There are so many layers. She has not lived at home for about three months. Child support was cut off even though for months her recovery has been costing three times the weekly contribution... I feel very isolated, and yet, my friends keep me going. I'm blessed that way. We are switching gears in her recovery, another story."

I suggested that Kayla go back to her old therapist. She had worked with Dr. Menni while she was in high school, and we both liked and trusted him. It seemed a logical next step since it was clear she still had emotional issues to work through. I could hear the excitement and relief in her positive response. I was delighted that Kayla wanted help.

I called Dr. Menni that night. He agreed to see Kayla and work with us on a sliding scale. He understood the addiction issue personally, explaining that he had addressed it in his own family. I felt relief and guarded optimism. Another angel was in my midst.

Following the social media attack in which Iris defended Kayla, Iris reached out to me with understandable concern. She was feeling "out of the loop" and wondered what provoked the vile public exchange she had witnessed. She asked to be informed.

My previous indiscretion had caused enough damage. Feeling gun-shy, I was not willing to risk causing more. I told Iris I was not at liberty to tell her and thanked her profusely for everything she was doing for Kayla.

Ever respectful, kind, and gracious, Iris accepted my response without argument. She said she knew how much love Kayla and I had for each other, and was angry that members of our family were being so insensitive and cruel. I was relieved and grateful for her continued support.

Days later, Iris sent an email in which she accused me of holding animosity toward Kayla, not doing enough for her, and not being forthright with my "agenda." She went on to say that she had seen positive changes in Kayla and that if Kayla were to continue living with her, she would need to charge rent.

Admittedly, I had been remiss in communicating consistently with Iris. Caught up in my world of woes, and unsure that I could think or act with clarity, I had avoided contact. Additionally, I was terrified Iris would kick Kayla out and worried obsessively about what I would do if that happened. I was paralyzed by fear and had chosen to avoid rather than confront. I ran from my perceived pain, and I was wrong.

Feeling embarrassed, ashamed, and weak, I responded by email:

> I'm sorry ...I respect that hosting Kayla is a responsibility you never asked for, and you have both my gratitude for taking her in and my apologies that our lives have unfolded in this way... (Kayla and my) relationship has become deeply damaged. She and I are working hard to come back to a point of mutual trust. Until such a time, I cannot allow her to come home, but I assure you it is our goal. I'm sorry our plans cannot be more concrete than that. In the meantime, I am glad you have nurtured discipline and responsibility in Kayla, and I think that it is entirely fair for you to charge her rent.... I continue to try to do what I believe is right for Kayla, Avery, and myself. It is only reasonable that I encourage you to do what you believe is right for you and Eva.
>
> I will do my best to answer any dangling questions you have.

I informed Iris of our plan to see Dr. Menni again.

Kindheartedly, Iris replied that she was angry with herself because she had been unable to fix the situation. She expressed great joy in recognizing the love between Kayla and me, and reassured me that trust would return. She also said Kayla had mentioned Dr. Menni and was excited to resume with him.

Relief swept over me.

A few nights later, Kayla showed up at my home. She was thoughtful, loving, and considerate. She had been locked out of Iris's house and uncertain when Iris or Eva might return to let her in. It was a stormy night. Wanting to wait in my house, she assured me she would leave as soon as Iris or Eva came back. By the time Iris returned, Kayla was fast asleep in my bed.

I allowed Kayla to stay, grateful to have her with me yet simultaneously unsettled and nervous. I couldn't help but wonder if she would leave with valued belongings she would sell for drugs. I slept uneasily.

In the morning, I sent Kayla back to Iris's house. Though she didn't want to go, and I very much wanted to let her stay, I wasn't comfortable leaving her alone while I was at work. Resigned to the reality of what had to happen, she left. My heart broke. We were both glad for the time we had spent together.

I wrote in my journal, "I am committing to trust. TRUST. What else is there? I can worry. I can fret. I can be annoyed, disappointed, frustrated. But in the end, it is what it is. If I can't change it, why eat myself up? Relax...breathe. I need validation. I need to give it to myself! Confident people don't wait for others to validate them. They move forward with resolve and if they make a mistake, they 'recalculate' and move on. I need to trust myself to be capable, smart, and 'good.' I will move through this. Stop judgment. Stop ridicule. Stop criticism. Be here now. Anything can change in a moment."

I ran the tape in my head, "No one is going to rescue you from yourself...you have to do it." I found myself repeating that message to Kayla as well.

Days later, Kayla called to tell me two of her car tires went flat. When I questioned her, she blamed the construction site near her job. She told me there was debris everywhere and that the flats weren't a surprise. I accepted her explanation. It wasn't the first time she had a flat tire, and it wouldn't be the last.

In celebration of her twentieth birthday, I took Kayla out for an all-you-can-eat sushi dinner. After the credit card issue, I swore I wouldn't spend a dime on anything but the professional help she needed, but I softened. I wanted to believe she had changed. I wanted my daughter back.

We had a lovely dinner with easy conversation. Later that night she posted on social media, "My day was okay until I got to see you. Then it became awesome =) I love you SO much Mommy. Thank you for a GREAT dinner and the best company I could ask for. I can't wait until everything is back to normal and I can show you that I'm a grown person and I can move back in and snuggle and be silly with you every night."

Oh how I yearned for her wish to come true! I smiled for the promise.

Two days later I was certain Kayla was using again, maybe still. *Had she ever stopped using drugs?* I reached out to Dr. Menni for direction. He told me to take her for a surprise drug test. I planned to take her to the lab the following morning, Saturday.

At 9:00 a.m. the next morning, I called Kayla and told her to get ready; I would pick her up at 10. When I revealed the reason, she got angry, mean, and loud. Eventually she admitted she was going to fail.

Feeling desperate, I demanded Kayla go to detox at once. It was time she got help through traditional means. She protested, screamed, and cried. Finally, she agreed.

In my journal I wrote, "Will I ever get to the place where I ride these waves with detachment? The swells swallow me and render me paralyzed. How do I navigate through?"

Rushing to action, Gabriel helped us locate several detox facilities whose services were covered by Kayla's insurance plan. Once again, I felt terror and loss. Emotionally exhausted, I made the first call. I was told there were no beds available and was instructed to call the following day. Other facilities had a similar response. We had to wait.

I was suffocating as I cycled through fears of losing my daughter and fears of going broke. I compelled myself not to go there. "One step at a time," I thought. "Just take the next step."

In my journal I wrote, "It will work out. She will heal and live a good life. What is the right choice? What is the next step? I'm always juggling, off balance. This is Sophie's Choice. Who do I save? Can I save myself? Can I save Avery? Can I save Kayla? Does she want to be saved? Dear God I hurt! Just please help me to get clear, to take the next step, to be whole."

Kayla stayed at my house Saturday night. I emailed a friend, venting, "Kayla is crying her eyes out. Here it is 9:15 p.m. and suddenly she needs cigarettes and a phone card and has no clean clothes and wants me to make it all better. Well, I can't and won't. I told her we'd deal with it tomorrow if they have a bed for her. Pisses me off. I am so tired of this. Yes, lessons, blah, blah, blah, but it hurts like hell and scares me so much more."

I felt deeply betrayed. I recognized a theme. My daughter betrayed me, as did various family members, and my friend/healer. As I thought about it, I remembered experiences of betrayal at every stage of my life since childhood. But the truth was, no one had done anything TO me. I knew others' behaviors had nothing to do with me. They were acting out their own struggles, not mine.

I figured out that my feelings of betrayal were directly connected to my need for validation and approval. As

I "performed" in hope of getting my needs met, disappointed expectations left me feeling dejected and betrayed. Ultimately, my perception of betrayal fueled my sense of failure, confirming my lack of self-worth and accelerating my self-loathing. It was a vicious cycle.

The message was loud and clear. Understanding my pattern offered another reminder to stop seeking outside validation and approval. I had to love and honor myself. It was time!

"Once I find it within," I wrote, "the 'second guessing' and desperation should subside."

CHAPTER SEVENTEEN:
MOTHER'S DAY

On the evening of Mother's Day, May 13, 2012, the detox facility had a bed available. Instead of celebrating the joys of motherhood, I spent the day preparing for my daughter's admission. We scrambled to get Kayla's clothes cleaned and gather the supplies she would need.

We arrived at the facility around 7:00 p.m. As we waited for insurance to approve her stay, Kayla paced nervously, barking at me as her body began to suffer the ravages of heroin withdrawal. She rapidly grew more and more impatient, angry, and mean.

I watched my tortured child writhe in pain as the drug began to play its evil hand. Swiftly delivering its cruel brand of torture, heroin pushed hard to bring itself back into favor. I was comforted to learn that once admitted, Kayla would be given something to ease her symptoms.

Knowing relapse was common, I wondered why anyone, having experienced withdrawal even once, would return to the beast. I was still a newborn in my understanding of addiction.

I hated seeing Kayla in so much pain. Nonetheless, my anger grew. Over and over, I replayed her lies. During her birthday dinner just days before, she fervently assured me she was clean. I felt so much joy reading the message she posted after dinner. It appeared to be pure manipulation.

Sitting in the waiting room, I felt sorry for myself. I felt impatient. I felt overwhelming sorrow and fear.

Other addicts and their families arrived and likewise awaited admission. As I watched the other parents, I had the startling realization that I was "one of them." All the judgment I had previously imposed on others poured inward. There I was, the parent of an addict.

Clearly, I didn't match the profile of my judgment. I wasn't the unfit parent I had demonized and condemned. Nor did my daughter match the stereotype of the addict I denounced. She wasn't a bad seed destined for no good because of her negligent, abusive, or degenerate parents.

I searched my mind for why I thought those thoughts. I realized my beliefs about addiction came from hearsay, propaganda, and fear. It was a harsh and startling truth. I was immediately humbled.

After waiting several hours, Kayla was processed for admission and taken from me. I had no idea what lay beyond the doors that closed behind her. I left my baby in the care of strangers. I slowly left the building and walked to my car, broken.

In the dark of night, I cried hard. I drove home. As if outside my own body, I didn't notice the roads I took or the turns I made. I was numb.

It had been a Mother's Day I wanted never to repeat and yet, I felt hope for my daughter. I was certain she would realize her transgressions and correct course. For that I was eternally grateful. As I lamented the way I had spent Mother's Day, my eldest son encouraged, "Your daughter is finally getting the treatment she needs. Under these circumstances, can you think of a better gift?"

It had all been too much. I tuned out my feelings. I went to bed. Since childhood I had been expert at going numb. Ironically, that was exactly what Kayla had done with drugs.

Insurance approved a total of six days' stay at the detox facility. People "in the know" were insisting Kayla needed at least a month of treatment. I tried to reconcile those incongruent realities and trust. In that moment, I was glad she was getting help. I was taking one day at a time.

While in detox, Kayla wasn't allowed to make outgoing calls unless she was with her counselor. I was given the numbers to two public phones and instructed to call during specified times if I wanted to speak to her. The phones served the entire ward so reaching Kayla was a gamble. I waited eagerly for those calling windows and dialed obsessively hoping to get through. When I did connect, Kayla was allowed ten minutes to talk.

Our first few conversations quickly deteriorated, with Kayla pleading to return home after her six-day detox. Each time I told her that was unlikely to happen, she lashed out, accusing me of being selfish, unfair, and irrational. Defensively, she emphasized how hard she was working and insisted that she deserved to live at home.

I felt beaten as I struggled to stay calm, rational, and realistic. Seeking guidance once again, I met with Dr. Menni. He helped me navigate my own path and plan for Kayla's release. Understanding my suffering, he urged me to actively surround myself with supportive people.

While I had people in my life who loved me, I felt most were not supportive in the way I wanted or needed. The list of people I could comfortably lean on was short. I was sad, overwhelmed, scared, and mostly alone.

In response to Kayla's rant, Dr. Menni advised me to "tell her that her impatience will not work for her, that she will need much more time for rehab (after detox), and that you are tired of her playing the victim role and then victimizing you." He further advised, "You need to be tough, and I might recommend a tough love group." Additionally, he suggested I go to a Nar Anon meeting.

It was hard not to feel sorry for myself and wallow in my own victimhood. As a child I learned to take on victim mentality for protection. As an adult, it only served to keep me stuck. I was not a victim!

I no longer believed things happened TO me. Instead, I wanted to trust things happened FOR me. I was learning. I reminded myself to take full responsibility for my life. As I moved through the realities of Kayla's addiction, I was given plenty of opportunities with which to practice.

Hearing my despair, a wise friend advised me to stay in the present moment as much as possible. She instructed me to take a deep breath, consider my condition in that moment, and realize that in that moment, I was fine. It was a grounding/calming exercise for which I needed regular reminders, but it helped.

My friend also suggested that despite the day-to-day horror, going through the nightmare was growing me and bringing me closer to my life purpose. She said she had already seen sweeping changes that had been a long time coming. Her words encouraged me. I held on.

Meanwhile, the financial burden was hitting a critical juncture. As I worried about paying bills, especially for Kayla's continued treatment, my stress level rose. I sent an email to someone I hoped would help:

> *Kayla is currently ... in a detox program. The cost to me is $101/day. She is also seeing Dr. Menni again. Following detox, she will participate in either inpatient or outpatient rehab as determined by the health insurance company, cost yet unknown. I've already spent more than $3,000 to get (Kayla) healthy.*

... I've just about exhausted all credit options and will be unable to sustain further treatment. This will be the only chance she has to get clean, and we have to make it stick, but I'm out of resources. Would you consider helping out?

I received no response. To quell my disappointment, I told myself, "At least I tried."

On the third day of Kayla's detox, I was able to speak with her counselor. I was eager to know what would come next. The counselor explained that insurance did not pay for in-patient rehab for "first timers." Following detox, Kayla would be sent to an Intensive Outpatient Program (IOP), three three-hour meetings a week, for up to ninety days. She would be responsible for getting herself to IOP at the appointed times. It was a voluntary program and insurance wasn't going to pay for it either.

According to the literature the counselor provided, IOP was designed to help addicts learn how to cope and problem solve without the use of substances. It was purported to help addicts avoid slipping back into active addiction due to cravings and urges. "The support of an IOP," the literature emphasized, "can be the difference between relapse and recovery for an addict early in the process."

Based on what people were telling me, I wondered how nine hours a week would be enough, but I hadn't been offered another option. I trusted that the medical and mental health professionals knew what they were doing. If nothing else, I was certain the random drug testing would help keep Kayla drug free. In addition, the recommended IOP program invited family to attend one session per week. I would get a firsthand view of the process.

By the fourth day, Kayla sounded much more rational. On the phone, she cheerfully described life in detox. She reported that each day she attended two AA/NA meetings and met one-on-one with her counselor. She said she had connected with many lovely people and described a few troublemakers as well. Her roommate, she said, was nice enough. She assured me the food was fine and said she especially liked the snacks that were available round the clock. She confirmed that she was feeling much better and was enthusiastic about staying clean. She told me all about the AA/NA program and was excited to continue attending meetings after she left detox.

Sharing an epiphany she had in therapy, Kayla said she realized the intense anger she had been directing toward her younger brother was misplaced. She was working to identify who/what was at the root of her issues. She affirmed that she loved her brother and wanted to make it right with him.

I was encouraged by Kayla's introspection and break-through. She was making progress. For a moment, I felt a little lighter.

About to run out of cigarettes, before we got off the phone Kayla pleaded with me to bring her a supply. She knew how I felt about her smoking. I hated the thought of contributing to her vulgar habit.

Though I abhorred cigarettes and resented having to purchase them, under the circumstances I felt it was the right thing to do. I went to CVS and bought two packs of Marlboro Lights. I brought them directly to the detox facility, eager for even a brief interaction with my daughter.

I parked the car, nervously approached the door to Kayla's ward, and rang the bell. After what seemed like an eternity, a technician cracked the door open and asked me my business. I stated my purpose and attempted to step forward. I was denied entrance. The technician took the cigarettes from me and assured me she would deliver them to Kayla. She closed the door abruptly, leaving me standing outside, dazed and disappointed. *I was right there! But I couldn't talk to my child.* I drove home feeling an overwhelming sense of despair.

On the fifth day, Friday, Kayla called from her counselor's office to tell me she forgave me. I wasn't sure why she needed to forgive me and felt immediately defensive. *What had I done requiring forgiveness? I was doing everything in my power to help! I was a loving, supportive parent! I wasn't the one needing to be forgiven!*

Continuing, Kayla listed others whom she had called to offer forgiveness. I knew the others and what they had done. I didn't like being included among them. Hearing their names, anger and resentment welled up inside me. I fought to remain calm and supportive.

Kayla explained that she forgave the others because she realized they were broken in their own right. She said she understood we each had our own demons to address. That, she declared, had nothing to do with her.

Despite my initial negative reaction, I completely supported Kayla's efforts to heal. I knew forgiveness was about the person doing the forgiving, not the person being forgiven. She sounded healthy and was making sense. I kept my feelings to myself and moved through them quickly.

I didn't think the process of forgiveness was as easy as she seemed to make it; however, I fully understood that holding on to anger ate us up inside. If Kayla was able to find forgiveness in her heart, she would be better for it. It was a step in the right direction.

Communication with Kayla's counselor had been scant and I felt ill prepared for her impending return. As Kayla's Saturday release loomed, I felt anger and fear rise again. I wanted answers. Did my daughter have a fighting chance to stay clean and sober? I desperately wanted to believe she did.

Despite her objections, Kayla finally accepted that she would return to Iris's house after detox. I was relieved by the change I heard in her attitude.

She knew she would have to earn permission to return home. She seemed prepared to take responsibility for her actions and do the work necessary to heal.

Late Friday night, Kayla called again from her therapist's office. She requested that I attend "Family Day" visitation at the facility the next day. Even though Kayla was due to be discharged, visitation was only permitted on Saturdays and she was eager for me to meet the people with whom she had been healing.

Rather than respond with enthusiasm, I felt annoyed and deferred any commitment. Visitation required I get up early and attend the "Weekend Co-Dependency Program" from 10:00 a.m. to 1:00 p.m. While Kayla's release was inevitable and expected, I had been looking forward to sleeping in.

My anxiety was through the roof and my body ached. I was exhausted, and since Avery would be with his father for the weekend, I yearned for the peaceful silence of being alone in my home. I yearned for the last bit of calm before the storm. I resented being asked to give up my "me" time.

As my displeasure subsided, I realized I was just making excuses. In truth, visiting made it all too real. I was still trying to deny Kayla's addiction and avoid being part of it. I had no idea what to expect.

"Family Day" was eye opening to say the least. Upon arrival at the appointed building, I was greeted and offered a beverage. I was then ushered into a large auditorium. Fifteen to twenty people sat randomly throughout the space. I sat away from the others. No one spoke.

A speaker/facilitator gave a brief welcome and then asked each of us to share our first name and why (for whom) we were there. I felt out of place and profoundly alone. I didn't want to be there. I didn't want to belong. I didn't want to participate. I said my name and why I was there.

I found myself sitting in judgment as I listened to introductions. Shockingly, some visitors were returning for the second or third time! I rationalized that I was better because my child was going to beat the odds. She was going to be healed after her first stay in detox. As Kayla had insisted, she wasn't "that bad." I wasn't going back.

With my whole being, I wanted to believe we wouldn't be back. I tried to convince myself we wouldn't be back. I pleaded with the Universe that we not go back. I wondered if I was looking at my future.

Lecture, video, and a question-and-answer period followed introductions. The Co-Dependency Program was designed to teach me about addiction and the harsh realities of loving my addict. While I learned things I never wanted to know, I was unable to absorb the majority of information offered. I considered the program to be thorough, yet irrelevant, and I resented having to waste my time. Denial was still instructing me.

When the presentation concluded, we were invited to visit our loved ones. Scant dialogue was exchanged as the group walked across campus to the detox building.

Once inside, Kayla greeted me with a big hug and a huge smile. Visitors were divided into two groups and, with our addicts, escorted to a room where we would attend a mandatory AA meeting. The large, non-descript meeting space contained a circle of chairs awaiting occupants.

The first to arrive, Kayla and I sat down. One by one, other recovering addicts filed in. Several other people from the lecture joined the circle. Once convened, a staff counselor asked that we go around the circle and introduce ourselves.

When it was Kayla's turn, she easily asserted, "I'm Kayla, and I'm an addict."

Despite having heard others repeat the same words, I was startled to hear Kayla say them. I regained my composure and followed with, "I'm Kayla's mother, Judi."

With introductions done, the counselor opened the discussion. One by one, attendees shared their fears, their struggles, and their stories. The format was foreign to me but seemed fluid and comfortable to the patients.

With tears streaming, one young man shared that his parents hated him and wanted nothing to do with him. He said when he called home, they would answer the phone, hear his voice, and immediately hang up. He felt rejected and unworthy. He questioned how he would keep going.

I offered an alternative viewpoint for him to consider. Perhaps, I suggested, his parents didn't feel hate, or if they did it was a mask. I asked him to consider that they loved him beyond words; it was just too hard for them to face the source of their pain. Speaking to him likely reminded them how much they feared losing him. Sometimes, I explained, it seemed easier to shut out our fears then to face them.

I told him about my own denial and inability to face the truth. I suggested that his parents might be resisting the truth as well. I was certain they couldn't bear to watch him destroy himself, and I had no doubt they were reeling from his drug-induced behaviors. I encouraged him to focus on healing his own demons and to trust that, in time, his parents would likely come around. He listened intently, thanked me for sharing my perspective, and seemed to shift ever so slightly.

After the meeting, Kayla and I joined many others who went outside to smoke and/or socialize. She had formed connections with a number of fellow patients, and she introduced me to her favorites. Several thanked me for my contribution to their meeting and shared about their own journeys.

That afternoon, I heard quite a few stories of recovery and relapse. I heard sorrowful accounts of devastated families and destroyed careers. A man in his forties told me he had relapsed after twenty years, losing his marriage and law career. Another young man told me that when he was seven years old, his mother would put a needle in her arm, then in his. I wept and wondered how any human being could overcome such trauma. I held faith that he would.

Kayla and I walked the park like grounds, and she told me about her week. In some ways it was as if she had been on vacation. She seemed renewed and refreshed, happy and hopeful.

During the nine hours I spent at the facility, a full complement of emotions had burst forth. As I listened to addicts' stories, I heard themes of self-loathing and unbearable emotional pain. It occurred to me that for so many, their extreme sensitivity and goodness was, ironically, what likely led them to addiction. Feeling the intense pain of life's inequities, they tried desperately to numb it.

Upon our departure, a staff member confirmed that insurance would not pay for continued inpatient services. She said Kayla would be assigned an IOP program early the following week. They would let us know. It was hard to believe they would release her without a plan in place. I was angry, yet resigned. I didn't have another option.

CHAPTER EIGHTEEN:
NEW LEASE ON LIFE

Kayla and I arrived home around 6:30 p.m., ate dinner, and talked. Kayla told me stories that made my stomach turn. Drug addiction wasn't for the faint of heart! I held tight to the fact that I had my daughter back.

As a "requirement" of recovery, Kayla had to attend at least one NA meeting per day for at least ninety days, "ninety in ninety." That evening, despite wanting to enjoy her time at home, she dutifully went to a ten o'clock meeting with a friend she'd made in detox. She was excited about the NA program, and I was excited for her.

Kayla said she was feeling very motivated and strong. She looked good and was making sense. My fears, however, were not about that day, or the next. I knew as the challenges, disappointments, and frustrations of real life found her; she would have to be vigilant in her commitment to sobriety. I was keeping my fingers crossed.

I permitted Kayla to sleep at my house that night. Her brother wasn't home and it felt good to have her close. I was encouraged by the hop in her step and her gleaming smile. And I was scared for the future. I tried to stay in the moment, telling myself, "One day at a time." Kayla was telling herself the same thing.

I sent a text to Iris saying Kayla was staying with me Saturday night and that she would return to her house on Sunday.

Iris texted back, "I guess since I haven't heard from her, she's staying with you. Tell her to get in touch with me and get her stuff out of my house."

Confused by her response, I assumed there was some kind of misunderstanding. I called Iris to clear things up. Her greeting and tone were unexpectedly harsh. Without the benefit of conversation, she made it clear that Kayla was no longer welcome.

While I couldn't blame Iris for her stand, the lack of warning left me stunned and disappointed. There was nothing to do. Iris had been an angel for months and owed me nothing. I was eternally grateful for all that she had done for us. I surrendered to the reality; Kayla was living with me again. I reasoned that it was just as well, found gratitude, and tried to believe it would be okay. Inevitably, however, Avery would be impacted.

The morning brought new challenges. Kayla was sick. Apparently common practice in detox, she had been given suboxone "...to remove the opiate addict's cravings for heroin..." Blocking the euphoric effects of heroin, suboxone presumably enabled withdrawal without the usual, painful, physical side effects. Now home, Kayla was going through withdrawal from suboxone which itself was potentially addictive.

I was furious that no one had warned me. It made no sense. *How was I supposed to handle her withdrawal? How could they release her like that? How could they not tell me?*

I was a disaster. I had no idea what I was looking at or how to properly support Kayla. I worried about how to support Avery. I wondered what surprise would slam me next. My body ached.

Kayla hadn't lived with her brother and me in months. I pondered appropriate rules and how to best enforce them. I wondered how to make my daughter responsible while protecting my son. I worried that no matter what I did; Avery would be adversely affected and unduly punished, again. I worried that chaos would return to my daily life. I worried that Kayla would slide back into addiction. Worry solved nothing and eroded my energy. I resolved to do everything in my power to make it work.

Having changed the house locks months prior, I made Kayla getting a key contingent on her behavior going forward. I felt a house key provided a reasonable incentive and had the potential to keep her in line.

We met with Dr. Menni to craft a list of rules and expectations for our new living arrangement. During our session, he reminded me, "You are not good at taking care of yourself." Through his words, I understood that it was imperative for me to abolish old, detrimental patterns. The following weeks would be crucial. As much as I was asking Kayla to change her ways, I knew I was equally responsible to change mine.

I wrote to a friend, "Tears and fears continue, but I'm trying hard to be optimistic and progress. I'm also trying to be proactive instead of letting the fear shut me down. This might be the real fight for me."

The challenges were growing, and I could feel myself falling prey to victim mentality. I questioned, "Don't I have enough on my plate?" and protested, "It's not fair" and, "I'm so tired of my life."

I found myself resenting Kayla for the hardship I had to endure as a result of her addiction. Troubles born of her irresponsible and desperate behaviors littered her path and consequently mine. As my anguish grew, it emerged in the form of accusation.

Each time I demanded she clean up her "mess," Kayla became enraged. Her responses were defensive, "I know Mom, you don't have to remind me," "Don't you think I get that?" "Stop shoving it in my face, I'm well aware of my mess."

Time and time again, familiar guilt and self-loathing easily replaced my anger. *Did she actually understand the devastation born of her behaviors? Was she aware of her mess? Was I just exacerbating her problems? Was I wrong?* I had a hard time believing her, yet self-doubt speckled my thinking.

I reached for my hard-held beliefs to give me courage. I believed there was a reason for everything, even if I never knew that reason. I believed the nightmare would grow me as a human and as a spirit. I believed that on the other side of pain was something better. I believed I would get through; I just had to find the way. I worked hard to honor my beliefs.

CHAPTER NINETEEN:
GO TO MEETINGS

Every irregular behavior set me off. I felt angry and suspicious all the time. Dr. Menni advised me to keep up my "intolerance" where Kayla was concerned. He also advised that I attend a Nar Anon meeting.

As I struggled to understand and navigate the path before me, "go to meetings" had become a dominant directive wherever I went. Whether I expressed a concern, asked a question, or released pent up emotion, experts and friends alike urged me to "go to meetings." People in recovery and people more ignorant about addiction than me repeated the same mandate, "go to meetings."

I resisted. I got angry. *How dare they tell me what to do!*

My rationalizations were powerful: "Why should I go to a meeting?" "I don't NEED a meeting!" "I'm not the addict!" "I don't have time!" "I hate being in groups, I'm an introvert!" "This is not MY problem!"

Slowly, very slowly, I recognized that indeed it was MY problem. Kayla's addiction was with me every minute of every day. I chronically obsessed and worried. The quality of my life had deteriorated. I was suffocating. *Wasn't my experience debilitating me in the same way substance debilitated the addict? Weren't meetings designed to help with just those issues?*

I was consumed by bitterness, writing, "In my agony, my pain, my depleted energy, and my overwhelm, now I have to find time for a stupid meeting?"

I continued to resist, but the voices were relentless. Even Kayla was demanding I go to meetings. She felt I needed to learn about her journey so I would stop hounding her unnecessarily.

As a relatively shy person, I was loath to step out alone. Additionally, I wasn't sure I really wanted more information. *Didn't I have enough? Couldn't I just go to bed?*

I understood the rationale. I was being pushed to make connections. Theoretically I would meet people who, like me, were also going through the nightmare. I would also meet people who had more experience than me and could offer guidance. I was repeatedly told I needed a support group and that meetings would help me learn more about the monster with which I was forced to cope. Presumably being part of such a community would comfort and grow me.

Even though Kayla had gone through detox, her behaviors continued to be reckless and unpredictable. I was constantly on alert. In truth, I really didn't know with what I was dealing.

Finally, I confronted my fear and resistance. *Was I afraid meetings would help, or terrified they wouldn't?* I conceded to go to a meeting.

I searched online. Meetings were available at a variety of locations and times, day and night, seven days a week. Some meetings were specifically open to "newcomers." I identified several meetings that would be suitable for me.

I let weeks pass. After spinning excuse after excuse, I rallied my strength, committed to try, and at 6:15 on a Thursday evening, I got in my car and drove twenty minutes to a church basement where a Nar Anon meeting would be held. I arrived plenty early.

Nervously, I approached the building and found my way to the appropriate entrance. I felt like I was in someone else's body, going through the motions of someone else's life. *How could this be my life?* I forced myself to open the door and go inside.

I made my way down the crooked steps, past the peeling paint, into a short hallway, looking for some sign that I was in the right place. Gasping for breath, I was a fish out of water wanting desperately to swim away. A kind woman appeared, greeted me, and invited me to sit in a small, damp room at the end of the next hall. Alone, I sat at the meeting table taking in the scent of mildew and looking at the yellowed decorations on the walls.

As I wondered what was to come, a man entered the room. He explained that he and his wife, the woman I had met in the hallway, would be running the meeting. Their son was in recovery, and the man told me they had been running meetings for years. It was their way of healing and giving back.

I was anticipating an informal gathering of people with similar challenges discussing struggles and strategies, comparing what worked and what didn't. I hoped for guidance, encouragement, and comfort. I wanted to feel empowered and optimistic.

At seven o'clock, the meeting was called to order. Going around the table, we introduced ourselves one by one. Attendees included a man whose daughter overdosed and died some years before, a man whose brother was actively in the throes of drug abuse, and a grandmother whose granddaughter was using. To my right sat a man who lived in my neighborhood. He harbored so much anger he scared me. His son was in rehab for the second or third time. Before the meeting had begun, he confided that his son had stolen his wife's diamond engagement ring, the final insult. He told me his wife was too grief stricken to attend the meeting with him. The woman to my left seemed calm and collected. Her addict was in recovery. I wondered why she was there. Lastly, there was a couple that, like me, was at their first meeting. Their daughter was in a facility, perhaps detox (they didn't use that word). They struggled to come to terms with what had already happened, as well as what would happen next and how to manage. In our pain, that couple and I connected. We were grappling with acceptance, gratitude, and terror.

I sobbed as I introduced myself, publicly acknowledging Kayla's addiction. There wasn't a lot of good news in that room. I felt gloom and despair overtake me.

After introductions, we read scripted passages, round robin, from the Nar Anon book. We took turns reading the Twelve Steps of Nar Anon as well. Through my tears I obediently choked out the words when it was my turn. Hearing them for the first time, I wasn't even sure I agreed with the words I read.

Use of the word "God" made me uncomfortable. The format reminded me of a religious service, even though the organization was nondenominational. I had long navigated through religious language, inserting my own interpretations, and finding nuggets of wisdom and support where I could. At that meeting, I found myself, once again, seeking the message meant for me.

I felt impatient. I wasn't interested in reading that stuff; I could read on my own. I wanted to hear how parents coped and how families survived. I wanted to hear stories of success. I wanted to know how to save my daughter. I wanted relief from my unyielding terror. I eagerly awaited that part of the meeting.

It never came.

When I sought advice from the group at large, I was told giving advice during the meeting was strictly prohibited. As the veteran attendees registered my panic, they suggested that more casual conversation would transpire between those who chose to stay and chat after the meeting.

At the meeting's conclusion, the young man next to me offered some "off the record" advice. His brother was actively using and wreaking havoc in his mother's home. Even though Kayla wasn't actively using, he had a good understanding of what was happening in mine. He suggested that I put things of value in a locked safe or get them out of the house altogether. He recommended that I install locks on bedroom and other doors to prohibit unsupervised access. He also urged me to attend at least a few more meetings saying, "It takes at least four to six meetings to know if this is the place for you."

I would hear that same suggestion again and again.

I spoke briefly with the couple who were also first timers. We hugged, acknowledging each other's pain and fear.

I bought the book.

I left.

I learned that meetings were not about saving the addicts. Indeed, they were about saving the brothers, the grandmothers, the parents, ME. What seemed prescribed and limited was a ritual proven to help millions of people. It was predictable and reliable, and gave attendees a platform on which to heal and grow.

Hearing about overdose, relapse after relapse, and years of drug abuse left me feeling sad and hopeless. Meetings didn't seem to be for me, though I acknowledged their power to help others. I was grateful the program had benefited so many.

With an enhanced sense of despair, I wondered what was next. I had been hoping for direction but felt, instead, increased heartache and worry. I felt betrayed by the lack of answers. I was angry I had wasted my precious energy.

I went home, reflected on the meeting, and read the Nar-Anon book. I had already been doing a lot of the personal work the literature espoused. The Twelve Steps, adapted from the AA model, were wonderful tools for self-growth and healing. As a life coach, I had unknowingly been working many of the same steps for years. I had identified my "higher power" and learned to trust it. I was constantly taking a "fearless moral inventory" of myself and had no problem admitting the "nature of my wrongs". I had been "making amends" to those I had harmed and was living my life through the lens of honesty to the best of my ability.

In addition, I was actively identifying my internal demons, shifting my perspective, taking responsibility for my own joy, forgiving myself, and learning to love myself without condition. Ironically, Kayla's addiction had been catalyzing and accelerating my growth. And there was much more work to do. Though I felt light years ahead in my personal work, I still wanted to know how to FIX my daughter.

Reluctantly, I started to acknowledge my impotence to compel Kayla to change. I knew the only ones we could ever change were ourselves, never another. If I was going to support my daughter through her challenge, one thing was certain; I had to continue pushing my own healing.

I found some of the Twelve Steps motivating and was happy to model the work. I began by making a list of the people for whom I held resentment. Surprisingly, it was a very long list! I identified why I was angry/hurt, then what part of me hurt or felt threatened, and finally, where/how I was responsible. It was eye opening. Just like the addict must, I knew I had to take full responsibility for my relationships, my actions, and my pain.

Over the following months I went to several other meetings. I discovered that while the general format was unchanged, each had its own flavor and offered something slightly different. In the therapist-run meeting, participants shared resources and tools they found helpful in their journeys. I embraced their vulnerability and generosity.

The support found at Al Anon/Nar Anon meetings was, in fact, invaluable. There was plenty of useful information flowing, but I had to be able to hear it. I also had to accept that there was no magic wand or quick fix. Each addict was on his/her own path, as were the people who loved him/her.

I still didn't feel meetings were a fit for me, but I understood why people urged me to go. I was grateful I did.

CHAPTER TWENTY:
A RESPITE

With an apparent respite (I prayed a permanent one) from Kayla's drug abuse, I re-engaged Katherine, my spiritual counselor. It was the end of May. "Being strong" had meant stuffing down much of my emotion at my body's expense. I needed to process it out of my body. Without imminent crisis to grab my attention, my emotions were erupting and overwhelming.

Katherine validated my feelings and pointed to my growth. "You are very aware of what is happening to you mentally, emotionally, and physically," she told me. "You realize what patterns are coming to the surface (e.g., you are looking for excuses). You are making decisions about what to do (just do one thing) instead of shutting down. And you didn't shut down."

Indeed, I had made big progress! Katherine suggested my feelings of overwhelm and failure came from wanting to do everything at once, fix everything instantaneously. She encouraged me to stay focused on one step at a time. Though I urgently wanted to mend my daughter's struggle, it wasn't realistic.

Further encouraging me to find my personal strength, Katherine reminded me to notice the "shoulds" that were

constantly replaying in my thoughts. "Should" was someone else talking in my head. As long as someone else was
directing my feelings, I was giving away my power.

I knew the first step toward changing anything was
to become aware. I was noticing my inner dialogue and
self-sabotaging ways. From a place of awareness, I knew
real change would happen.

"You have done so much already," Katherine wrote to
me, "I pray for the day when you are able to embrace, really
embrace, the beauty of your soul. I know it's coming. I feel
blessed to be a small part of your process."

I was tearful as I read her words. I admired Katherine
and trusted her fully. Despite the hardships and pain I had
been experiencing, I was doing my work, and I was making
progress. Though I didn't know how it would work, I intuitively understood that healing my own wounds would
help Kayla.

I wrote in my journal, "So I knew the lessons in this
nightmare would be profound, and indeed they are. As they
are still unfolding, I know already that finding myself - my
heart, my spirit, my internal strength - are integral to this
process. I know that honoring/valuing/loving self is imperative. Taking out judgment, noise, and chatter are helpful. I'm
learning self-reliance and detaching from others' opinions.
It's like I'm breaking out of a cocoon - METAMORPHOSIS."

On the morning of May 31, I found a suboxone wrapper on the kitchen floor and a cut straw in the living room. Both, I had learned, were indicative of drug abuse. Though suboxone had been given to Kayla in detox, it was classified as a narcotic and could be abused. The straw was a vehicle through which to snort drugs.

Panicked, I confronted Kayla. Her reaction was an explosion of defensiveness, accusation, and excuses. She posted a vile rant on social media that included, "I am working my ass off doing something that is NOT easy, that most of you will NEVER understand! I'm not gonna fucking use today. And that's a fucking miracle at this point!"

Kayla also texted, "You need to give me some fucking credit for the hard, fucking work that I've been doing. This hasn't been easy AT ALL. You really just made me want to go out and use when really that didn't need to happen like that."

It was hard to know what to believe or how to react, but I knew I didn't want to live with fear, hostility, and blame. I remained pretty calm in the face of Kayla's outburst. I didn't raise my voice. I simply outlined what I had found and what I expected from her. Looking like a bomb had exploded, I felt her room was a sign of her continued illness.

I told her she had to clean it. Truly, I maintained, no one in her right mind would choose to live in such filth.

I reached out to Dr. Menni. Once again, I felt like I was in free fall. My head was spinning. *Was I going to cause my daughter's relapse? How could I avoid pushing her back to drugs? And how could I prevent my own emotional decline?*

That evening, Kayla was scheduled for an evaluation at IOP (two weeks after her release from detox). Dr. Menni felt confident they would determine whether or not she was using. Based on what I had shared, he suspected she was.

To make life even more stressful, angry rants were once again posted on social media. In that public forum, people unloaded their disgust with Kayla's abhorrent behaviors. Among the complaints, Kayla was accused of lacking respect, gratitude, and decency. I was sickened by the spectacle and devastated by relationships turned sour.

Overwhelming anxiety was consuming me. Kayla's behavior instigated chronic worry, but I found myself obsessing over the mundane. Bills needed paying, the house needed cleaning, and I had responsibilities to tend. At some point during my frenzy, I caught myself, paused, and identified action steps I could take. Progress!

Yearning for peace and companionship, I wrote to a friend, "Overriding is this sense of being alone and sad. Not physically alone but alone in my life."

I continued to cycle through thoughts of wanting a man in my life. While that preoccupation was painful, it provided a desired distraction.

Kayla sent me an email:

Mom,

At (detox), one of our groups was about stress and anger management when it comes to talking to others who don't quite understand the things we're going through, drug related or not. So instead of blowing up over, or underreacting and letting my emotions get the best of me, I'm writing you this letter to get my thoughts out clearly and calmly in an appropriate way.

I want you to read up on PAWS (Post Acute Withdrawal Syndrome) and get an understanding on it because for at least the next 90 days and probably up to 18 months, that is what I will be experiencing. It does become less and less with time, but you must understand that today, I am only 19 days clean and serene, and that is very miniscule. I am still fragile, and my emotions are coming back full force. I'm on edge, there is a lot going on, and I'm tired and trying to focus on my recovery above all else.

That's exactly what I need to be doing, and anyone involved with the program will tell you, I need to put my recovery first above all other things in my life. At this time, that includes my family and friends and home. I can only do so much, and that's not to say that I won't pitch in or I won't make my family a priority, it just means that right now my first priority is me.

I have been going to at least one meeting every single day, when I can even two or three meetings. And that's really important. IOP is not going to save my life, either is therapy or work or school or my family. NA meetings are what are going to keep me away from drugs. Having a network of clean and sober friends to hang out with and talk to, gaining experience with having CLEAN fun, and continuing to go to meetings are what I need.

The suboxone wrapper and straw you found today does not surprise me, I have those types of things floating around in my purse, in my room, etc. I know I need to clean my room, and every day I do a little bit, but I'm honestly scared. I have empty dope bags in my room, I have straws, I have a whole bunch of crap I used with, and every time I think about tackling it, I become terrified.

I will get there. I will gain that strength, and until then I will continue to do it a little at a time. But the only way I'm going to be able to do it is by going to meetings and talking to my people. Maybe I need a friend to help me. Ethan offered, although I'm not sure how much I want him to do that, but these people that I'm becoming close with KNOW what it's like to be in the early stages and have to clean up your drug mess. And truly, only addicts can help other addicts.

If I'm sitting at home all the time, instead of going out and being active in my community, I'm going to relapse. It's as simple as that. That's when the voice of my disease kicks in the loudest, when I'm sitting doing nothing at home, or worse, cleaning up drug shit. I desperately want this. I want sobriety. I want to be a part of this program. But it takes TIME.

My drug use was a symptom, and removing that symptom doesn't change the disease, I'm still the same person, possibly even a lot more insane. There is much that I need to work on, and by going to the amount of meetings I'm going to, and hanging out with my clean people, I'm working on it.

I'm not asking you to understand, I don't know if you ever will understand, and that's okay. I just want you to have some understanding. I'm getting over be-ing sick, and I found out it's not uncommon to become VERY sick with infections, viruses, etc., right after kicking dope. My immune system is at its weakest right now. There will be more sinus infections, more doctor visits, and more emotional breakdowns.

When that happens, I need you to realize that this is me moving forward, which is a lot harder than going backwards and using. Nothing I do is a personal attack on you. It is a combination of PAWS and learning how to do EVERYTHING in my life again without the use of drugs. It's hard, tiring, and takes its toll on me. But I want this, so I'm not going to stop going to meet-ings, and I'm not going to stop trying, and just for today, every time I wake up, I'm not gonna use and I'm gonna take it each day at a time, because that's the only way I'm going to succeed. But my recovery comes first. Above all things.

I would really like for you to support me with that and be proud of me instead of fighting with me. I've come a long way, and I have an even longer way to go, and a little positive reinforcement couldn't hurt the cause.

Kayla

It was a lot to absorb. I heard the things I wanted to hear..." I want sobriety," "Nothing I do is a personal attack on you," "I'm not gonna use," "I'm going to succeed." I was heartened by her honesty and her request for support. I acknowledged I still didn't understand the monster called addiction.

I forwarded the letter to Dr. Menni, "Please tell me what I'm supposed to think/feel/do?" I pleaded.

He responded that it was a nice letter but to let Kayla know it was a two-way street. We would discuss it further in his office. I was so grateful for his willingness to mediate. His counsel was invaluable to me.

I told Kayla I appreciated her thoughtful letter. I would look into PAWS and try to understand and respect what she was experiencing. I offered to help her clean the drug reminders out of her room, and I praised her for her efforts. I also told her that she had to meet me half way, respecting my needs as well and participating in the household.

After reading about PAWS, I sent Kayla an email:

Dear Kayla,

I looked up PAWS. It is not a lot different from my day-to-day existence. The big difference is that your coping mechanism is to do drugs. Of course I would like you to find a more healthy way to cope and never want to see you go back to drugs, ever. At the same time, I will not allow you to use your recovery as an excuse to continue to disrespect and hurt me. Your drug addiction has affected the rest of the family, not just you. Part of your recovery is to take responsibility and to make amends. Making amends includes living in this house with respect for me and your brother. Disobeying my rules and requests is not ok.

NO FRIENDS HERE without my permission and me home

No boys in your room, period

Clean your room and the middle room by (insert date here)

Clean up after yourself...particularly kitchen: cabinets and drawers closed, dishes washed/in dishwasher, counter wiped down, food closed and put away properly

No smoking by the house (street only)
Cigarettes go in the outside trash or toilet
Lock the door when you come in at night
Lights out when you are not using them
Do not use my towels. Do your laundry, which includes your towels.

You may NOT go in my drawers/closet or other personal possessions.

Do not use my things...no matter how tempting
No personal belongings in the living room
Fold blankets and clean up living room
NO FOOD in any other part of the house but kitchen and dining room!!!

In addition, you should be responsible to clean some part of the house...like the front bathroom and/or the kitchen floor.

Additionally,
Wake yourself up and get to work on time EVERY day (9:30 a.m.)
Go to IOP
Go to meetings

According to PAWS, Kayla's behavior was within the realm of normal. Nonetheless, it took great effort not to react to her mood swings, irresponsibility, filthy habits, and aggressive speech. The possibility of her returning to drugs and stealing from Avery and me was a constant threat. I yearned for a sense of safety and peace in my home and in my heart.

Another week went by and new challenges surfaced. When Avery got home from school, Kayla had a boy in her bedroom. Not bad enough, she brought him back at midnight while I slept. She was blatantly ignoring my requests.

I knew I had to impose consequences but didn't know what was appropriate. I couldn't bring myself to throw her out. I reasoned "the punishment didn't fit the crime," but her complete lack of consideration was intolerable. I wanted to shut down.

When I contacted Dr. Menni, he advised, "I think her total disregard for your rules is unacceptable. I would pack her bags, leave them in front of her room and tell her 'You either follow the rules or you're out, no excuses.' This is self-preservation for you and you're not helping her by allowing her to do whatever she pleases. This is highly disrespectful to you. I know this is difficult, but saying fuck you to you will also lead to saying fuck it to staying clean. I'm pretty clear about this."

As Kayla's defiant behavior accelerated, Dr. Menni encouraged me to look at my own behavior. I was feeling abused. I was acting the victim. As long as I was weak, Kayla would take advantage of me.

"I'm not criticizing," Dr. Menni told me, "just trying to get you to see that you hold much more power than you exercise."

Dr. Menni further explained that my unwillingness to take the hard steps (put her bags at the curb) was enabling Kayla. She was displaying a sense of entitlement and was walking all over me. His powerful words, "Only Kayla can recover," resonated.

Still, I was ill prepared to throw my child to the street. I continued to make excuses and stuff the pain just far enough down to ignore it. Like a cancer, it ate at me.

Despite my encouragement, Kayla didn't want to celebrate the milestone of her thirtieth day in sobriety. She maintained that she had seen too many people relapse after thirty days, and it troubled her.

I struggled to shake off her words, "Too many people relapse after thirty days." As I felt my anxiety rise, I reminded myself to return to the present moment. Worrying drained my energy and accomplished nothing.

In session with Dr. Menni, Kayla continued to lash out at me. With a talent for hitting me squarely where my insecurities lay, she ridiculed me, saying I was "just self-pitying" and accusing me of wanting to make her miserable. I was disappointed that Dr. Menni didn't step in to defend me, but respected that he was the expert and knew what was best.

It had been one month since Kayla's release from detox and two weeks since she had gone for the IOP evaluation.

Finally, we received approval for admission to an IOP program. Claiming she had managed fine without it for a month, Kayla lobbied hard not to go.

Since Kayla was attending NA meetings regularly, the three-hour meeting wasn't terribly compelling; however, mandatory drug testing was. It would give me much needed peace of mind. Despite the significant cost, Dr. Menni and I agreed that Kayla's attendance was non-negotiable.

The evening Kayla was scheduled to start, she texted that she was unable to go to IOP because her car had been towed while she was at work. I nearly lost my mind until her boss, Lucy, got on the phone with me. Apparently Kayla's car had been towed due to a number of unpaid tickets she'd accrued. Lucy interceded and eventually remedied the situation, but not in time for IOP.

Kayla's IOP start date was rescheduled.

With utmost compassion, knowing I was consumed with fear, Lucy texted me later that evening. She wanted me to know Kayla was doing quite well at work. I was heartened by her words and appreciated her thoughtful effort.

Kayla also sought to assuage my concern. She explained that she had been parking illegally since she sold her parking pass for drug money. While deeply disturbed by her confession, I was gratified by her honesty. I viewed it as a healthy step toward taking responsibility for her past and cleaning her mess.

Reluctantly, Kayla attended the next available IOP session and several more after that. Resistant from the beginning, her disdain for the program grew rapidly. After a couple of weeks, she pleaded with me to let her stop. She promised she would faithfully attend NA meetings which she not only preferred but also enjoyed.

I had attended an IOP meeting with Kayla and experienced firsthand what she disliked. I couldn't disagree with her assessment. I was spending a lot of money for a drug test.

I consulted with Dr. Menni. We agreed that if she stopped going to IOP, Kayla would have to faithfully attend daily AA/NA meetings. In addition, she would be expected to be "exemplary in her cleaning," showing responsibility and respect in the house.

Unexpectedly, Dr. Menni sent me the following email:

Judi,

You will get through this. I have faith that we're on the right track. Your job is to take care of your own reactions. I know this is hard for you and wish you had more support. But you do have to remind yourself what a very good person you are and how Kayla's choices are NOT about you at this point.

Dr. Menni

Tears escaped my eyes as I read his words. Dr. Menni understood my despair, frustration, and exhaustion. I appreciated his reminder that Kayla was traveling her own path and that ultimately, I was only responsible for my own path. I was grateful to have his support.

As the following week unfolded, little changed. I was beside myself as I watched Kayla oversleep, spend money she couldn't afford to spend, and continue to ignore cleaning and curfew rules. Once again Dr. Menni suggested packing her bags.

Toward the end of June, my mom threw a surprise party for my dad on the occasion of his eightieth birthday. Despite family conflicts, the kids and I wouldn't have missed it for the world. Having all three of my children together was a special gift for me and for my parents.

At the restaurant, we sat with my cousin Isaac. He had driven six hours with his mother and sister (my aunt and other cousin) to celebrate with us. I had a wonderful relationship with Isaac who had himself been an addict for the better part of thirty years. Clean and sober for almost ten years, I considered him a miracle and an inspiration. He was a voice of reason, often providing me with wisdom and guidance as I struggled through the twists and turns of Kayla's addiction.

Deeply respectful of Kayla's journey and mine, Isaac was always careful not to give advice or cast judgment. When I felt I could handle no more, Isaac was the one to whom I turned to "talk me off the ledge." He held me gently, listened intently, and when he could, he offered alternate perspectives for what I observed.

Prior to the party, Isaac agreed to chat with Kayla to "get a feel for her thought process and progress." Meeting for the first time, he and Kayla hit it off immediately. During their conversation, Isaac expressed his need to attend a meeting. He asked Kayla if he could join her that night. Kayla was delighted to receive the deep understanding and camaraderie of a family member.

Only in town for two days, with his addiction well under control, Isaac's request surprised me. When I questioned him, he confessed he didn't need a meeting. He was hoping to bond with Kayla, show his support, and perhaps introduce her to some new thoughts.

Knowing Isaac had been where Kayla was, she trusted him, and so did I. I was grateful for his willingness, love, and support. I was hopeful his influence would have a positive impact.

Isaac accompanied Kayla to an evening meeting. The next day, he gently relayed his bleak observations. He said Kayla still had a victim mindset. From what he heard and saw, it was clear she wasn't taking responsibility for her life or her choices. In his experience, that wouldn't bode well for her staying clean. He had encouraged her to continue attending daily meetings, emphasizing the lifeline they could provide. He offered his support. There was nothing more he could do.

I hoped she would change her ways. I hoped she would use him as a resource. She did neither.

CHAPTER TWENTY-ONE:
SUMMER

Summer progressed. Kayla's volatility and oppositional attitude persisted. I tried to do my work and maintain my life. I was perpetually anxious about finances, getting a teaching job, and supporting my family. I tried not to worry about Kayla, though she was never far from my thoughts. I felt lonely and tired, sad, angry, and scared.

I worked hard to focus on the good in my life. Among other things, I had friends and family who were abundantly supportive (my dad was no longer keeping his distance). I had a roof over my head and food on my table. I had daily work and a car to get me there. And, as far as I knew, my daughter was clean. Listing my gratitude forced me to focus on what was working and delivered me to the present moment. In that moment, I was okay.

By mid-August my concerns fixed on Kayla's social/sexual choices. The professionals at the detox facility strongly advised against addicts engaging in intimate relationships for at least two years after getting clean. They insisted that energy and focus should be spent solely on growing resolve to stay clean and working the AA/NA program.

It was disturbing to watch Kayla obsessively crave and seek male attention. When I expressed my concern, she dismissed it, refuting any emotional attachment. She claimed no attachment meant no risk. Based on my experience, I believed she was drowning in denial.

As I reflected on Kayla's obsession for men in her life, I saw my mirror. Though I wasn't sleeping with anyone, my mind was habitually occupied with thoughts of men, past and future. The men I had chosen were emotionally unavailable and like Kayla, I was in denial about the real issue at hand.

Little by little, the truth was becoming clear. Kayla and I both needed to acknowledge our bad choices with men and learn to love ourselves. I was certain that once I honored and loved myself, I would attract men who were caring and available. Perhaps more importantly, once I truly loved myself, I would enjoy my own company. I would no longer NEED a man; rather, I would CHOOSE to be in relationship.

High anxiety and physical pain pushed me to seek permanent relief. Believing emotional wounds created my pain, I was driven to heal. I wanted to be whole and authentically happy. I found numerous, free, online lectures and materials about spiritual and emotional healing, and I was seeing Katherine monthly.

Nurturing, wise, and kind, Katherine advised me to stop resisting the feelings that wanted to emerge. She told me fear, anxiety, and panic were obstacles to my healing. As long as I resisted, I would stay stuck. If I allowed the feelings to pass, she explained, I would be able to clear the patterns and release what no longer served me.

Even when I felt relatively good about my progress, I was unable to ignore others' opinions. I often felt judged, criticized, and wrong. Katherine praised me for the hard work I was doing to heal and addressed my sense of failure. She explained that people judged others as a way to make themselves feel better. Judgment was a vehicle through which people could numb their own sense of failure and avoid healing. She further explained that by doing my work, I became an energetic trigger. For those who were not working to heal their emotional wounds, there might be a subconscious effort to hold me back. Conversely, my healing efforts would energetically inspire those who were ready to do their own work.

Awareness was crucial. Katherine instructed, "Be a coach for yourself. You'll still have reactions but you will move through them faster and faster, and their effect on you and your life will become less and less."

I practiced being aware of my feelings and watched my triggers. Triggers, I knew, highlighted parts of me needing to be healed. When strong emotion arose, I practiced responding rather than reacting, reflecting rather than escaping, allowing rather than resisting. I practiced gratitude and being present. I toggled between being strong and feeling frail.

Exhausted by Kayla's outbursts and abuse, I stepped gingerly in my own home. Avoiding her attacks, however, was nearly as exhausting as enduring them. Despite my frustrations and concerns, knowing Kayla was going to work each day kept me believing she was on the right track. In order to sleep at night, I grabbed any evidence available.

Issues continued to emerge. Kayla continued to ignore the rules I had set forth: clean your room, come home before midnight, smoke by the street, throw the butts in the trash pail, etc. Locked out of the house several times, she complained vigorously, pleading for her own key. Without a minimal display of responsible behavior, I refused to provide one.

In session with Dr. Menni, Kayla blamed me as she bemoaned that we didn't communicate with each other. She called me a hoarder and a bad role model. I was angry that she was making me her scapegoat instead of taking responsibility for her own life. I journaled, "I need to let her find her way and stop trying so hard to save her from herself."

By the end of August, Kayla had become extremely moody and volatile. She proclaimed that all of her friends were "dirt bags," thus causing her to be upset all the time. She refused to elaborate.

On Saturday, August 25, I found heroin wrappers on Kayla's bed. When I confronted her, she insisted she had pulled the wrappers from the side of her bed where they had been stuck. It was a plausible excuse, but alarms were ringing.

When Kayla decided she didn't want to continue talking to Dr. Menni, I insisted she submit to a drug test. I bought a kit at the local pharmacy.

I had been advised to administer the test as a surprise. If she was using, I was told, Kayla could use a variety of methods to "trick" the test. A few days later, the "surprise" drug test turned out negative.

While highly suspicious, I desperately wanted to believe Kayla was clean. The "proof" was in my hand. I would later learn the only way to ensure an accurate reading was to actually watch her pee into the cup.

As chores beckoned for my attention, I was happy to focus my energy tending to them. One afternoon, ready to mow the lawn, I opened the shed to retrieve the mower. The gas can was gone. There was no use searching; I had no doubt it had been stolen nor by whom.

Kayla had been spending time with a neighborhood boy who was also "in recovery," and I didn't trust him.

Unfortunately, I had become familiar with the desperation born of drug addiction. Together they spelled trouble.

I questioned Kayla immediately. She passionately denied any knowledge of the stolen gas can, suggesting perhaps I had misplaced it. *Misplaced the gas can? No, this time I knew I wasn't losing my mind.* I called the police. If nothing else, I wanted to send Kayla and her friend a strong message that I was not going to remain an easy target.

As I shared my story with the officer, I wondered whose life I was living. I felt guilty for reporting such an inconsequential problem and apologized several times for bothering him. He assured me it was okay and told me I was doing the right thing.

Unsurprisingly, with no real evidence, the police were unable to take action. Nonetheless, making the report helped me feel empowered. It wasn't easy to call the police. It wasn't easy to accuse my daughter and her cohorts. But I had suffered too much loss already. I was no longer willing to look the other way. Progress.

As August concluded, I was convinced Kayla was using again. I reached out to my cousin Isaac. He advised me to test her again. I procrastinated.

CHAPTER TWENTY-TWO:
HERE WE GO AGAIN

In September, as the school year began, I prepared to return to substitute teaching. It felt like a consolation prize. I was grateful for a job, but it barely paid enough to cover my bills. I wanted to teach in my own classroom.

I berated myself for wasting time and money earning a master's degree I wasn't using. I felt like a complete failure in every corner of my life. As trouble with Kayla accelerated, however, I questioned whether I had the strength or focus to run a classroom of my own.

I wrote to a friend, "I am not currently sure whether (Kayla) is clean or not. It is a constant and devastating stress on me and on Avery. She makes choices that I am not comfortable with, but then, the whole recovery thing is a foreign life. Some days I see my little girl in there, but most days I just see an abusive, troubled, manipulative young woman for whom I can do little. I try to accept what is. Drug tests and looking over my shoulder have become a way of life."

I toggled between rage and sadness, blame and guilt, disgust and concern. Nothing was clear, especially how I felt. The pounding sense of loss came in waves. Steadily, things had disappeared; the silver dollars my grandfather gave me when I was a little girl; my lifetime collection of wheat pennies; necklaces; earrings; a cherished, handmade, pendant; sterling silver platters and bowls; and more.

I hid my cash (though Kayla often found it).

I felt anger. I felt sad. I felt terrified. I felt violated. I fought the truth. Denial still came easily. *Wasn't she cured?* It seemed as if I had learned nothing about addiction. In fact, I had learned more than I realized.

Finally, I had had enough and was ready to act. *How could I have been so foolish?* I told Kayla she had to return to detox or leave my home. As my heart tore open and bled into my throat, I gagged with revulsion for her. My strength became tangible but my sorrow untold.

Perplexingly, in moments of clarity (that she was using drugs) and strength (more like self-righteousness), I viewed my daughter as a hideous monster and fully condemned her. Sometimes I even convinced myself I no longer cared for her. It was as if I forgot I loved her more than life itself.

Of course, therein laid the greatest pain. I was fighting with myself, throwing punches at my own perceived failures, and suffering the most devastating sense of loss imaginable. I was torn apart by conflicting feelings. I felt fury over Kayla's heinous behaviors and agonized over my impotence to save her. I fought her egregious actions, and felt guilt for not preventing or curing her addiction. My hopes and dreams for her happy future were fractured as I observed the horrific life she was living.

There was no glory or pride in the life of an addict. That had become clear. At some point, Kayla's only choice became survival. Indeed, the terrorist hijacked the plane and headed for the tall building. There was no turning back. There was only one focus for an addict, where to get the next fix.

I wrote to a friend, "It's weird...I'm kind of on autopilot. I was very strong, yet I am in denial on some level. Either that or I am coming to accept things for what they are and for what I have to do. Sucks, sucks, sucks."

Mercifully, Kayla agreed to return to detox. A treasured family member, another angel in our lives, generously provided the money to sustain Kayla's readmission.

At Dr. Menni's urging, I reached out to the person whose support Kayla craved most. By phone, I explained the situation, hoping for support and insight. Cutting me off mid-sentence, the person asked me to hand the phone to Kayla. I watched her body register shock, then pain, as the words echoed through the receiver, "You're on your own kid."

Summarily cut off by this person of import, Kayla was shattered. I was appalled but sadly, not surprised. So went the seesaw of emotion.

Kayla went to work the next day. To her credit, she called the detox facility as promised. She was told they could take her late the next day (Saturday) or Sunday morning. I wanted her out of my home immediately.

No longer the ignorant optimist, I couldn't shake the sense that after detox Kayla would likely relapse again. If she did, I would have no choice but to throw her out. Each time I thought it couldn't hurt more, it did. Watching my baby kill herself brought me to unparalleled depths of despair.

On Saturday, September 8, I wrote to a friend, "I'm one part numb, one part angry, and two parts very sad and afraid. 'My little girl...' that is all that keeps running through my head. I don't have any answers right now. Today, when I said I'd rather bring her tonight than tomorrow, she said she absolutely was NOT going tonight because she doesn't want to be there all night in process. I told her she doesn't get to choose since I'm involved too. She said 'just drop me off, I don't need you there with me.' I may just do that. Maybe she needs to get a feel for independence. The saddest part is the lack of hope. I just feel like I'm going through a script, and we will be back. And I can't."

On Sunday I found myself looking at the familiar walls of the detox admissions lobby. Insurance approved Kayla for just four days. An impossible slap in the face, I knew that four days was not enough to make real strides in the fight against addiction. Ultimately, insurance approved one more day for a total of five.

"I am a mess." I wrote, "The sad thing is, I don't think she is going to get what she needs.... and we will be back to square one again. Next time I will have to kick her out and mourn again, only worse. I hate this life."

Though I didn't fully understand about "people, places, and things," a reference to an addict's familiar drug triggers, I resolved to thoroughly clean Kayla's room while she was away. It seemed imperative that she return to a clean, healthy environment if she was to have any chance of recovery.

My dear friend (another angel) offered to help me clean. I enthusiastically welcomed Paige's company, support, and direction. We ripped up the carpet and painted the walls. While it was wonderful to have a respite from being physically alone, I remained alone in my heart. Cleaning that piece of Kayla's mess felt useful and was somewhat cathartic. The fear was overwhelming.

Somehow, I managed to move through the days. I continued to put on a brave face, apply for jobs, and distract myself with the task of writing cover letters and resumes. Each time I was rejected, I grew more hopeless about finding a "real" job. Despite my perceived failures, I tried to set goals, find balance, and love myself.

By email, Katherine advised:

> *In my opinion, the greatest frustration comes from the feeling of not knowing what to do; that every action seems exhausting; that it feels like whichever way you turn, it is wrong. The tendency is to shut down rather than feel that frustration and the whirling around our minds do as a response to it.*
>
> *So, what to do? In my experience, taking one step opens the door to longer lasting change. It is extremely hard to take that first step and to make the decision of what that first step should be. Try to clear yourself from judgment and see if any thoughts rise to the surface concerning what you could do to move in the direction of making your life a little easier right now. Don't resist any thoughts that come up and don't judge them. This is not about making a decision, so you don't have to DO anything. I am just interested in learning what your deeper self is feeling.*
>
> *If you start to engage in thinking about what comes up, you'll start to figure out reasons about why what you thought is impossible, or too hard, or simply no good. Try to avoid that. Better that we talk about it together. If it is easier for you, journal. Let's see where this takes you. I know that you're scared and*

that asking you to do this will probably bring up fear.
Breathe through it. There's nothing that you have to do
in response to what comes up right now.

I went to see Katherine the next day. She helped me navigate the terrain of my feelings.

CHAPTER TWENTY-THREE

TOUGH LOVE

During Kayla's brief stay, I was reminded that detox provided addicts with medical care and supervision as they were weaned from the physical ravages of their drug of choice. Additionally, addicts were given daily, private counseling and introduced/reintroduced to AA/NA and the Twelve Steps.

Detox was only a first step. There were glaring limitations to the program. For example: Detox did NOT take the addict through the emotional and mental aspects of withdrawal, only the physical. It did NOT teach the addict how to take responsibility, how to cope, or how to proceed with life. It did NOT accompany addicts beyond the few days of treatment. It was a start, but not a finish. Once released from detox, addicts had an uphill battle to stay clean.

No longer a first-time offender, Kayla was strongly advised to go to rehab following detox. Almost without consideration, she adamantly refused. Not knowing what else to do, I allowed her to come home.

Within two days of completing her second detox, Kayla relapsed again. Needing drug money, she sold her $1000 MacBook to a pawnshop for $50. Given to her as a high school graduation gift, that computer had been Kayla's lifeline. Selling it was an ultimate act of desperation.

Impossible to digest, Kayla's action was a terrifying and damning confirmation of her dire condition. I cursed the agony that brought her to that point. I hated what I knew. It was the last straw. Denial was no longer an option. Complacency was no longer possible. Kayla was an addict, and she needed help I couldn't provide.

I demanded Kayla return to detox. When she refused, I called the facility to ask for advice. The man on the phone suggested I offer Kayla an ultimatum: have a conversation with the therapist or find another place to live.

Given her choices, Kayla reluctantly agreed to "have a conversation." That rainy evening, we drove to the facility in silence. I anticipated leaving her there for yet another round of detox. I had become all too familiar with the process.

Upon our arrival, the young man with whom I had spoken, a counselor, took Kayla to an office out of my view. She admitted to him that she was using again. He advised her to check herself in. When she refused to stay, I had no choice but to refuse to bring her home. With support and direction from the counselor, I stood my ground.

Enraged and defiant, Kayla disappeared into the wet, dark night. We were a twenty-five-minute car ride from home, and it was late. I drove home alone without knowing my daughter's whereabouts. It was a long, sleepless night.

I was scheduled to work my first subbing job of the year the next morning. As I was leaving the house, Kayla appeared at my front door. She pleaded with me to let her in. Resolved, I refused and left her standing at the curb as I drove away. My heart was heavy and my mind full with fear. My first taste of "tough love" was bitter and agonizing.

With nowhere to go, Kayla frantically texted throughout the day. She insisted she wanted to stay clean and told me how determined she was as a result of being left out in the cold. I fought tears as I read, "Being on the street is hard. I'm cold and hungry, and I have to pee. I have no place to go. I'm scared."

After a time, I had to stop reading Kayla's texts. While she had incited my every emotion, she was still making demands, refusing to go for treatment, and showing no humility. Her pleas yanked at my heart, but I knew I had to stand strong to save her life. There could be no bargaining.

Still, in my journal I wrote, "I feel like I want to give (Kayla) another chance to do it right. She is broken. But this drug, heroin, it is a monster. It becomes the master. But I don't feel like she's lying this time. I feel like she wants to be clean. I feel like she understands the consequence. Can I dare to hope? Can I be so bold as to believe my baby can beat the odds? I want to!"

Kayla returned to detox.

Two days later I found myself sitting through another three-hour lecture that would allow me access to my child. I was no longer a newcomer, nor was I resisting or judging. I understood the co-dependency about which they spoke. I understood the seesaw of life with an addict. I understood about enabling and denial. I heard the information offered.

As Kayla's third admission to detox wound down, I was asked to meet with Kayla and her therapist. In her office, the therapist calmly explained that Kayla no longer had a choice about going to rehab. She said the speed with which Kayla had relapsed was absolute proof that she needed more substantial help.

Acknowledging her need, Kayla agreed to go, with conditions. She insisted she remain in our home state.

The therapist calmly explained that staying within reach of "people, places, and things" from her drug days would guarantee failure. Her best chance at recovery laid in getting away from everything that was familiar. Our state was not an option.

Kayla got up abruptly and left the room.

Already familiar with my financial limitations, the therapist had anticipated my concerns. She had been in contact with an organization that helped in situations like ours. Through his non-profit organization, a man named Scott was going to arrange and pay for Kayla's flight to Fort Lauderdale, Florida. In addition, he would help place her at a rehab where she would receive a scholarship for any remaining cost after insurance.

Two more angels, the detox therapist and Scott, had entered my life. My emotions were a scramble. I was grateful, terrified, sad, relieved, and humbled. My daughter would get the help she needed. She would be 1500 miles away, and she would have a chance at survival. I would be spared additional debt.

By the end of the day, Kayla conceded to go to Florida.

Scott called me to discuss the details of Kayla's trip. After detox she would go to Sea Waves Rehabilitation Center (not the real name). He had already booked her flight.

On the phone, I asked Scott a million questions. He patiently answered each to my satisfaction. He had been in recovery for eight years and understood the process intimately. He explained that there were no guarantees, but assured me we were taking the right next step. He told me about his own journey and compassionately shared that he had hurt his mom deeply in the process. Though he had been the addict, he had a keen sense of what I was going through.

Scott was kind, gentle, and direct. His story gave me hope. His guidance gave me strength. His counsel kept me sane.

Trying to envision what was to come, I asked about Kayla's living arrangements and what she would experience on a daily basis. I wanted to know how rehab would help and what happened after rehab. Every answer left me wanting more. In truth, I wanted reassurance that Kayla would be okay. I wanted to be told there was no need to worry, that in a month my daughter would return to me good as new.

I worried out loud about Kayla being alone and so far away. Scott encouraged me to stay strong and cultivate resolve. He implored me to maintain a posture of tough love in order to save her life.

Though I had practiced tough love that night at detox when Kayla refused to admit herself, and the following morning when she pleaded for a bathroom and warmth, I fought the foreign concept at a cellular level. My motherly instinct was to nurture and protect my children. I had always encouraged them, trying to give just enough assistance and support to help them succeed. I was a parent who reasoned and negotiated in order to teach compromise and self-reliance. Tough love required I be strict and unsympathetic. It meant doing the opposite of what made sense to me. It meant watching Kayla suffer the consequences of her actions no matter how harsh. It meant risking her life in order to save her life.

Scott asserted, "Statistics have shown that Kayla has a better chance of survival if you don't help her. She is more likely to die if you do."

With that single statement, Scott convinced me to toe the line of tough love. Though it took every ounce of strength for me to maintain the recommended posture, knowing it was a matter of life and death was powerfully motivating.

CHAPTER TWENTY-FOUR:
THE NEXT RIGHT STEP

Kayla was scheduled to leave detox and fly to Florida on the twenty-fourth of September. That same day, I was scheduled to interview for a replacement teaching position at a local elementary school. I left early to pick up Kayla at detox. I brought her home to pack her things while I went to the interview. After the interview, I returned home, loaded Kayla and her belongings into the car, and was on the road to the airport at 3:00 p.m.

We were both nervous and exhausted, but resigned and resolved. Kayla was clean and getting help. I was eternally grateful.

During the hour and a half drive, Kayla casually mentioned that she was "surprised you didn't notice my hand."

Ill prepared for what Kayla was about to share, I questioned, "Why would I notice your hand?"

"It's better now," she replied, "but when you brought me to (detox) it was swollen. I thought for sure you'd notice."

Thinking she had been injured and I had somehow been remiss, I tried to subdue my guilt as I asked, "Why was it swollen?"

"Because that's where I was shooting the drugs," she revealed, nonchalantly.

OH. MY. GOD!

Panic, denial, searing pain, renewed fear, and disgust coursed through my body simultaneously. I tried to convince myself I had heard wrong. I was instantly nauseated.

Until that point, Kayla had prided herself on not injecting her drugs. She defended her "good health," explaining that injecting, or "shooting" drugs, signaled loss of control and "hard core drug use." She had consistently emphasized that she was in control.

As a matter of self-preservation (maybe self-delusion), I had been holding fast to Kayla's assertions. I told myself she had a passing problem, not that serious because she wasn't shooting. Believing her assertion kept me ignorant.

In the car that day, Kayla's confession exposed the severity of her problem. She had crossed the line she had drawn. She was a hard-core drug addict.

Dizzy from the brick hitting my forehead, I tried hard not to react. Tears seeped out of my eyes. "Shooting up." "Hard-core." "Junkie." The awful words echoed through my mind.

I always hated the word "junkie." It conjured images of derelicts sitting in dark, abandoned houses in some distant inner-city ghetto. It was a disturbing, sticky image of boarded up windows, crumbling sidewalks, and darkness. In my mind I saw life straining through cracks, desperately trying to survive. It was smoke-filled spaces and dirty mattresses, and the acrid scent of human waste. I imagined half dead, faceless humans moaning for their next fix. I did not consider those junkies had mothers who loved them. I could not envision my daughter amongst them.

I regrouped. I told myself the past was the past and the future held promise. Kayla was on her way to get help. She would be okay. She had to be.

Kayla and I tried to make conversation. Since her therapists had all pointed to "abandonment issues" as a source for her pain, I suggested she spend time working through them while in rehab. I encouraged her to be brutally honest with herself so that she could heal.

To my surprise, Kayla turned the tables on me. She demanded that my "bad men decisions" were the problem. She accused me of setting a bad example.

I was devastated by her accusation and felt it was unfounded and mean. While emotionally unavailable men had unconsciously hurt me, I didn't date "bad" men. I fought the anger, then the self-doubt and guilt. *Had I been a bad example? Was I responsible for Kayla's addiction?*

(Kayla's comments would linger in my thoughts and help me more fully awaken to the unhealthy choices I had made. Ultimately, I would heal enough to choose differently.)

As if reading from a list called "How to Shock My Mom," Kayla then shared that she tried to kill herself several times.

Furthermore, she told me she didn't know if she had a desire to live. Without wanting to live, I wondered how she could ever get healthy. I prayed rehab would help her. She was a mess.

I knew Kayla needed me to be strong. I needed me to be strong as well. Balancing heartache and fear with hope and support was tricky. I called upon my reserves, knowing the love I had for my daughter was absolute. We were taking the right next step.

Directionally challenged and unfamiliar with airport parking, I accidentally parked in "economy" instead of "short term." Confidently, Kayla took the lead, directing us to the shuttle that would take us to the terminal.

A short ride later, we were checking in. Due to the nature of Kayla's trip, I was permitted a "gate pass," enabling me to accompany Kayla in the waiting area until boarding. Periodically breaking the silence, we made superficial conversation as we nervously passed the time.

When Kayla was called to board, we hugged tightly and said goodbye. I whispered words of encouragement and told her I loved her. I didn't want to let go. Reluctantly, I released my grip. Courageously, she turned and began her decent down the jetway.

Swallowing my tears, I watched until Kayla disappeared from my sight, and then I watched a little longer. Unable to contain my emotion, I began to shake uncontrollably. Surrounded by people, I was alone with my pain. I waited a few minutes, working hard to stifle the agony, then made my way out of the airport, moving as if escaping a fire. I was suffocating.

I arrived outside, the journey a blur. I turned my focus toward finding my way back to the car. A quick shuttle ride and short walk later, I found my Honda where I had left it.

Collapsing into the driver's seat, I was able to release the intense emotions I had stifled. I sobbed uncontrollably for what seemed a lifetime. The pain was unbearable. I ached for myself, and I ached for Kayla. I knew I had to accept reality, and Kayla had to figure things out without me.

I drove, alone with my thoughts.

I got miserably lost. I asked for help. I got back on track.

I wondered if my driving experience was a metaphor for my life.

When I arrived home, discouraged and exhausted, Avery comforted me. He had been living the nightmare too, and he knew the toll it had taken on me. I cried in his arms.

Kayla called a couple of hours later to tell me she landed safely. A "tech" (residential recovery technician) from the rehab had been waiting for her at the airport. She was in a van en route to Sea Waves where she would reside for the next thirty days. They would be confiscating her phone, she told me, and I would not hear from her for two weeks. Once she got phone privileges, she would be allowed ten minutes a day to call me from the public phone.

In many ways I felt relief, and at a deep level I mourned. My child was in the care of others, out of reach, out of touch, gone.

I hoped Kayla would find the courage to feel her pain and face the agony that ultimately brought her to rehab. If she didn't face her demons and the pain of what she had created, I knew she would continue trying to numb it. I prayed for her recovery.

Two weeks later, I found myself arranging my days to receive her calls.

CHAPTER TWENTY-FIVE:
ADJUSTING

With the best of intentions, aching for support, connection, and distraction, I decided to attend the family celebration of Rosh Hashanah. With wounds still fresh and my emotions raw, it didn't take long for trouble to erupt. Almost as soon as I had arrived, I left, angry, hurt, and in tears. It was a foolish effort.

I was inconsolable. Adding to the insult of missing my extended family, I would also miss seeing my eldest son. I had planned to pick him up at the end of his workday and bring him to join the family. Though I looked forward to our time together, I was in no condition to visit. I called Gabriel, explained what had happened, and told him to take the train back to his apartment.

I drove home to lick my wounds. On my way, I called Paige. I needed help sorting through the emotion that was billowing out. She rushed to my house and helped me process through my anguish. I felt challenged and stressed in every area of my life. There was no respite and no escape. I resolved again that I had enough on my plate, and I pledged not to engage with family. I had to protect myself. I had to find relief wherever possible.

Leo became slightly more present in my life. A mixed blessing, he provided occasional companionship that was void of emotional substance or promise. Without my knowledge, our relationship conspired to reinforce my loneliness.

Every day I fought an internal battle wondering if time spent with Leo was worth the resulting pain and disappointment. In truth, I believed no one else would want me. *Did Leo want me? I didn't want me!* Over and over, I rationalized that it was better than nothing. I held onto a bad, sporadic relationship instead of facing what seemed like the most painful of realities: I had to love myself. I felt broken and dejected.

I wrote in my journal, "My struggles in relationship are a reflection of my struggles inside."

CHAPTER TWENTY-SIX

REHAB

From the beginning, various people warned me not to allow Kayla home after rehab. They said it would be too soon and that her next step should be "halfway." I didn't know what "halfway" was and pushed the warnings aside. I had put Kayla on a plane to Florida with an understanding she would return in a month. I was not going back on my word. I wanted my baby back.

Within days, I missed Kayla terribly; not drug addict Kayla, but the real Kayla. I cried a lot, terrified of the inevitable next wave of pain. I tried hard to be optimistic and stay out of the future. I was finally coming to accept that I could not save her from herself, but I hoped rehab could.

As usual, Kayla gave permission for her counselor to speak freely with me. During our first conversation, I asked a million questions, trying to understand how rehab worked and how my daughter spent her time. I wanted to know how they would cure her.

Living in a restricted, supervised environment, Kayla and a roommate shared an apartment. Each morning residents were taken by van to "The Center," where they attended a variety of classes designed to help them live drug free, healthy lives. Kayla was learning how to maintain healthy finances, create manageable schedules, and develop good communication. A range of additional offerings encouraged residents to develop healthy interests, hobbies, and coping skills to help manage the stressors that would inevitably arise. Yoga, meditation, and nutrition classes were among those choices. Kayla attended daily group and private therapy sessions. Residents also attended daily AA/NA meetings in the greater Fort Lauderdale area.

Each week Kayla was given a cash stipend for food. Along with the other residents, she was then taken to the supermarket where she purchased supplies. The intention was to integrate residents into normal life, teaching them to budget, be good shoppers, and prepare their own food. Most days she prepared lunch and dinner.

Not only did Kayla find preparing meals enjoyable, she also discovered she had great talent in the kitchen. Being her mother's daughter, she had trouble cooking for just one, thus, staff and residents often benefited from her expertise. Though Kayla suffered social anxiety and kept largely to herself, food became a conduit through which to build relationships.

Sea Waves provided a number of weekly outings for residents. On Fridays they were taken to the beach; Saturdays to "Golden Corral Buffet" and the movies; Sundays they enjoyed a bar-b-que by the pool. All activities were supervised closely. Additional privileges were earned after certain time markers. When not engaged in programmed activities, Kayla "hung out" by the pool, soaking in the tropical sun.

Learning about Kayla's daily schedule triggered me to feel angry, then jealous. It sounded like she was on vacation at a lovely, inclusive resort. *I needed a vacation too! Hadn't I earned one?* As I struggled with my emotions, the counselor explained the rehabilitation philosophy: Recovery required intense focus. In a distraction-free, nurturing environment, Kayla would be able to immerse herself in the program and heal.

I tried to trust.

As that first week wore on, I wondered if Kayla was doing the work needed to heal. *Was she working through her issues? Was she getting the help she needed? Were they making her better? Was she done with drugs?* Unable to shake my worry, my stress grew.

Several months prior, Kayla had convinced me to let her adopt a Maine Coon cat. The cat was wreaking havoc in my home. With Kayla gone, the full responsibility of his care fell to me. As an animal lover with three female cats and a dog in the house, I tried to make it work, but Kayla's boy cat was not using the litter box. He had done irreversible damage to the carpets and floors, and no attempted remedy worked.

Twisting over the decision to rehome Kayla's cat, I began putting out feelers. Just as I began to lose hope of finding him a new home, a family who had recently lost their beloved Maine Coon contacted me. It was clear they would offer him a very loving environment. They were willing to take him immediately.

The couple arrived at my house late afternoon. The husband brought in a transport crate and placed it on the foyer floor, door open. As if knowing he was going home, the cat calmly walked in and lay down. It seemed his new family was meant to be. Before leaving, with kindness and utmost generosity, the wife extended an invitation for us to visit whenever we wanted.

Knowing Kayla could see "her cat" again lessened my anguish slightly. As I watched the truck pull out of my driveway, I was torn apart by conflicting emotions. Relieved to see the cat leave my house and go to a loving home, I was watching a part of Kayla disappear. She loved that cat. By sending him away, I felt like I was giving up on her. Tears flowed freely. I knew the couple were angels sent. Gratitude and trust had to prevail.

The car would be my next focus. A continued financial burden, I had to sell it, but first it needed some work. Not only had Kayla been driving on bald tires, but she also left it a filthy mess. The notion of cleaning it sickened me to in-activity. *She injected drugs in that car.* I procrastinated.

I received a parking ticket in the mail. It was the second, maybe third. Because the car was registered in my name, I had to pay the fine. Even with Kayla in Florida, cruel re-minders of her illness persisted.

A friend wrote, "I hope you can rejoice a little in knowing, at least for now, (Kayla) is safe and being given help. If she is not taking it, there is nothing you can do about that other than pray that she opens herself up to being helped."

My friend urged me to focus my energy in a positive di-rection rather than on fear and worry. It was good advice.

I replied, "I am trying hard to accept that (Kayla) created this, and she will have to figure it out. I cannot make it work for her anymore. In fact, I think I did a poor job of making it work for her in the first place or we wouldn't be here."

The lack of drama and quiet house was soothing. I be-gan to question my decision to allow Kayla back after thirty days. While I missed her terribly, I didn't miss the mess and the drugs and the confrontations. *Why wasn't there a hand-book?* I didn't know the right answer.

As the weeks unfolded, I busied myself in my life. I at-tended a CoDA meeting with a friend. We both hoped to learn more about codependency and enabling behaviors we knew were unhealthy. We met some nice people and nev-er returned.

For a change of scenery, I went to the gym regularly. Besides providing a meditative space, working out helped relieve some of my physical stress, albeit temporarily. I craved the endorphins produced from exercise.

I was grateful for my dear, caring, generous friends, and for the distractions and comfort they provided. To get me out of my head and house, they often treated me to dinner, drinks, or lunch. I felt, as I was, blessed.

I was asked to teach a demo lesson, the next step in the interview process for the replacement teaching position. I spent many hours perfecting a lesson plan and bolstering my confidence. I appreciated the opportunity and redirected focus.

CHAPTER TWENTY-SEVEN

A JOB

Finally, with determination to make Kayla's car sale ready, I confronted my demons and the arduous chore of cleaning. Within minutes, I found heroin wrappers and other paraphernalia in the cab. I sat in the car and sobbed. It served as a harsh reminder of the truth I was trying to forget.

Opening the trunk, I found various stolen items Kayla was unable to pawn: a silver bread dish, a vase, an old camera, and sundry electronics that had become obsolete, therefore valueless. I ached for what wasn't there. I soothed myself, rationalizing that if I didn't know what was lost, I didn't need it in the first place. That mind trick worked for a minute.

I told myself cleaning the car was a healthy step, but my heart suffered. I lamented the lost stuff and felt the violation, but mostly I mourned for my daughter. I was looking at evidence of desperation borne of an illness that could kill her. Stuff, I reasoned, could be replaced but not my child. What I found in her car reinforced what I was finally understanding: Kayla would do anything to support her habit. The drug had been in control.

Knowing the remaining filth and cigarette residue would make the car impossible to sell, I arranged to have it professionally detailed at a local shop. With the gas tank almost empty, I stopped to fill up on my way. The battery died. A friend came to give it a jump. Despite having an appointment, the detailing shop closed early without notice. Clearly, I was being blocked, or redirected, or both.

Riding the wave of determination, I drove to my auto repair shop to have the tires replaced. When I arrived that late afternoon, Joey, the owner, was there to greet me. Over the years, Joey had been a compassionate ear and fierce supporter. We often talked about our kids, comparing notes on our trials and tribulations. His genuine concern, combined with my exhaustion from months of anguish and the terror of continued addiction, primed the pump of my rumbling volcano. When he asked about Kayla, my emotions erupted.

In his own way, Joey encouraged me to stay in the moment. He reminded me Kayla was clean and getting help. Going to the future was an excessive energy drain. He was another angel in my life.

I realized the fear was always with me, conscious or not. Nonetheless, I knew I had to push forward. I had to keep putting one foot in front of the other. I had to take the next right step.

Joey helped me get the car sale-ready. He fixed what needed fixing, and he knew someone who could do the detailing. He thought he found a buyer, but after a few weeks that buyer fell through. He helped me create and place an ad, and taught me how to field inquiries. He had my back. I was grateful.

Despite my conviction that selling the car was the right thing to do, I needed regular reassurance. Joey helped me work through the guilt I felt. He helped me work through the fear. He helped me stay strong and determined.

I moved forward, pushing through the issues of my day-to-day life, attending to work and chores, and doing my spiritual work. I wanted to shut down, but I didn't. Deep down I believed Kayla would energetically feel my determination, my improving health, and my progress. I believed my energy would positively motivate her own.

I was offered the replacement job. I accepted. It was temporary, but it was a start.

I received a letter from my parents imploring me to settle the family unrest. As much as I hated the situation and how it affected them, my own survival compelled me to hold true to myself.

I responded with an apology for any pain my behavior inflicted and reasserted my boundaries. I had no idea what the reaction would be. I felt both empowered and awful. My old pattern was to stuff my feelings, appease others, and suffer. Taking a stand was new to me, and it felt right. It was a matter of survival. I wished no one else had to suffer as a result.

On October 10, 2012, I started my new teaching job. The learning curve was steep, and I found myself routinely working twelve-hour days. I was thrilled to be earning a living wage and connecting to kids in "my own classroom." As I pushed far beyond my comfort zone, I was exhausted, scared, and excited.

My days were demanding. Each morning I left for work by 7:00 and returned home to make dinner around 7 p.m. Exhausted, I would fall into bed shortly thereafter, only to begin again the next day. The rigor provided little time to think about much else.

CHAPTER TWENTY-EIGHT

HURRICANE SANDY

Kayla was offered two additional weeks in rehab. Though her counselor and I pushed hard for her agreement, she consented to only five days. She would be returning home in a week and while she sounded good, I had grave concerns.

Kayla's counselor warned me about the pitfalls of her returning to "people, places, and things" too soon. Despite my concern and the credible argument to keep her in Florida, compelling Kayla to stay didn't feel right. Neither of us had considered the possibility nor had we prepared for such a step. I was certain forcing her to stay under those conditions would push her back to drugs. I booked and paid for her flight home.

As I mentally prepared for Kayla's impending return, my dear and abundantly supportive confident and friend abruptly removed herself from my life. She felt allowing Kayla to return home was an egregious mistake she couldn't bear to watch. It was an unbearable blow and devastating loss.

Hurricane Sandy was moving north after hitting Cuba as a Category 3. It was expected to pummel the east coast of Florida the day before Kayla's flight home. Kayla was living a short distance from the ocean and I held my breath while I prayed for her safety. Meanwhile, Kayla prepared for her departure.

Sandy's rage lessened as it passed over Florida but gained strength as it moved further north. Nonetheless, Kayla's flight took off on time.

With mixed emotions and considerable trepidation, I went to meet Kayla at the airport. My body tensed with anticipation but as soon as I spotted her, it relaxed with delight. Relief set in as we connected. Indeed, it was fantastic to see her. She looked good. We hugged for a long time.

The day after Kayla returned home, Sandy hit us with great force, causing massive power outages and widespread damage. We lost power for only fifteen hours, but other homes, schools, and businesses in the area were not so fortunate. Downed trees blocked roads and lay on rooftops. The region was shut down.

Kayla mused about having experienced Sandy twice. Unable to leave our house, Kayla, Avery, and I passed the time playing board games, talking, eating, and catching up. It was good to have my daughter back, clear headed and optimistic. For one glorious week, we thoroughly enjoyed each other's company.

I went back to work, and Kayla went back to drugs.

As the truth emerged, my heart split open once again. Knowing what had to be done, I reached out to Scott who generously arranged another flight to Florida and another stay at Sea Waves. Kayla would have to detox as well as recover.

Delivering the news of her necessary return to Florida, Kayla spoke the reality before I could, "I know I'm not going to be coming home this time." With clarity and resolve, Kayla packed "her life."

On the way to the airport, we got stuck in horrific traffic and missed the flight. I thought my head would explode from the pressure. Frantically, I called Scott from the road. He was calm, compassionate, and reassuring. By the time we returned home, he had the details of Kayla's reservation for a flight the next day.

While missing the flight was impossibly stressful, I felt grateful for one more night with my daughter. I wondered if I would ever see her again once she returned to Florida.

Two weeks following her return home, on the tenth of November, my heart vanished on the jetway along with Kayla. I cried and cursed the reality, then headed home. I didn't get lost.

CHAPTER TWENTY-NINE:
REHAB PART II

Kayla called to tell me she had arrived safely in Fort Lauderdale. I knew the drill. Her phone would be taken, and she would not have phone privileges for two weeks. I reminded myself that Kayla was in the only place that might save her life.

I knew much more about Sea Waves than I did the first time. During Kayla's two weeks at home, she had gushed about the owners, Jess and George. They were recovered addicts who became very successful in their lives. Driven by their deeply personal passion, they opened Sea Waves. Through the rehab, Kayla told me, they were giving back in gratitude for their blessings.

Kayla provided example after example of how Jess and George went above and beyond to help their clients succeed. That was certainly true for how they were helping Kayla. I was grateful for all they were doing and prayed it was enough.

In my journal I wrote, "Yesterday I put Kayla back on a plane to Florida. I don't know if or when she might come back to me. It is clear that until she has significant clean time behind her, she cannot live here. So, I am struggling to find peace within myself as I miss my baby terribly. I know this is best for her."

Punishing loss and sorrow hit me in relentless waves. During the hurricane week I had been given the gift of my smart, generous, kind, compassionate daughter. I was reminded of the joy and wonder she brought to my life, and of the strong connection we shared. Her relapse shook me to my core.

While my new job kept me busy and distracted, wanting to quell the pain pushed me to continue my spiritual work. I was determined to find self-love and peace, despite the nightmare. I went to see Katherine the following week.

In the days following my session with Katherine, I found myself crying unpredictably and often. She advised, "Just try to be present as much as you can. Pay attention to your feelings and let them lead you back to your thoughts. Try to catch your thoughts when they fly through your head. ... You are definitely on track and solidly in the groove. It may not feel that way all the time, but it's true. As time goes on, you will be aware of your progress more and more."

My life had become a Tetris game. Difficulties dropped in and I scrambled to make them fit. Sometimes I managed to resolve crises and they disappeared, but with each resolution, new crises appeared and the pace accelerated. I tried to keep up.

As the winter holidays approached, my emotions darkened and my sensitivities amplified. Through most of my life, the holidays had delivered sadness and dismay. Living with the black cloud of Kayla's drug abuse, relapse, and uncertain future, along with my family disputes, I was facing an especially challenging time.

I received an invitation to join the family for Thanksgiving. My emotions were still too fragile. I acknowledged the kindness extended and declined.

Dear friends graciously invited Avery and me to join their holiday celebration. While my heart ached and I yearned to be left alone, I knew it was a gift I best not refuse. We were fortunate to have such loving friends.

In my journal I wrote, "I want to feel accepted and somehow normal. I feel anything but normal. I feel strange. I feel like I don't quite know where my feet are, let alone my next step. I want to know, deep in my soul, that it's all the way it should be."

I counted my blessings. Energy and optimism came in spurts. There was no proof of progress, only trust.

With her phone privileges reinstated, Kayla called two weeks after her return to rehab. She sounded good and said she was happy. She reflected on her brief time at home and emphasized that her relapse proved she could not come back. I was relieved she wasn't blaming me; still, my heart ached with the reality. I hoped and prayed she was working through her demons.

I didn't know how her life would unfold, where she would live, or how she would survive in Florida. I chose not to dwell while she was in rehab. I still felt like a newcomer to the ways of addiction and recovery. As I wondered if I would ever feel different, I told myself I would rather not.

After residing at Sea Waves for a month, on Christmas day Kayla moved to Phase II of the treatment program. As I understood it, Phase II provided a framework within which residents transitioned to life in the real world. While there was staff on site, Phase II residents were given more free-dom to come and go on their own. They were expected to find jobs and provide for themselves.

Phase II residents attended IOP at The Center several nights a week. Kayla would no longer receive a food sti-pend, nor would she have access to the beach outings, bar-b-ques, or movie trips she had grown accustomed to. She would continue to be randomly drug tested and subject to curfew, and as before, she was required to attend daily AA/NA meetings for which Sea Waves provided transport.

As Kayla entered the next step of recovery, she seized her new responsibilities with enthusiasm and determina-tion. Each morning she got up early, rode a bus to town, and scoured the area for a job. Within days she was hired as a "gift shop attendant" at a beachfront business.

One day on the phone Kayla marveled, "Here I am, a drug addict, living in paradise." The paradox had not eluded me.

I was thrilled for Kayla's progress and anxious about the environment in which she was living. Paradise also meant party central. Fort Lauderdale was a destination and with bars everywhere, it was known for spring break mayhem and vacationing frivolity. With all that partying in her midst, I wondered how she would stay clean. Temptations were everywhere.

I had a long talk with my wise cousin Isaac. I bemoaned that getting clean in party central was counterintuitive and much too challenging. I demanded he provide logic I could grasp. Certain there was a flaw in the program, I insisted Kayla should remain secluded until her cravings for drugs were gone and her troubles healed.

I was aware of my projection. I wanted to be secluded until my pain was erased.

In his gentle, loving way, Isaac provided a succinct reality check. He said getting clean wasn't about the where; rather, it was about an internal resolve, a change in thinking, and a desire to live differently. "If you can be clean amidst the parties," he said, "you can be clean."

Isaac also reminded me that rarely was a location void of drugs and alcohol. "Most people can't live in a monastery up on a mountain," he cajoled. "Jude, this is real life. If she wants to get high, she will."

Isaac's words echoed in my mind, their truth callously mocking me. If Kayla wanted sobriety, she was going to have to love herself more than she loved the escape. She was going to have to do the hard work on her own. I couldn't do it for her.

Speaking from experience, Isaac shared his recovery process. He said at some point his focus shifted and he stopped thinking about drugs. Addicts and dealers stopped appearing to him like "shiny pennies," and he got on with his life.

Impatiently I yearned for Kayla to arrive at that same juncture. She was vulnerable, and I was raw. *Would she ever get to that point? Would I ever escape the nightmare? How long did I have to wait? What else did we have to endure?*

Kayla trained for a week at her new job. In the second week, management failed to put her on the schedule. She assumed it was a fluke until, in the third week, she was only scheduled for two days. Distressed, she realized she couldn't sustain her life with so few working hours and the week-to-week uncertainty. She tendered her resignation.

Once again Kayla was seeking employment. Time moved quickly and her stay at Sea Waves was coming to a swift conclusion. She had no job and no place to live.

My thoughts were dark and my body ached. I was a chronic combination of fear and sadness. I withdrew, choosing to talk to very few people. Once again communicating was just too hard. Isolation took hold.

So much of my life was upside down. I was working twelve hours a day. I spent most of my weekends in bed, stricken with stress headaches and exhaustion. The extra income I was earning helped me catch up on bills but didn't afford me any extras. Cooking, cleaning, and other demands were more than I could manage.

What was I doing? Where was I going? I struggled to find respite from my fears. One minute I had a head of steam, made decisions, moved forward; the next minute I felt overwhelmed, hopeless, and despondent.

As an important key to healing, Katherine had been encouraging me to tap into my creative. She suggested I turn to my art and to nature when I didn't know what else to do. She maintained that when in the creative, answers would come.

I began painting a portrait of my grandfather. I began weaving. It had been a long time since I focused on my art. I walked in nature and listened to the birds and the trees. I brought my camera and framed pictures through the lens. I found peace in my creative. I felt grounded. I moved forward.

I continued to attend yoga classes and worked on quieting my mind with meditation. Sometimes I spontaneously burst into tears. Katherine explained that in those moments I was connecting to the real me, the beautiful me, and that the tears were a release of the old. She saw my progress even when I could not.

Indeed, I was changing. I didn't always feel good, but I heard the whispers of transformation.

CHAPTER THIRTY:

HALFWAY

It was the end of January 2013. In a blink, Kayla's time in rehab was concluding. Processing her release, a woman from Sea Waves called to tell me Kayla would be leaving the following day. I became instantly frantic. *Where would she go? What was next? How would she survive? Was she ready? Was she healed?*

Matter-of-factly, the woman explained that Kayla's next step would be a "halfway house," where supervision and structure provided the framework for clean and sober living. It was an environment designed to help addicts adjust to real life in general society.

Halfway sounded a lot like Phase II of rehab; however, instead of insurance footing the bill, Kayla would be responsible for the weekly rental payment. Anxiously, I questioned how we were to find such a place. The woman assured me she was actively seeking a placement, "But," she lamented, "there don't seem to be any openings."

I was a nervous wreck.

The next morning the woman from Sea Waves called to say she "found a bed." Upon request she provided a phone number with which to contact Camilla, the owner/operator of Internal Changes Halfway House (name changed).

Without delay, I dialed the phone, hoping to gather information and reassurance. I had no idea what questions to ask.

On the other end of the phone, a woman with a thick accent walked a fine line between abundant kindness and compassion, and utmost professionalism and detachment. She explained that her all female halfway house was comprised of separate apartments of various size. Kayla would be placed in a three-person apartment and share a bedroom.

Internal Changes required tenants to maintain a clean and respectful environment, and abide by strict rules. Kayla would be subject to random drug tests twice a week, mandatory weekly house meetings, and strict curfews. She would be required to attend ninety AA/NA meetings in ninety days, with an expectation that after ninety days she would continue to attend meetings.

Additionally, staff approval would be required for any medication Kayla required, even over the counter remedies. Entertaining men on the premises was forbidden and smoking inside prohibited. Kayla would be expected to get a job and secure a sponsor immediately.

Camilla made it abundantly clear that she had zero tolerance for non-conformity. Failure to conform meant immediate eviction. I was happy to hear she ran a tight ship. I believed Kayla had a good shot at recovery in such an environment.

As if removing the cork from a champagne bottle, my questions spilled forth. *Was the neighborhood safe?* Well, it wasn't the worst, but it also wasn't the best. *Was she close to the bus line or potential work?* She would have to walk a mile to the bus stop. It was possible that she would find a job within a couple of miles. *What was a sponsor?* Kayla would connect with a female member of NA who was living the program of recovery for at least a year, preferably longer, and was willing to build a supportive relationship with her. Kayla would go to her sponsor for support when she felt insecure in her recovery. The sponsor would also guide and support Kayla as she worked through the Twelve Steps of NA. *Where would she find a sponsor?* Kayla would find such a person in "the rooms" of NA (at meetings).

Though no one could provide the promise I sought, I still yearned for a guarantee that my daughter would be okay. Asking question after question, I wanted to keep Camilla on the phone as long as possible. In some way, I believed her answers could ease my fear. When I ran out of questions, I thanked Camilla and said goodbye.

Since Kayla didn't have a job and hadn't worked more than a few days at the gift shop, I agreed to pay her security deposit and first two weeks of rent. Camilla felt that would give Kayla enough time to find a job and begin paying her own bills.

I was terrified for Kayla. I was terrified for me. Ultimately, I had no choice but to trust that Internal Changes was the right living opportunity. Since it was the only bed available, the alternative was the street. I was grateful for Camilla's pragmatic guidance and wisdom. I wept.

Carrying the same suitcases with which she had arrived at rehab, Kayla was delivered to halfway. Once settled in, she called me to make clear she wasn't happy. With her resistance palpable, all I could do was listen and suggest she shift perspective, give it a chance, and find humility.

Without a counselor providing balance for Kayla's complaints and outbursts, it was hard to decipher the truth. She was far away, on her own, and no doubt afraid. While I was frustrated and racked with concern, in many ways the distance made it easier. After each call I would hang up the phone, take a deep breath, and hope for the best. There was nothing more I could do.

By her second week in halfway, a local burger restaurant hired Kayla. She was excited about her new minimum wage job, but she continued to complain venomously about her living situation. She said she felt out of place and hated being there. She grumbled about how mean the other women were. In addition, she was completely freaked out by her daily contact with palmetto bugs.

"I feel like I was just thrown into a place where I don't know anyone or where anything is, and I'm expected to act like an adult," Kayla texted.

"That is kind of the way it is," I responded, "except you weren't thrown. Survival had its cost. You will get through. You need patience and that determination you are so good at."

Evidenced by her ability to successfully negotiate drug addiction, I knew Kayla had a full complement of useful skills. She was determined, resourceful, fearless, clever, and more. I was certain that using those same skills in a sober life would take her far. I pointed out her strengths, hopeful she would come to recognize them in herself, tap in, and succeed in her recovery.

For people in recovery, making ends meet was a mammoth challenge. Before starting her new job, Kayla complained that her paychecks would be used, almost entirely, for rent. She questioned how she would buy food. Fortunately, Florida had a wonderful food stamp program for which Kayla qualified. She had filed the paperwork before she left rehab but hadn't yet been approved.

I urged Kayla to be patient. We didn't know how long it would take for her benefit to begin, but help was within reach. I was grateful to the state of Florida for their anticipated assistance. I encouraged Kayla to stay in gratitude as well.

In the meantime, Kayla asked me to provide a buffer. I sent her $30 and told her to make it last. She balked at the paltry sum. I suggested inexpensive eating options like peanut butter, pasta, and beans. I reminded her she was entitled to one meal during each shift she worked. I was confident she wouldn't starve.

Food wasn't my only concern, however. During her time in Phase II, Kayla had secretly begun dating a man I nicknamed "Boston." Ten years Kayla's senior, Boston had also been a resident at Sea Waves. Nothing about him seemed healthy.

Despite the deafening warnings clamoring to be heard, Kayla chattered about the wonderful relationship she had with Boston. She gushed about his kindness and listed the many things they had in common. She sent pictures of the two of them lying on the beach together, and elaborated that she was finally having fun and incredibly happy.

Three weeks after Kayla moved to halfway, I received a phone call from Camilla. Kayla had packed her bags again and presumably moved into an apartment with Boston. Camilla delivered the news as tactfully as possible. She explained that since her arrival, Kayla had been consistently hostile and angry, rude and volatile, resistant and combative. Under the cover of night, Kayla had gathered her things and left the premises. There was nothing Camilla could do. She was calling me as a courtesy.

As the blood drained from my head and my world spun, I managed to ask Camilla about the eventuality of Kayla returning. I was certain the relationship with Boston would fail. Camilla was non-committal. I went numb.

Shortly after I spoke to Camilla, Kayla also called. She declared that she "just couldn't stand the way (I) was treated at halfway." She insisted the rules were ridiculous, and the girls with whom she lived were awful. She said she was happy with Boston, and they were going to make it work. Giddy with the illusions of love, she shared that they had even purchased "this cute Forman Grill and are cooking together."

Kayla assured me she was making good decisions and was happy. Nothing I said would change her mind. I held my breath.

Three days later, in the middle of the night, I received a hysterical phone call. Kayla was alone, on the street, battered, and scared. Boston got violent and threw her, and her belongings, out. She didn't know where to turn.

I was 1500 miles away. I urged Kayla to reach out to Internal Changes and beg for her bed back.

Camilla objected to taking Kayla back, but Georgia, the house mom, fought for Kayla's return. Camilla reluctantly agreed. By the next morning, Kayla was once again living at Internal Changes.

Kayla's attitude changed.

Despite her periodic complaints, Kayla finally seemed to be adjusting to halfway and the rigors of her life in Florida. At least that's what I wanted to believe.

In a note to Dr. Menni I wrote, "Kayla is in Florida, living in a halfway house and working at a restaurant. She seems to have turned a corner in her recovery and sounds better every day. It has been quite a ride to say the least! She celebrated 100 days clean this week. Her thinking is still a bit scary at times, but I know that with each day it will get better. I miss her terribly...but now I have hope that she will come back to me whole one day."

My enthusiasm and sense of relief for Kayla's "recovery" became consuming. I bathed in a tub of optimism, convincing myself the worst was over and Kayla was cured.

Perhaps to remind, or maybe to reassure myself; perhaps to share joy, or maybe to ignore the real potential for relapse; perhaps to make it true, or maybe to dispel truth; I often referred to Kayla as "a miracle," "a success," and "healed." When Kayla heard me use such accolades, she would balk and reprimand me. She would remind me she had to take "one day at a time." Meant to be encouraging and empowering, my words were apparently harmful.

One day when I announced Kayla's addiction was a thing of the past, she became angry and hostile. She implored me to be grateful for the day we were in and stay out of the future. That was good advice for that moment and every moment! Nonetheless, her rebuke made me uneasy. It was like going into a marriage planning the divorce. *Was she planning to go back to drugs? Were my words going to accelerate her fall? Was Kayla going to die?*

Based on a prominent AA philosophy, addicts were repeatedly instructed to only take "one day at a time." The theory, as I understood it, was that anything beyond the present day could be overwhelming. Kayla was still dealing with cravings and reminders, and stresses and struggles; not to mention the mess she had left in her wake. She had to stay present in order to survive. Overwhelm created despair and it was too easy for despair to lead to relapse. *Wasn't that exactly how I was coping...staying in the moment, staying out of the future?*

I stopped referring to her success. I stopped applauding her recovery. I reigned in my expectations and held my breath. I still hoped her recovery was permanent. I reminded myself, "one day at a time."

CHAPTER THIRTY-ONE:
NOTHING IN ISOLATION

Around the same time Kayla moved to halfway, an email arrived in my inbox imploring me to right my wrongs with the family. The sender wrote, "It seems as if you would rather jeopardize all relationships...this family wants to help." Accusing me of shutting out the sincere understanding and love my family was willing to pour forth to "help" me, the sender urged me to fix my "broken" relationships, "Your parents are getting older... think of the joy it would bring to them to know that we will all be together as a family, today and long after they are gone."

While I knew the letter was written with the most honorable of intentions, I felt it was biased, and filled with admonitions and expectations. I was hurt by how little was actually understood about me or my struggle, and I was annoyed by the guilt provoking claims (but guilt was something I had to agree to).

Maintaining that the family had to "walk on egg shells" with me, the sender went on, "It is necessary for us to reflect on our faults and inadequacies. We must admit when we have been defeated or at least feel as if we were defeated."

Defeated? No, they had it all wrong. My actions were protective. I was finally honoring my needs. I felt neither defeated nor inadequate in that regard.

The email was a reminder that family and friends don't always understand or embrace our transformation. As we grow, they often fight to keep us static. I wondered why, if my family felt so enamored of me, did they continue to overlook who I was? And why did they want my company if they didn't like me? At times, it was very confusing, but my determination to move forward was strong.

As I wrote my response with honesty and confidence, I realized how much I had actually changed. The old me would have agreed to the guilt and would have suffered the shame. I would have tried, at my own expense, to make everyone else happy.

I replied:

> *There are a number of points on which I'd like to re-*
> *spond. First, Mom and I have a good relationship at*
> *this point, one that has taken a lot of work, reflection,*
> *and respect. It is not perfect, but it is genuine on my*
> *part and I believe on hers, and I treasure it.*
>
> *Next, I have heard the 'walking on eggshells' remark*
> *all my life. I've finally come to realize that this is a*
> *good thing. It means you are honoring my boundaries,*

boundaries that, whether or not you understand or approve, are in place because they are necessary for my well-being.

...I don't feel a need to defend myself. It always takes two in any relationship. I am more than willing to accept a portion of that relationship equation (regarding the conflicts at hand). The fact is, at this point, the most I anticipate is the ability to be in the same room without pain... Done is done, the future unknown.

Without any disrespect intended, not one person in this family has an inkling of what I have been through the last two years. We all deal with pain differently and I make no apologies for the way I've dealt with mine. If the family does not accept that, so be it. I do not dwell on it, nor do I seek sympathy or anything else. I do not presume to tell anyone else what is best for them, but when it comes to me, I am doing the best I can with what I have.

My siblings planned an anniversary celebration for our parents' fifty-sixth. I agreed to attend. I received a note saying they were glad I would be there. I replied with a thank you for the kind note. It was a start.

CHAPTER THIRTY-TWO:
IN A CHRYSALIS

It was mid-March and my replacement position was ending. All too familiar, my insecurities about the future were rising. I had been applying for full time teaching jobs to no avail, and I hated the thought of subbing again. It felt so humiliating and deflating after having my own classroom.

I was beyond exhausted and needed a break. I sought refuge in an unhealthy space.

Providing just enough contact to kept me off balance, Leo and I had begun seeing each other more regularly. Though I was evolving to genuinely like my own company, I still craved male companionship. Despite frequent disappointment, I yearned for the comfort of Leo's company and embrace. My feelings for him had not subsided.

As I pondered my twisted yearning and angst over Leo, I came to a startling realization. HE was MY addiction, my drug of choice. I thought about him constantly, even though I knew he was bad for me. Each reunion provided less joy, each departure left me feeling more desperate, and the craving to be back in his company was unbearable.

From the beginning, as I sought to understand my daughter's affliction, I realized I had limited ability. I did not have an addictive personality or leaning, making the logic (or lack thereof) of addiction nearly impossible to understand. I often said things like, "You know what a mess it makes of your life, just stop," and, "Why would you ever go back to that life knowing what you know?"

With the realization that Leo was my addiction, I began to glean an understanding of what Kayla had gone through. It was startling to realize the depth of difficulty embedded in recovery. Emotional cravings were hard enough, and with the addition of physical cravings, it was clearly a monstrous struggle.

At halfway Kayla volunteered to help in any way she could. She was finding joy and fulfillment through her contributions. As an added benefit, she was making connections and starting to fit in.

Kayla found a sponsor who supported and encouraged her, and guided her through the challenges of the Twelve Step program. With great determination and focus, Kayla routinely met with Eden to unearth the truths that would help her heal. Sometimes completing multiple steps in one session, Kayla excitedly reported that she felt invigorated by the work. Constantly seeking evidence to support my desire for her full recovery, I believed her exemplary progress provided a guarantee.

We spoke regularly, if not nightly. Kayla loved her job and felt she had found her calling in the restaurant industry. She already had aspirations to become a line cook and eventually move into management. Well-liked and appreciated, her managers validated her potential.

With Kayla's improved attitude, optimistic outlook, and significant homesickness, I booked her on a flight home for an April visit. We eagerly counted the weeks, then days, until her arrival.

As the acute stressors of Kayla's condition diminished, my personal issues gained strength. My body ached as a result of a prolonged, severe fibromyalgia flare. Going back to subbing was hard on my ego and on my bank account. I was grappling with how to proceed in work and relationship. My self-esteem was in hiding, and I felt frightened, frail, and alone. Fighting depression, I was once again caught in a "work-nap-eat-sleep" cycle.

Writing to Katherine, I wondered, "Maybe this is how the caterpillar feels when he is in the chrysalis waiting to become a butterfly. I just wish I knew if I was fooling myself." It was difficult to keep trusting when I couldn't see evidence of progress. (How quickly I forgot.)

Katherine replied, "Change is hard - can't see around the curves but that's where the new beginnings are."

I continued taking the next step.

I attended my parents' anniversary party. Cordiality felt comfortable, and everyone got along. I was happy to be there for my parents' sake and glad to reduce the collective stress.

In session with Katherine the following week, she helped me fortify a sense of optimism and return to trusting my evolution. She validated my feelings and encouraged me to keep allowing them to come "up and out."

A few days later I emailed, "Please tell me how I'm supposed to find the joy??? I have a much better toolbox now, but it seems to be hard to open."

The seesaw of emotion had become familiar.

Katherine continued to encourage me to do what made sense in the moment, to stay away from "should," and to feel what I felt. Again and again, she validated my journey and my progress.

Meanwhile, Kayla's car was a noose tightening around my neck. A daily reminder of the painful past, I dreaded the eventual impact the sale would have on Kayla. Nonetheless, it had to be sold. I was resolved to do what I had to do.

With little interest generated from previous ads, Leo helped me create and place a new one. I was beginning to accept that I would have to take a substantial loss on the car. I gathered my strength.

While I was consumed with getting through each day, my challenges did not unfold in isolation. It was no surprise that the one person closest to me was also struggling to survive. Avery's ability to cope was weakening.

Given the intensity of stress in our home, I had been in regular contact with Avery's school personnel for some time. Complaining he didn't feel well, he had been missing a lot of school. When he attended, I received reports that he was sleeping in class or non-participant. I was actively seeking solutions to help him thrive, to no avail.

I tried everything within reason and budget to help my son, but by the end of March we had a full-blown crisis on hand. Directed by the school to make some calls, I was able to secure free professional services from the county, including in-home therapy. I felt grateful for the help and guidance we would receive.

Unfortunately, not everyone felt the gratitude I felt. One individual called my actions "heinous" and accused me of jeopardizing Avery's future. I was criticized for my "inability to parent" and berated for my ignorance. Despite the anger and cruel criticism thrust at me, there was no offer of help or alternate solution.

Another birthday came and went. I didn't celebrate.

CHAPTER THIRTY-THREE:
VISIT HOME

Eager for her April visit to begin, Kayla arrived at the Fort Lauderdale airport hours ahead of her evening flight. An hour before the scheduled departure, she called to tell me the flight had been delayed. As the new departure time approached, she phoned again with news of another delay, then another.

Through our mutual, enormous frustration, I did my best to keep Kayla calm and help her process the information she was receiving. Late that night, after waiting at the airport for many tense hours, Kayla received confirmation that her flight home had been cancelled. She was given a voucher to sleep at a nearby hotel and scheduled to board a flight that would arrive at an alternate airport first thing the following morning.

Exhausted, disappointed, and frightened, Kayla gathered her things. Seeing her dismay, a man offered to help. He had also been disappointed by the cancelled flight and, like Kayla, had been given a voucher to overnight at the same hotel. Additionally, he was scheduled to depart on the same morning flight.

Despite my significant concern for Kayla's safety, the stranger turned out to be an angel. He paid for the taxi they shared to the hotel and accompanied Kayla back to the airport the next morning. They enjoyed breakfast together, boarded the plane, and never saw each other again.

Finally, my daughter was on her way home!

I could barely contain myself when I spotted Kayla walking toward me at the airport. I thirsted for our time together. As if in slow motion, we moved swiftly toward each other. For the first time in six months, I had my beautiful child in my arms. I didn't want to let go.

During her abbreviated stay, Kayla would spend a night with her big brother, enjoy time with her grandparents, and visit dear friends. I was glad for her connection with others, but selfishly, I wanted her all to myself. I savored her company and actively dreaded her departure.

Four days later, at five o'clock in the morning, we arrived at the one gate, local airport where Kayla would board a plane that would take her back to Florida. Without hesitation, Kayla requested I be given a gate pass. She easily explained that she was in recovery and at risk. While my emotions were overflowing, I felt proud of her confident posture. During her time in Florida, she had gained a level of independence I admired.

Over and over, I reminded myself Kayla was not returning to Florida an addict; rather, she was in recovery, clean,
and productive. She was returning to halfway and a job.
She was reestablishing her life.

Waiting for the boarding call, I choked back tears. Kayla
remained brave and resigned, musing at my extreme emotion. I couldn't fathom what she had been through, nor the
courage she needed to live in Florida alone. The agony of
our long-distance relationship was overwhelming. I reminded myself I had been given the gift of her recovery. My
little girl was alive.

Despite missing her family terribly, Kayla concluded
that Florida was where she needed to be. I agreed. We made
small talk, awaiting and resisting the passage of time.

The boarding call came and we hugged goodbye. I
watched Kayla bravely walk onto the tarmac and climb the
stairs leading to the plane door. As she disappeared onto
the aircraft, I bawled uncontrollably.

Once settled in her seat, Kayla texted, "I love you Mom.
I'll be back before you know it, and I'll be even better of a
person. Growing more every day."

I stood at the window, watching and crying. I tried hard
not to make a spectacle of myself. There was an elephant
standing on my chest and I struggled to breathe. A kind
airport worker led me upstairs to the "observation deck,"
where I watched the plane take off.

I stood dazed, grateful, and heartbroken, waving as if
Kayla could see me.

I trusted that Kayla was healing and held her texted sentiment close. She was growing. I had my daughter back. As I mourned her departure, I counted my blessings. Gratitude reminded me of my good fortune.

Despite Kayla's resolve, going back to Florida had its challenges. As we both went back to the cadence of our lives, missing the family became unbearable for her, and her loneliness amplified. Missing her intensely, I felt much the same.

Through text and talk we worked our way through the struggles of being so far apart. "It will all be good Kay," I bolstered. "We are where we are meant to be today. We don't know what tomorrow will bring."

I worked hard to believe my own words and repeated the sentiment often.

Obsessively seeking assurance that Kayla was well, I texted and phoned frequently. When I didn't receive a timely response, my thoughts went dark. I imagined her with a needle in her arm or worse. Panic and terror were regular companions.

I knew better than to imagine the worst. Kayla was healthy and worry only depleted me. Up and down went the seesaw of my emotions.

Our frequent communication was filled with sentiment and gratitude. Kayla often credited me with giving her the attributes I admired most: her optimism, her love of people, her work ethic, and her spiritual groundedness. Kayla's determination inspired me. Besides kicking drugs, she was on her own, 1500 miles from home, and paying her own bills. She persevered.

CHAPTER THIRTY-FOUR:
DAILY CHALLENGES

In halfway, Kayla lived with women who were also struggling to transform their lives. Though she yearned for deep connections, friendships forged were tenuous at best. Too often "friends" went back to drugs, leaving Kayla sad and discouraged.

With so many treatment centers in the Fort Lauderdale area, there was a huge demand for employment by people in recovery. The restaurant industry seemed to be a magnet for them. Consequently, even the friendships Kayla forged at work were often with people who had a similar past.

One afternoon at work, Kayla discovered a co-worker/friend shooting up in his car. Distressed, Kayla texted, "I know I can't save him and that he has to do it when he's ready, but I'm having a hard time not telling someone. He looks awful and thank God I was just disgusted when I saw it, but I really care about him and at the end of the day, I don't want to see him die."

My mind raced with fear, then sorrow, then fear again. I was grateful it wasn't my child, grateful for her disgust, grateful for her concern, and simultaneously aware that he was someone's son, someone's brother, someone's friend. Indeed, he was Kayla's friend.

I ruminated on the past, my anxiety rising. It could have been Kayla in that car! Just a short time ago it was Kayla! I thought, "There but for the grace of God..." I counted my blessings. I regained composure.

Kayla toiled over her friend's relapse, finally confronting him with what she knew. She urged him to go back to treatment and understood his resistance. He feared losing all that he had achieved. He had a job, an apartment, and a car. *Why on Earth would he pick up again?*

As Kayla reasoned with her friend, an idea was born. Desperate to have a vehicle, Kayla would assume his car payments. She would use his car while he was in treatment, and when he repaid her, she would return his car to him. In her view, it was a win-win solution. She was giddy with anticipation.

Relaying the details of their plan, Kayla assured me, "We have to work out the kinks, but I wouldn't mind having a car for the summer. But we'll see."

Though danger was written all over her proposed arrangement, I tried not to react emotionally. I conveyed my most pressing concern, "Kayla, that was his heroin den!" I expressed my strong disapproval and released the subject. Predictably, Kayla cast my warning aside. I assuaged my fear, telling myself it was unlikely their plan would become reality.

Needing a car had become fodder for regular, significant tirades. Working long hours and walking two miles each way to work, Kayla often returned to halfway after midnight. As the summer months in Florida encroached, the heat was also taking its toll. She begged me to let her have "her" car.

I hated that Kayla was walking home exhausted and in the dark, and worried for her safety. Nonetheless, I reminded myself it was her mess to clean. I had to stay firm. Tough love was saving her life.

In response to Kayla's explosive demands for a car, I would calmly invite her to make a budget and save for one. Not having the financial means to help her helped me stay strong. Despite her heart wrenching pleas, I insisted she make it happen on her own. I ached in sympathy for her struggle.

Kayla cycled through meltdowns and demands. I reasoned that she WANTED a car but didn't NEED one. She begged me to let her come home where "her car" sat idle.

Irrational thinking continued to permeate Kayla's rants. Her old companions, "entitlement" and "victimhood," intensified their presence. Hearing them step forward terrified me. As long as Kayla believed herself a victim, I knew she was at risk for relapse.

CHAPTER THIRTY-FIVE:
KAYLA'S BIRTHDAY

Saddened that I would be unable to join Kayla on her birthday, I plotted from afar to make her day special. For years, rather than a birthday cake, I had been providing her favorite Italian delicacy, cannolis. I pushed into high gear searching for a way to orchestrate a surprise delivery. I imagined the joy and sense of love she would feel upon receipt.

I wrote to a friend, "I have visions of cannolis arriving at her door...would be such a treat to her."

I failed.

I found out Avery would not graduate high school as planned.

I was requested for a subbing job working one on one with a boy who accidentally stabbed me in the eye with a pencil.

I lost my wallet.

I felt off balance, ungrounded, and vacuous. I couldn't seem to land anywhere. I wasn't happy or sad, eager or disinterested, motivated or unmotivated. I was in limbo. My inability to find a next step was unnerving.

Before I knew it, overwhelm set in. I felt depressed and alone again. I concluded I needed fun in my life, something to look forward to and feel good about, something that was just for me. I wasn't sure what fun looked like, and it was impossible to identify when I felt so awful. I allowed myself to feel what I felt and stayed open to solutions.

One of the greatest horrors plaguing people in recovery was the lingering mess they created while using. Legal troubles were common. On the eighth of May, a summons addressed to Kayla arrived in the mail.

Certain Kayla would want to run from her responsibilities, I franticly texted, "Baby, there is a summons in the mail for you. My heart is in my throat. What should I do with it? Returning it to sender will just delay. I can send it to you, or I can open it and tell you what it says. You know ignoring it will only make it worse. You have seen that happen (a reference to friends who went to jail for not responding to summonses)."

While I knew it was not mine to decide or handle, I spun over how to protect my child from the pain and consequences of her past. I was in overdrive trying to think of a solution. I considered every contingency.

Despite receiving my text while at work, Kayla responded immediately. Without hesitation, eager to face the truth of her past and settle it, she asked me to open her mail and tell her what it said.

I felt proud of her resolve, confidence, and commitment; nonetheless, I was nauseated by the thought of legal trouble. Maybe it was me who wanted to run. I insisted we open it together and asked that she call me when she was free.

That evening, relief came swiftly. The summons turned out to be for jury duty! We laughed and cried; the crisis was averted for the time being. I was quite aware a new crisis could arise at any moment.

To her credit, Kayla understood how much her past triggered and stressed me. On the heels of the summons, she texted, "I may not be recovered, but I know right from wrong, and I know when to reach out for help when I need it. Don't worry Mom."

Indeed, Kayla was proving herself to be strong and independent. She was working hard, advancing at her job, finally making friends, and doing her spiritual (Twelve Step) work. At halfway, she was emerging as a leader. She seemed to be in a good place.

"I'm so happy with my life," Kayla texted. "Two new girls knocked on my apartment door this morning and asked if I could lead them in prayer. It feels so good to do the right thing. I might still think about getting high sometimes, but I want my recovery more than I ever want to get high. I love my life today."

I embraced her sentiment as best I could. All we had was the moment we were in. The more I settled into that moment, the more I relaxed and found joy. My daughter was healthy and safe. She loved her life. She seemed a model of healthy recovery. At the same time, I couldn't deny that seeing the word "high" in her communication sent me reeling. I acknowledged the trigger and chose not to dwell. As Kayla relayed her excitement, I let my heart expand.

No sooner had I settled into Kayla's enthusiasm then the script changed. Chaos returned. Such was the roller coaster of recovery and consequently of my life.

"It feels impossible to clean up the mess," Kayla texted. "I can't make more money at a job like this and to get a better job, I need a car, but I can't get a car, I need money. It doesn't work."

I tried hard to bolster her resolve, to coach her to find spirit, and to guide her toward healthy coping. Using the language of her Twelve Steps, I encouraged, "Put your faith in a higher power," "Trust," "Stop thinking so much," "One step at a time," "Meditate." I was suggesting she use the same tools I was learning to rely on. Those were my bedrock.

At work on her birthday, Kayla's co-workers showered her with balloons and cupcakes. Though I was unable to secure a cannoli delivery, I sent a small gift so she would have something to open. She had a good day.

Three days later, with my children scattered, Mother's Day dispensed an emotional challenge. I turned to gratitude. I was grateful to have kids whom I loved deeply and who unquestionably loved me. I chose to enjoy the day, focusing my attention on my mother. My relationship with Mom had grown from troubled to supportive, from adversarial to compassionate. A silver lining resulting from the nightmare, I was abundantly thankful for the gift of my mother. And, I wasn't sitting in the waiting room at detox! I joined my family at my brother's house.

I got food poisoning from the bagged salad. I lost two days of work.

I wrote to Katherine, "I'm still struggling through in general. It's been a month fraught with challenges. The good news is, I'm still standing."

Tired of walking "everywhere" and aggravated by the restrictions resulting from not having a car, Kayla's obsession, along with her indignation, grew. The Florida heat and torrential rains accelerated her misery. Her demands got louder.

Every conversation digressed into a plea for a car. Kayla complained vehemently about her lack of funds, lack of mobility, lack of credit, and lack of resources. She contended she had no ability to shift her situation.

I told Kayla that as much as it hurt, it was about cleaning up her mess and paying her dues. I didn't have the answers, but others had been where she was and successfully figured it out. I encouraged her to talk to people in recovery. I encouraged her to call Isaac for suggestions. She balked at every suggestion I made.

Refusing to take action toward a healthy solution, Kayla battered me with texts: "I'm working myself into the ground," "I need a life," "When will any of this pay off?" "This all sucks," "I'm tired of (fill in the blank)."

Kayla's rants were wearing me down. Despite believing she had to do for herself, I ached for her substantial struggle. The physical difficulties she faced were enormous. I felt guilty for my inability/unwillingness to help. I wanted to help. I accepted that I couldn't help.

Unyielding, Kayla's whining, pleading, and demanding pounded my emotions. I held strong, successfully resisting the bait Kayla offered. I was working through my guilt. Over and over, I strained to forgive myself for the pain I perceived I was causing.

"Can you guilt my father into buying me a car?" Kayla inquired one day.

Kayla had to work through her challenge. It was not within my ability or my intention to help her buy a car. I was absolutely not willing to ask her father. Such a request would only serve to agitate and disappoint us both.

"Your uncle thinks you can find a car for a thousand dollars. Call him and ask how and what to look for," I suggested.

Her sarcasm bled through the phone, "Good thing I have a thousand dollars. Oh wait..."

I remained reasonable, rational, and calm, once again inviting Kayla to save her money. I reminded her that we had already discussed the issue to death. I remained focused on her independence; emphasizing that she had to make it happen, no one else.

"I don't want anyone to do it for me, but I think I've earned it by now," Kayla charged.

And there they were again, the demands of entitlement and victimhood, an addict's best friends. It had been seven months, but red flags continued to flap in the turbulent wind.

CHAPTER THIRTY-SIX:

MISERY

I missed Kayla and was eager to see where she lived and worked. In early June, I decided I would go to Florida. I planned a five-day trip for the end of July. I made hotel reservations close to the beach and reserved a rental car. It was the first "vacation" I would have in many years.

Kayla secured approval to stay with me in the hotel, provided she "dropped" (was drug tested) at least once during my visit. Though she would still have to work, we anticipated plenty of time together. We discussed possible adventures.

My excitement ran amuck. As I announced my vacation plans, I boasted to my friends about how well Kayla was doing. I proudly referred to her as a "miracle."

Kayla and I began our countdown.

For the most part, Kayla seemed to be making sound judgments, and I supported her choices. She was managing the disappointments and frustrations of daily life remarkably well. However, the empty promises of advancement at work were mounting, and the scheduled wage increases were slow to come. Camilla raised Kayla's rent by $25.00 a week, and her roommates were on a carousel of relapse.

Given her busy work schedule, Kayla went to NA or AA meetings when she could fit them in. She had surpassed the mandate of ninety meetings in ninety days and was comfortable going less often. She felt the "local" meeting was filled with too many newly recovered addicts, and she preferred not to expose herself to the inherent risks they brought.

One evening, as one more roommate returned to drugs, Kayla texted, "I don't want to be a drug addict anymore. I just want to be a normal fucking person. I'm so tired of this shit…. Everyone I get close to relapses and fucking dies. I don't want to be surrounded by it anymore. Five relapses in the past two days at my house."

It was one more of the monumental challenges Kayla faced each day. How, I wondered, do addicts ever stay clean? With so many major obstacles in their way, the odds seemed too great. I continued to believe Kayla was the miracle.

I scrambled for wisdom. I searched for words of encouragement. *What do I say to a twenty-one-year-old who is watching people die?* I validated her pain and her challenge, and reminded her she had great strength and determination, a generous, caring personality, and a bright future toward which she was working. I tried to raise her confidence and dissuade her despair.

Seeking to shift Kayla's focus, I pointed out the good that surrounded her. I encouraged her to find gratitude. "Mistakes take time to heal. You are doing it," I emphasized.

"I don't want to do this anymore," Kayla pleaded.

"I'm sorry baby," I responded. "Hold onto your success as much as possible. It's a hard road you chose, and you are a happy outcome. You are a success story. You are a model for what can be. You will not be surrounded by this forever. You will move on. You are stronger than you think. You have a light inside that glows as inspiration for others. I love you."

Panicked that Kayla could be the next relapse, I was trying to convince myself she would be okay as much as I was trying to convince her. There was a mirror in what I said as well. I, too, was stronger than I thought and had a light that inspired others. I fought to stay confident, optimistic, and forward moving.

I reminded us both, "This too shall pass." I repeated that phrase often. It reminded me, as my father did throughout my life, that nothing lasts forever. Maybe relief was around the corner.

As Kayla felt more and more overwhelmed, she texted, "I don't know how to do all of this. I've never been an adult before."

Hearing her agony, sparked my own. Being an adult was hard enough under the best circumstances. Alone in Florida, Kayla's struggles were amplified. It was easy to grab onto despair.

I bolstered my resolve and mustered my strength. Kayla had to take responsibility, push through, and do what was necessary to succeed. I couldn't do it for Kayla, but I could definitely take full responsibility for myself.

"You are learning and doing a great job," I told her. "I don't always know how either. It's a process."

Kayla and I were each other's mirrors. Navigating life was one big adventure. Being an adult required courage and determination. Like Kayla, sometimes I felt it was just too hard, and I wanted to give up. I wanted someone to fix it for me. I had to do it for myself. I had to take one step at a time.

As Kayla backed off her demands for a car, she accelerated her demands to leave Florida. "I want to come home," she texted. "I could get a job and buy a car and pay my shit a lot faster."

I couldn't blame Kayla for working herself into a full-fledged pity party, but I also couldn't coddle her. I was her rock, the one she turned to with her frustrations. Not having a car, empty promises at work, relapses and aggravation at halfway, a sense of isolation, and missing family conspired to push her over the edge. I had great empathy.

I acknowledged the magnitude of Kayla's challenges, but a voice deep inside told me there was a bigger problem brewing. I tried to focus on what was working. Kayla was still clean. I pushed the negative thoughts aside.

I was in constant battle with myself. Tough love incited a strange amalgam of opposing feelings. For Kayla's highest good, the actions I had to take contradicted my motherly instincts. While I wanted desperately to say "yes," I had to keep saying "no," hoping Kayla would connect with her own strength and resolve, and stay clean.

I questioned every thought, every decision, and every communication. The voice of dissent was steady, but I remained committed to Kayla's recovery. I stayed strong. I told her she could not come home yet.

Kayla demanded, "WHEN?"

I knew the first two years held the most profound challenges and risks for a recovering addict. While there was nothing written in stone, two years seemed a reasonable target. The more I said no, the more Kayla argued and insisted.

As Kayla argued, I routinely heard the addict rise up. If she was going to survive, she had to take full responsibility. She had to admit her mess and fix it. No one owed her anything. I knew she had what it took.

I hid my despair as best I could, reminding myself I was saving Kayla's life. The guilt, the grief, and my desire to rescue Kayla from her pain were unbearable. Still, as her words triggered deep fear, I strengthened my resolve. I could not rush in to fix things for her. I could not enable. I had to stay strong.

CHAPTER THIRTY-SEVEN:

RACHEL

I didn't know anyone who escaped life's challenges, who fully eluded stress, or who avoided the pain inherent in fear, loss, and disappointment. Stress and pain seemed to be natural byproducts of living. Even great healers had suffered. Certainly, no one consciously chose to endure the ravages of life.

As I sought my own healthy coping solutions, I often wondered why so many people chose unhealthy options. Drug and alcohol abuse, working too much, shopping too much, eating too much or too little, cutting, gambling, etc. were ways people tried to run from and numb their pain. How, I wondered, did people learn to manage pain differently? How did they replace destructive behavior with options that nourished them?

Kayla continued to smoke like a chimney and threw herself into work. Clearly, work and cigarettes were preferable to drugs; however, if she was going to stay away from drugs permanently, I believed she had to find healthy alternatives. She needed a "go to" that didn't depend on anyone else for success and didn't adversely impact the quality of her life.

For most of Kayla's life, dance had been her passion and her release. After high school graduation, dance opportunities dried up, leaving her without a good emotional outlet.

Even while dancing, however, she worked and smoked too much. As I listened to Kayla's angst fifteen hundred miles away, I knew she had to find healthy ways to manage and release her extreme emotions.

Fully understanding the need for healthy coping skills, when on premises, Camilla provided halfway residents with impromptu yoga and meditation sessions. Kayla valued and enjoyed those sessions, but they were not pursuits she wanted to continue on her own. She agreed she needed something but rejected most of my suggestions: jogging, writing, reading, drawing, nature, and yoga and meditation. Those were the things that helped me. We brainstormed ideas, seeking something that would appeal to Kayla.

One of the most talented people I knew, Kayla's creativity pushed well beyond dance to drama, visual arts, poetry, and music. One day she mentioned a desire to play the ukulele. She said she had previously played one and really enjoyed it.

"They're easy to learn, and I think it would ease a lot of my stress!" Kayla offered.

"That," I thought, "I can provide!"

I jumped to action, scouring reviews on line, researching vendors, and comparing prices. Within days, a ukulele was en route to Kayla. It felt good to find something I could do to help.

Kayla's emotions continued to bounce up and down. When Sea Waves asked her to return to the rehab as a speaker, she felt honored and thrilled. Their invitation helped

Kayla realize how far she had come and how well she was doing. She looked forward to conveying hope to the residents both in word and by example. Her confidence soared.

Kayla had formed a deep friendship with a beautiful young woman named Rachel. Residing in halfway together, they found connection in their similar backgrounds and views on life. As real friendships require, they shared meaningful concerns, triumphs, and fears, as well as adventures and fun. Rachel even invited Kayla to her family's home for a holiday meal.

Rachel was often in the room with Kayla when I phoned. Rachel and I spoke several times, sharing well beyond cordial conversation between strangers. She had an infectious joy about her, and oozed kindness and generosity. As they laughed and "played" together, Rachel and Kayla sent me "selfies" and texts. Rachel's smile matched her personality; she could light up a room.

Though Rachel and I hadn't met in person, she crawled right into my heart next to Kayla's childhood friends. It took no time before Rachel had become "one of mine." We even spoke several times on our own. I was eager to meet her when I arrived in Florida.

By the end of the month, another emotional bomb exploded. Kayla texted, "Rachel relapsed. I hate living in halfway."

Hearing the news, I felt like I had driven into a cement wall. I knew my pain was small compared to Kayla's. *How could this happen?*

Once again, the paradox of recovery showed its hand. The very system designed to encourage sobriety was infested with dangerous influences and destructive temptations. At halfway, residents were vulnerable, struggling, and united in fighting the demon. At AA/NA meetings, addicts working to stay clean sought strength and support from one another. All the while, so many were teetering on the edge of relapse.

In theory, success bred success. Examples of long-term sobriety gave hope and confidence to the newly recovered. Sadly, the opposite was equally possible, with one relapse giving way to others. Whenever Kayla reported relapses, my heart raced with renewed fear for her. When Kayla told me Rachel relapsed, the world grew darker, and my worry reached new depths.

Relapse and death were all too common occurrences in Kayla's young life. Though she yearned to be out of that pain-ridden community, she needed it to survive.

CHAPTER THIRTY-EIGHT:
CONNOR

Admittedly, my coping skills weren't always the best. As I continued searching for a man to ease my pain, I perused online dating sites. I didn't find anyone of interest, but several men contacted me. Ironically, they had one common characteristic; they were each in recovery.

The repeated "coincidence" was more than curious (I didn't believe in coincidence). With each contact, fear reflexively rose in my body. I already had more connection to addiction than I wanted. I wasn't looking for more.

As each man revealed his past, I watched the ugly shadow of judgment sneak in through the back door of my thoughts. Judging someone for his past, however, felt too much like condemning my own daughter. Although I wanted to run, I felt I owed it to myself, and to Kayla, to allow for possibility.

Though nice enough, none of the men with whom I spoke were "right for me." Nonetheless, each provided a unique glimpse into the world where my daughter lived. Each enriched my understanding of addiction. The insights were both a blessing and a curse.

It became painfully evident no one would be "right for me" until I learned to love myself. In my journal I wrote, "I'm learning to respect and honor myself. I do have a light

253

that shines brilliantly, and when it is time, I will attract a wonderful man…one who accepts me."

Contrarily I wrote, "Sometimes I feel like I'll go crazy being alone any longer, but being alone is not a physical characteristic. It's in my psyche. I feel alone even when surrounded by people."

In moments of despair, despite my affirmations and periodic clarity, my thoughts turned to the familiar… Leo. Though mostly fantasy, he had been my focus for a long time. It was hard to break the cycle.

While I made every effort to stay out of Kayla's mess, her past periodically showed up. Sometimes my house phone would ring, delivering a jarring call from a collection agency. I usually stated that Kayla no longer lived with me and quickly ended the call. One day, a particularly aggressive agent caught me off guard. Mindlessly, I gave him Kayla's phone number. Immediately realizing what I had done, I called her in warning.

I firmly believed that cleaning up her mess meant Kayla had to repay her debts. I was also well aware that she was barely making ends meet. As long as she was struggling financially, it would be impossible for her to address her albatross. It was a real catch 22.

Financial stability was essential before Kayla could make amends for her past. She also needed to heal. To that end, she often considered the big questions about life and death. One evening she texted, "Mother Earth is my higher power. I don't believe in a man in the sky; it's just not real in my head. But Mother Earth and the collective consciousness of the Universe are. So when I talk about God, that's what I mean."

I had been exploring the topic of life and death all my life. Kayla and I spent long hours discussing our ideology. Holding similar beliefs, I was happy and excited to support her assertion. When she forgot, I would remind her, and when she wanted more, we would continue to explore together. I believed finding meaning in life gave way to purpose.

As we settled into July, Kayla excitedly reported that she "met a boy." Connor was a new hire at the restaurant where Kayla worked. Residing at a nearby men's halfway house, they had much in common. She gushed, "I met someone. He's really sweet...I have never met anyone as considerate and just caring as he is... only problem is, he only has ninety days, so I'm taking things real slow."

It was nice to hear Kayla's enthusiasm. I wanted her to feel "like a normal person" and was eager for her to have some fun. However, given what I knew about recovery and the recommendation to stay out of romantic relationship for at least two years, red flags were rising once again.

I couldn't blame Kayla for wanting male companionship or a romantic connection. *Wasn't that what I wanted, too?* But relationships were a challenge even under the best of circumstances. They muddied thinking, tempted danger, and distracted focus. Sometimes they caused us to make dumb decisions and take foolish actions.

Observing Kayla's recovery to that point, I noticed that each day made a significant difference in how she processed her challenges, viewed risk, and managed emotions. Her thinking and decision-making had become clearer and more rational with time. Ninety days was like infancy in the ways of recovery.

"That does not make me happy," I told Kayla. "He still has dope brain…I don't want to burst your bubble, but he is still in a sick head."

In my opinion, Kayla's choice to pursue a relationship was irresponsible and short sighted. I worried that Connor would bring her down. I encouraged her to remember herself at ninety days. I reminded her that at that point in her recovery, she was just turning the corner from volatile and angry to willing and humble.

Kayla assured me she knew the risks and was eyes wide open. She reiterated that she was "taking it slow." Over the following weeks, Connor was all she talked about.

Connor had a car and a computer.

CHAPTER THIRTY-NINE:
SOLD

B ecause of Kayla's exemplary progress, Camilla suggested she move from halfway to three-quarter housing. With less restriction, three quarter was the next logical step toward a fully independent life. Since all of the women in three-quarter had substantial clean time, the turnover due to relapse would subside.

Kayla felt great about the offer and the confirmation of her progress. Unfortunately, however, with the three-quarter residence a mile further from her job, she would need a car to get to work. She complained bitterly about her conundrum and resurrected her demands.

Unbeknownst to Kayla, for more than two months I had been trying to sell "her" car. Exhausted by the process, I had seriously considered keeping it for her, but I reminded myself of both the financial burden and that it had been her drug den. She had too many memories wrapped up in that car—people, places, and things. Besides, she had to earn her own wheels. She had to take responsibility and find her own way. Tough love.

After more than a dozen inquiries and test drives, I had what appeared to be a serious buyer. Understandably cautious, the prospective buyer requested I prove the integrity of the car. With a multipoint inspection from the dealership and a new, "passed" inspection sticker, they would agree to the price.

I had already dropped my asking price over $1500. I was horrified by the thought of spending more money but needed the car out of my possession. It needed a new battery, which I purchased. It was otherwise in good shape.

Over a period of a few stressful weeks, I jumped the remaining hurdles. Finally, the car was sold. As I watched the new owner drive away, I filled with raw emotion. I was thrilled and relieved that the sale was complete, and excited for new life to be breathed into a vehicle that had served us well. At the same time, as I endured another piece of Kayla depart, tears streamed down my cheeks.

Kayla was going to be shocked, disappointed, and furious. As I ruminated about the right time to tell her, my anxiety rose and my heart ached. *I did the right thing.*

A few weeks before my trip to Florida, Kayla texted, "I have eight months now, I'm cured."

Despite her lighthearted optimism, Kayla's declaration scared me. In the past she had consistently insisted addicts were never "cured," only "in recovery." Though her words held a grave warning, I desperately wanted to own them. *Was she cured? Please let that be true!*

As my trip to Florida neared, Kayla texted a considerate warning. Knowing my triggers well, she wanted me to know she had lost a lot of weight since I had seen her last. Indeed, just hearing the words caused my stomach to churn and my mind to race to heroin abuse.

My fearful reaction came swiftly and I demanded an explanation. Kayla assured me that long, hard hours at work were at cause. Remembering she was routinely drug tested, I was able to accept her explanation and calm down.

With scant chance to subdue my anxiety, Kayla sent another startling text stating, "I'm going to start looking at apartments close to my job. I can't deal with the halfway anymore. I've been here long enough."

I didn't disagree but wondered if an apartment was the right answer. I acknowledged that three-quarter housing was too far from her job but still believed Kayla needed a structure through which to be held accountable. The thought of her completely on her own was terrifying.

Kayla's house mom, the woman responsible for Kayla's second chance at Internal Changes, lived with her boyfriend in a small, three-bedroom ranch down the road. Knowing Kayla wanted to leave halfway and seeking to defray her own rental costs, Georgia offered Kayla a deal. For $130 a week, $45 less than Kayla was paying for halfway, Kayla could rent a bedroom in Georgia's house. The three adults would share the common areas: living room, kitchen, and bathroom.

Kayla became excitedly obsessed with the proposed opportunity. She envisioned freedom, financial gain, and a slight reprieve from the long walks to and from work. Perhaps most importantly, Kayla saw relief from life next to the revolving door of relapse.

Every cell in my body was screaming "bad idea." My stomach felt queasy. Something was way off. I deferred the discussion until we could speak face to face. We had a lot to talk about.

As the days passed, Kayla and I deliriously counted down to my visit. Back and forth, we texted each detail and time marker, "Only eight days," "I know," "Five days," "Can't wait," "Three days till I wrap my arms around you," "I get a hug in two days," "I KNOW, SO SOON, SO EXCITED."

With the convenience of Connor's car, a new world had opened up to Kayla. The night before I arrived in Fort Lauderdale, Kayla and Connor went to a Dave Matthew's Band concert. Kayla was absolutely giddy.

Calling from the show, Kayla shared that they were seated in the "sober section." As the concert progressed, she relayed how surprised she was that sobriety could be so much fun. After the concert, Kayla texted, "I got wasted at the show. Just kidding. I didn't."

"Not funny," I demanded, smiling at the playfulness in Kayla's tone.

"Shot up love. Totally love drunk," Kayla replied.

CHAPTER THIRTY-NINE: SOLD

Kayla's play-on-words was clever but biting. I was not ready to hear drug references and maybe never would be.

CHAPTER FORTY:
VACATION

Kayla was still asleep when I texted that my flight had arrived early. Only a five-minute cab ride from the airport, by the time I deplaned, Kayla was waiting for me. Looking down from the top of the escalator, I spotted her waving. The sweeping sense of delight and relief I felt left me breathless. I leapt off the escalator, wrapped my arms around my baby, and held tight. She looked good!

We picked up the rental car and set off for our five-day adventure. Our first stop was Kayla's apartment at Internal Changes. I was eager to see where she was living and to meet Camilla.

Not at all what I envisioned, I was surprised to discover that the powerful woman with whom I had spoken on the phone; the woman who had to be convinced to take my daughter back all those months ago; the woman who helped Kayla survive every day with strict rules, firm guidance, and a loving heart; was a petite, beautiful, young person with a warm and generous smile. Her wisdom belied her youth.

We hugged tightly, and talked briefly about Kayla and gratitude. From the bottom of my heart, I thanked Camilla for the care and support she was providing my daughter. Words failed to adequately express what I felt.

After meeting Camilla, Kayla and I crossed the street and entered her apartment. She eagerly showed me around. It was bigger than I expected, equipped with all the comforts of home. Her roommates were out, and there was little to suggest any individual personality. The walls were notably bare.

In the bedroom she shared, Kayla and I sat on her bed and talked. I presented her with a wall hanging I had created. Weaving her favorite colors into a tapestry, I hoped it would remind her of my unconditional love and comfort her across the miles. She was thrilled to receive my gift.

As I looked around seeking the perfect spot to hang the tapestry, Kayla informed me that putting nails in the walls was forbidden. Feeling disappointed, I urged her to ask for permission. Not only did Camilla grant special permission, she sent her husband to do the hanging!

With the weaving hung, we were eager to check into our motel, make plans, and begin our vacation. Kayla packed a few things and we headed out. It was a ten-minute drive.

To our great surprise and amusement, we arrived to discover the motel was located directly behind the Sea Waves residence! *Coincidence? I don't think so!* We checked in, found our way upstairs, and entered the ample room that would be our home for five days. Inside we found a small, adequate kitchenette and a decadent, king size bed.

Excitedly, I presented Kayla with the cannoli's I had narrowly gotten past airport security. Searching my bags, the guard had threatened to throw away the frozen delectable. I told him my story and pleaded that he allow me to deliver the treat to my daughter. I even offered him a taste. Finally, after consulting another guard, with strong admonitions, he let me through.

Kayla grabbed a spoon, stretched across the bed, and dug in. Watching her delight, I felt euphoric. Spoon in hand; I joined her on the bed. As we savored the heavenly dessert, we sketched out a plan for our time together.

Kayla would have to work two of the five days I would be there, but our time together would be ample. She was eager to show me the area in which she had been living. She had selected several destinations she was sure I would enjoy.

Having never been to the Everglades, we were both eager to explore its unique wildlife and beauty. Our first destination was a wildlife park on the Seminole Reservation. We took in the sights and sounds as we drove, stopping to snap pictures along the way. We talked and laughed and enjoyed easy camaraderie.

At the park, we toured the grounds, taking in both an airboat and swamp buggy ride. We were hoping to spot wild alligators and get a sense of their primal fierceness. We saw a few pair of eyes breeching the waters, and we viewed gators in captivity. As it turned out, summer days in Florida were even too hot for alligators.

Though mildly entertaining, our gator sightings failed to meet our expectations. Disappointed, we resolved to search for the primitive beast along "Alligator Alley" on the way back to the motel. We were determined to see an alligator in the wild.

Canals flanked the roadway. We stopped at every available pull off/recreation area. We knew alligators trolled the murky waters and hoped for even a brief glimpse. We saw a spectacular array of native birds and beautiful scenery, but no beast. Feeling let down, as we sat on the dock at the last possible stop, a magnificent, wild creature approached. We were filled with excitement and joy. We named him "Gordon."

Back at the motel we reviewed the many pictures I had captured with my camera. We laughed and re-experienced our fun. It had been a great day!

Delivering Kayla to work the next morning, I was eager to meet the co-workers about whom she had so often spoken. It was good to put faces to names and to get a feel for the environment in which Kayla spent so many hours. I lingered as long as possible, then left Kayla to her ten-hour shift.

With the whole day ahead of me, I was faced with a choice; I could hide back at the motel, or I could step out of my comfort zone and explore. Even at home I rarely stepped out on my own. Away for the first time by myself, despite feeling incredibly nervous, I felt opportunity knocking.

I mustered my courage and resolve, and headed to the beach. I walked for miles, enjoying the sights and sounds, and collecting coral and shells that had washed ashore. I breathed in the salt air and mused over the antics of families on vacation. I was expanding, and felt proud and liberated.

With hours left before I could retrieve Kayla, I returned to the motel room for a much-needed nap. Eager to be with my daughter, upon waking I brushed my hair, washed my face, and headed to the restaurant. I brought my journal, prepared to entertain myself while she finished her shift.

It was fun to watch Kayla seamlessly connect with customers and staff. She was good at her job, and it showed. Her manager, Trudy, was kind enough to sit and chat with me. She praised Kayla for her excellent work and raved about the "great gal" she was.

Also in recovery, Trudy had many years of clean living behind her. She told me about her recovery process and patiently answered my many questions. She seemed to have her priorities in order, and I was glad she could be a positive influence for Kayla.

When she wasn't busy, Kayla joined the conversation. Among other things, we talked about boys and relationship. With Kayla listening, Trudy emphasized that it was a bad idea to be in relationship during one's first year in recovery. Furthermore, she stressed, "The last thing a girl in recovery should do is move in with a guy." Trudy had learned from experience. She had learned the hard way. I urged Kayla to accept the lesson without having to live it.

Kayla squirmed a bit, well aware of the targeted nature of our conversation. She insisted she was proceeding slowly in her relationship with Connor. She agreed that moving in with a boy was a bad idea and affirmed that she had no such intention.

Eventually Trudy went back to the demands of her job, and Kayla completed her shift. It was nice to spend time with Trudy. Kayla had spoken fondly of her managers and I understood why. I felt good about the guidance Trudy was offering.

That evening, I met Connor. He was pleasant but reeked of the bad attitude indicative of addiction. He joined us for dinner and lingered for some time after. Tired from the day of sun and emotion, I wanted to go back to the motel room and relax. Despite my limited time in Florida, Kayla chose to go out with Connor rather than return with me. Her obsession with Connor was alarming.

While I tried to be patient and understanding, I was aggravated and distressed. I was insulted by Kayla's choice to spend time away from me. In addition, fear was rising. I had given my word to Camilla that Kayla would be safe. I didn't trust Connor.

The next day, Kayla and I drove to Las Olas Boulevard. She was certain I would enjoy the many art galleries in the area, and she was right. As we walked around viewing the collections, we discussed the pieces we loved and those we found distasteful. We philosophized about what made certain art appealing to some but not to others. It was fun to experience the works through each other's eyes.

Later that day, Kayla, Connor, and I went to the beach together. My idea of beach fun was to scavenge for treasure. Their idea was to cuddle on a blanket. Once again, I found myself walking the beach alone.

When we all had enough sand and sun, we headed back to Connor's car. At the crosswalk, waiting for the light to change green, Kayla remarked, "I really want my car."

My body tightened and my jaw clenched. I could no longer keep the secret. Without fanfare, I confessed that I sold the car.

I watched Kayla's body go limp with disappointment as she grasped my words. My heart ached with guilt and compassion. I wanted to shield her from that truth. I wanted to protect her from the hard life she was living. I wanted to keep her safe from disappointment and pain. Those wishes were not in my power to fulfill.

In a split second, Kayla was lashing out in anger, accusation, and ultimately in despair. Then, as she slowly came to terms with the news, she indicated acceptance. She acknowledged that if she wanted a car, she would have to earn one. She took responsibility. I was relieved and grateful.

Kayla, Connor, and I decided to purchase dinner "to go" and return to the motel to eat. Sitting in the courtyard, I noticed a dramatic swing in Kayla's mood and attitude. She was complaining, blaming, and arguing. Perhaps triggered by news of "her car" being sold, she was clearly broadcasting her continued sense of entitlement and victimhood. She listed her hardships and bemoaned their unfairness.

Working in a restaurant that served beer and wine, Kayla lamented her inability to drink alcohol. She argued that she was at a disadvantage and worried it would impede her opportunities for promotion. "Besides," she defended, "it's not like drinking is like shooting heroin. I can handle alcohol."

Horror welled up in my throat. I insisted alcohol was a drug and that she must stay away. There was no wiggle room! Feeling desperate, I relayed Isaac's story: Every time he thought he could take "a drink," he spiraled back to drugs in no time. I demanded it was too great a risk.

Kayla argued that it was necessary to drink alcohol in her line of work. She protested that she wasn't Isaac and asserted that she resented the comparison. In an effort to make peace, we agreed to disagree.

Once again, instead of staying with me after dinner, Kayla disappeared into the night with Connor. I guess I shouldn't have been surprised. My sense of hurt, anger, and terror amplified. *What if she starts using again? What if something happens to her? What if she doesn't come back?* I soothed my concerns with reminders that Kayla would be drug test-ed at halfway. She had been living without me for almost a year. I had to relinquish my desire to control. I had to trust.

In spite of Kayla's foul mood and inconsiderate behavior, I began to dread my impending departure. Separated by 1500 miles, I missed Kayla relentlessly, but there was more. The fantasy of "my healthy child" was rapidly deteriorating. My spider senses were on high alert, and leaving would authorize my imagination to run rampant.

More balanced than when I had seen her last, I tried to convince myself Kayla was healthy, healing, and working hard. I tried to see past what I knew intuitively. The danger signs were posted.

The next morning, I confronted Kayla with how I was feeling. I told her that given my short stay in Florida, I found her choice to be with her boyfriend every day insulting. I explained that all I wanted was to spend time with her, and I felt she was deliberately avoiding me. I said I was bothered by her impatience with my concerns for her safety. I told her I was wondering why I was there.

Kayla texted from work, "I'm sorry Mom. As you can see, I'm very frustrated. And you being here really makes me miss home."

My heart ached as I responded, "I've been very upset all day. I love you Kayla. I wish I could make your life easy. That is not in my power and it hurts me to my core. So does hearing you talk about drinking."

"I don't even want to drink. I just want to be normal," she answered.

Her statement was half true.

Heavy hearted, five days after I had arrived, I boarded a plane back home. I ran out of tissues before the plane took off. I was lucky enough to sit next to a kind and compassionate man who worked hard to engage me in conversation, providing comfort and distraction.

Kayla handled my departure with grace. Perhaps she felt relief, ready to return to her life without my hovering. She texted, "It's going to be okay."

I responded, "As long as you're okay, I'm okay."

I yearned for my daughter's good health. As a result of my visit, I was even more anxious about her recovery. I had no idea when I would see Kayla again or under what circumstance. To combat my anxiety, I reminded myself to stay in the moment, not borrow trouble, and trust.

My motherly intuition illuminated a hotbed of trouble on the rise.

Following my visit, Kayla and I texted each other frequently. We spoke when our schedules allowed, usually once a day. Normal life resumed for us both, but there was nothing normal about the journey we were on. I continued focusing on my own path, working through my obstacles, and accepting that I had no control over Kayla. No matter what the outcome, I knew I had to be okay.

It didn't take long before Kayla and I ached to be near each other again. In conversation, I tried to stay strong. When she complained about her challenges, I reassured her. I told her she was on the right path and to keep putting one foot in front of the other. I urged her to focus only on the moment, not on perceived hardships in the future. I repeatedly told her I loved her and secretly wished my words could convey how much. Once again, the messages I delivered to Kayla were messages I needed also.

CHAPTER FORTY-ONE:
MOVING ON

Suffering what felt like Post Traumatic Stress Disorder (PTSD), the slightest reminders of Kayla's addiction sent me reeling. Failure to answer her phone or call me back in a timely manner caused me to become irrationally anxious. References to weight loss, urgency for money, illness, or anything potentially drug related caused me to fill with fear and anguish. A shift in her tone or hint of defensiveness could instantly trigger me.

Even though Kayla was clean, the reminders of sick thinking were clearly present. To her credit, she tried to understand and respect my sometimes-extreme overreactions. Likewise, I tried hard to recognize when they were in play.

Despite Kayla's growing resistance, I vowed to continue guiding her as best I could. I loved her fiercely. That would never change.

A week after my return home from Florida, Kayla decided she would move into Georgia's house. Her logic seemed reasonable.

"She's offering me my own room," Kayla explained, "and it would basically be like living by myself for five days a week. (Georgia and her boyfriend both worked around the clock, five days a week, at their halfway jobs.) It's a little closer to work and cheaper rent. I would be renting a room in someone's house, but I'd be in a safe place."

Kayla insisted that Georgia was "clean and responsible," and would hold her to a high standard (no pun intended). She trusted the woman who had fought for her return to halfway after she ran away with Boston. She viewed Georgia as a model of healthy recovery.

Kayla's optimistic conviction was in direct opposition to my grave concern. I was certain Kayla's sobriety would be in jeopardy. When Georgia and her boyfriend were home, Kayla would have to acclimate to their ways and accommodate their wishes. The boyfriend was a complete unknown. With no curfew, drug tests, or ready support system, her resolve would have to be stronger than ever. After my trip to Florida, I didn't believe it was.

Trying to be objective, I considered the facts. Kayla had been clean for eight months. Georgia and her boyfriend had many years of clean time, and they both held supervisory positions at halfway houses. *Surely to hold those positions they had to demonstrate clean living!* Kayla believed the environment would be healthier than halfway, and she felt confident she had proven her ability to stay clean. She would be away from the chronic relapse of roommates and saving money.

In truth, Kayla didn't need my approval. After expressing my concerns, I had no choice but to accept her decision. I squelched my worries and rallied around her next chapter with enthusiasm. She would move mid-August.

As Kayla took what seemed like a giant leap toward normal adult life, she was jubilant. She said she felt like the weight of the world had been lifted from her shoulders. Georgia even told her she could have a puppy.

On the first of August, Kayla's mood was bright. She was ecstatically looking forward to her new living arrangements. She excitedly reported that Connor got a new, better job, and she joyfully daydreamed about getting a puppy. (I actively discouraged her from considering a puppy. Adopting a pet was a huge commitment and responsibility. Kayla was in no position to guarantee a dog's security. First she had to guarantee her own.)

After two days of no communication, on the third of August, Kayla texted that she hated her life and was working too hard. She followed with, "I want to come home." Then she went silent again.

A new pattern had emerged: days of considerable joy and enthusiasm, followed by days of silence, followed by messages of despair. I worked hard to detach, to allow, and to support Kayla the best I could. Change was hard, and I assumed Kayla's mood swings were a reaction to her impending move.

I missed my baby and felt, as I was, helpless. Kayla's exclamations of anguish challenged my resolve to keep her in Florida. However, as I searched for the "right" answer, my conclusion was always the same; stay the course to save her life.

Tough love was torture.

It was both a blessing and a curse to have Kayla residing so far out of my reach. Knowing she was alone, about to move, and struggling, was hard on my emotions. I wanted to help. At the same time, in order for her to grow and thrive, I knew she had to move through her challenges on her own.

In an effort to ease her burden, I allowed Kayla to "borrow" the $300 security deposit I had paid when she moved to halfway. It was a small act through which I could provide some relief.

I called Camilla and asked her to release the money to Kayla. During our conversation, Camilla praised Kayla and expressed her sincere hope for Kayla's bright future. Easing my concern, Camilla voiced support for Kayla's decision to move in with Georgia. Camilla's kind words amplified how much I missed my daughter. I held tight to her progress.

I followed up by sending Camilla a "written" request via text, asking her to release the money. In the note, I added, "Thank you for all you've done for Kayla. It was really good to meet you. I pray that this next leg of Kayla's journey is a healthy one. I'm glad you got to know the real Kayla."

Camilla responded, "I also feel blessed to have met such a wonderful young lady! Even though she's moved out, I'm still here for both of you any time, day or night!"

My heart expanded. I felt honored and blessed to have Camilla in our lives. I had no doubt she was an angel sent to us. She continued to provide me with a sense of peace and direction. I knew she would help Kayla in ways I was unable.

On August 9, 2013, Kayla successfully moved out of halfway and into Georgia's house. She was proud and filled with the excitement of progress. I was cautiously optimistic.

Two days later, she joyfully texted, "I have nine months today!"

We shared celebratory texts.

"Nine months," I thought, "The time it takes to grow a baby." Indeed, Kayla was birthing a new life, and I prayed she would stay the course.

I was eager to hear every detail of Kayla's new living arrangement. During the first week we texted often and continued to speak on the phone when able. By the second week, the phone went completely silent. Texts slowed to a trickle. Her occasional communications were brief and evasive. I rationalized that she was busy connecting with her new roommates, adjusting to the new rhythm of her surroundings, and going to work; but my darkest imaginings took over. Fear settled in.

I ran to my toolbox: stay in the moment; don't borrow trouble; I only have control over me, nobody else; Kayla is on her own path; all things have a purpose. Each time I went dark, I pulled myself back. I focused on my next action, went to my creative, sought distraction. I had cycled through fear more times than I could count. I had to find the light. I had to be the light.

A week after Kayla went silent, she re-emerged, admitting that she had been avoiding me. She knew I wouldn't approve; Connor had moved in with her.

Hearing her confession, my face flushed with rage as I struggled to digest the news. I was angry she hid the truth, angry at the truth she had hidden, and angry that her judgment could be so bad. During my July visit, we had serious conversations about the pitfalls of relationship. Her manager had emphasized the dangers of living with a man too soon, and we discussed the potential damage that could result. We talked about the importance of focusing all of her energy on healing. Kayla had listened and agreed. She assured me living with a boy wasn't her plan. She said all the right things. *Had she already been planning to have Connor move in with her? Was she blatantly lying?*

I struggled to remain calm. I responded simply, "When you feel a need to hide the truth, it is a big red flag. I'm disappointed. I pray you stay healthy Kay. That is all."

For many, relationship muddied the waters of self-care. Kayla was scarcely on the shores of self-discovery and far from the depths of self-love. I had experienced Connor's unhealthy thinking first hand. At best, living with Connor significantly complicated her recovery. At worst, their living arrangement put Kayla in jeopardy of relapse. Though I tried, I failed to find a single positive direction from which to perceive her choice.

Kayla pleaded with me to be happy for her happiness. She asserted that sharing rent meant she could save for a car, and she urged me to validate her forward thinking. Once again, she gushed about Connor, telling me how absolutely amazing he was. She affirmed how far she had come on her journey and insisted she was making sound decisions.

Lying was a "using" behavior, even lies of omission. She had lied about her intentions and lied about her living arrangement. Despite staying clean for nine months, Kayla's choice to live with Connor highlighted sick thinking. The more she defended, the more evident the danger.

Four people in various stages of recovery were living in Georgia's small house. Logic told me if Georgia and her boyfriend were making good decisions, they never would have allowed Connor to move in. If they wanted to keep Kayla safe, they would have helped her see the risks inherent in her thinking. They would have encouraged her to focus on step work and sobriety. Instead, they had advocated for Connor to move in.

Unsurprisingly, Kayla was pulling away from me more and more. Though distance made them difficult to confirm or deny, I was sure the lies were accelerating. All I could do was wait, pray, and accept whatever might come.

Despite my best efforts, fear was boiling over. I felt sick. With no power to change the situation, I knew I had to trust and stay in the moment.

CHAPTER FORTY-TWO:
PUPPIES

Kayla worked long hours and spent most of her free time with Connor. Contact had become infrequent and limited. When we did speak, I tried to remain supportive and encouraging, accentuating anything positive.

Having grown up with dogs and cats, Kayla missed the unconditional love shared with a pet. She missed our dog, Lacey, whom she leaned on for comfort through much of her childhood. When Georgia adopted a puppy, Kayla was thrilled. She eagerly agreed to help with the puppy's care and training, and embraced every moment she could spend with it.

I was far from delighted. With Georgia and her boyfriend gone most of the week, daily care and the chore of housetraining fell to Kayla. The dog was full of energy and needed a great deal of exercise and attention. I felt it unfair and presumptuous to leave Kayla in charge.

I worked hard to let go judgment, pushing myself to respect that Kayla was responsible for her own choices. Nonetheless, I voiced my concerns. Kayla accused me of "yelling at her all the time."

It was not my nature to agree for the sake of agreeing, but anything shy of agreement pushed Kayla further away.

She was furious at me for thinking the puppy was a bad idea. Defensive and accusatory, once again she berated me for not supporting her happiness.

In defeat, I told Kayla, "I will stop having an opinion. I'm not sure what you want. It feels shallow." I shut up and shut down. A welcome, familiar friend, shutdown allowed me to crawl back inside myself and block (or pretend to block) the pain.

Before August concluded, another young man moved into Georgia's small home. Fresh out of rehab, he occupied the remaining bedroom. Adding to the growing chaos, Georgia adopted a second puppy. Georgia's boyfriend was becoming volatile and loud, and Kayla was starting to crack. Her "safe" environment had rapidly deteriorated.

Vile nightmares returned to my troubled sleep. I woke gasping for breath after watching my daughter shoot drugs into her veins. While grateful to wake, I was reminded the real nightmare was far from over. I texted Kayla, "I had nightmares all night that you relapsed. Please don't!"

The demands of two puppies in an overcrowded house were taking their toll. With the novelty having worn off, Kayla became frustrated by the burden bestowed on her. After working a twelve-hour shift, coming home to puppy messes and needs was overwhelming.

As the stress of her living situation increased, Kayla preyed on my vulnerabilities, demanding she be allowed to return home. When I continued to refuse, she charged, "You want me to relapse?"

It was evident Kayla was trying to run from her problems again. I knew several things for certain:

Wherever she went, there she'd be. Problems resided within and followed us wherever we ran.

Bailing her out would only prolong her struggle.

She had to address the chaos and find solutions to the problems she created.

I loved Kayla enough to deny what she, what WE wanted most. Tough love had to prevail.

I was reminded of the Dr. Seuss book "A Fish Out of Water." In it, the boy's new pet goldfish wanted to eat and eat and eat, but giving it what it wanted put it in jeopardy. To take proper care of the goldfish, the instructions read: "Never feed him a lot. Never more than a spot! Or something may happen. You never know what."

Though I very much wanted to, I couldn't feed Kayla what she wanted. Unlike the assertion in Dr. Seuss' book, I assuredly knew what would happen. Instead, I chose to feed her emotional support, encouragement, and guidance. I was powerless to accommodate her ravenous appetite. I was powerless to change her situation.

Despite my conviction that Kayla had to take charge of her own situation, I lived in fear that I would inadvertently do or say something that would push her back to drugs. I was experiencing a tornado of emotion that thrashed me this way and that, at times causing me to lose all sense of direction.

Occasionally the winds would subside, setting me down in stillness. In the clarity of those moments, I understood Kayla's addiction was not my fault, nor was it a result of her living environment. Regardless of what life threw her way, Kayla had to find her own desire, determination, and will to stay clean and move forward. She had to choose life over death.

In my journal I wrote, "The situation with Kayla is my most powerful teacher. I'm concerned for her well-being, but I don't have to live her struggle. I don't have to make it my own."

I wanted to improve the quality of my days and find happiness in my life. I worked hard to release Kayla to her own path. I worked hard to relinquish my guilt, fear, and anger. Where I wanted to change Kayla's life, I found a mirror reflecting what I needed to change in my own.

From the beginning, the nightmare pushed me to create personal boundaries. It taught me to disengage from detrimental conversations, to avoid toxic or difficult people, to remove myself from unhealthy and/or uncomfortable circumstances, and to provide essential self-care. I learned that being kind and helpful didn't have to mean sacrificing myself.

I finally understood I could not choose for others. My role was not to fix anyone but myself. I had to respect that each human had her own journey with her own lessons and timetable. The more I released what was not mine, the more I was able to find peace. The more I found peace, the more I could be of use to those for whom I cared.

I had spent most of my life wallowing in low self-esteem and self-loathing, second guessing decisions, and seeking validation from others. As the nightmare continued, my ability to trust my intuition and make sound decisions improved. I was learning to believe in myself. I was letting go of what others thought.

A welcome byproduct, as my sense of self shifted, other parts of my life also improved. I became dissatisfied with complacency. I was becoming empowered, strong, and ambitious. I was determined to make a difference in the world and was gaining the confidence I needed to do so.

CHAPTER FORTY-THREE:
CRAZY TALK

Kayla and Gabriel had always been as close as siblings could be. As they grew older, they became good friends. The first weekend in September, Gabriel flew to Florida for a brief visit. Beyond excited for their time together, Kayla took the weekend off from work. They stayed together at a hotel near the beach.

Gabriel's decision to visit Kayla felt like a nod in the direction of Kayla's good health. I was delighted by the bond they shared and excited for their reunion. At the same time, I was eager for Gabriel's feedback. He would unwittingly be "boots on the ground," able to fill me in on what was really happening. I hoped for good news.

Upon his return, I picked Gabriel up at the airport. In short order, he confirmed that he thought Kayla was still clean. Lamentably, however, his description of what he'd observed at her house painted a grim picture in my mind. The quarters sounded claustrophobic and awful, and the people with whom she lived sounded derelict. I wondered how such an environment could be conducive to forming good habits or for making good decisions.

I felt my nerves catch fire.

By late September, Kayla's view of paradise lost its shine. The dogs, the people, the abuse, and the filth were too much. Kayla complained that Georgia's boyfriend was "a loud racist who drank and got nasty." She said she was beginning to fear for her safety.

Living in a small room with Connor had also become problematic. Connor's moods had become unpredictable, causing Kayla to ride an emotional rollercoaster. Certain his mood swings were a product of the environment in which they were living, Kayla was convinced they needed to leave Florida and find a place of their own.

Maintaining that Connor was the only thing making her happy, Kayla intensified her plea to come home. She obsessed about moving north, vowing they would hitchhike if they had to. With or without my help, she insisted, they would make it happen in the next few months.

As Connor pressured Kayla, Kayla pressured me. I continued to encourage her to make a plan and save money. Despite her initial enthusiasm, she hadn't saved a dime since moving into Georgia's house. As much as I wanted Kayla healthy, whole, and home, and because I wanted her healthy, whole, and home, I stood my ground. If she wanted out badly enough, she would make a plan and start saving.

I tried not to react to Kayla's crazy talk. The less I responded, the more she increased the intensity. One evening she demanded, "How can you banish me 1500 miles away?"

I implored Kayla to change her perspective. "Kayla," I pleaded, "think about why you are in Florida and how you got there. Connect with gratitude and work toward coming home if that's what is best for you. You have to have a plan. I feel like while you were working with Eden (her sponsor) you were able to see things differently. You were happier. It's about where you focus. Find the good."

Rational thought fell on deaf ears. Nonetheless, hearing my own words helped me reaffirm the only real choice. Kayla was creating her own misery. If she wanted change, she would have to choose differently. If she wanted to move north, she would have to make it happen without my help.

While I listened to Kayla's rants, I felt her pain deeply, and I worked at separating hers from my own. I reiterated the tools I thought might help her: Twelve Step work, gratitude, meditation, yoga, art, music, and nature. I implored her to look deep inside and stop running from herself. I urged her to stop avoiding the truth. I suggested she move back to halfway. I grasped what faith I could that she would move past the irrationality and take the next right step.

Kayla pushed back harder, sending multiple texts:

"Mom, I'm really struggling and need your help. I know you can't help me or don't want to help me or maybe it's a combination of the two, but I don't know who else to turn to. I don't have anyone else."

"I'm unbearably miserable."

"I want to kill myself."

"I get that I'm a fuck up and you don't want me anymore, but it took the last year of my life to get clean and show you

I can change and I'm pretty sure I've done that so I'm not spending another month in Florida."

Breathing deeply with each assault, I strengthened my resolve. I reminded Kayla she had to take responsibility in order to move forward. I pointed to her past behaviors and what had helped her triumph. I told her how much I loved her and repeated, "Make a plan, save some money, prove you are ready, face your demons."

Over and over, she pulled at my heartstrings, and then she stopped answering my texts. It was as if she was punishing me. I bolstered my resolve. I reminded her I loved her. I reminded myself I was saving her life.

The texts began again, pounding me relentlessly. Clearly Kayla was unhinged.

"I'm miserable...I'm done with Florida. If Connor and I come north we could both get jobs where I used to work... we could probably afford an apartment within a month. I need to get out of Georgia's house. I hate her boyfriend. He's a racist, the dogs are a burden, and the house is filthy. I don't wanna be here anymore."

I could only respond, "I love you."

My father had been admitted to the hospital. I was worried for his health, and my patience with Kayla was wearing thin. I demanded Kayla stop the barrage of threats and accusations, and do something different. I suggested she get a second job, urging her to stop running from her responsibilities.

I informed Kayla of her grandfather's condition and repeatedly asked that she call him. Since the days were never promised, I knew if something happened, Kayla would be inconsolable. Additionally, I knew her call would lift my father's spirits.

Kayla assured me she would call. It was another broken promise.

CHAPTER FORTY-FOUR:
PROMETHEUS

Kayla's drug buddy from home had also been recovering in Fort Lauderdale. Living nearby, Jessie provided Kayla with a sense of familiarity, emotional comfort, and camaraderie. While I worried that their old habits could be easily reignited, I understood Jessie's value in Kayla's life.

Early in October Kayla told me Jessie packed up and moved back home. A mixed blessing, I prayed Jessie would stay strong and healthy. I also prayed for Kayla's strength. To some degree, Jessie had been Kayla's emotional safety net and suddenly, she was gone.

Kayla's rant to come home accelerated, "Mom, I will buy a plane ticket when I get paid and I will get my old job back and take the bus. I just want to come home."

"You have to have a plan, Kay," I responded. "I keep telling you this. You can't come back to hopes. I need to know you have a structure and a plan. You are running away and where you go, you will follow."

"As long as I'm working a shit job, that's just not going to happen. I would do so much better at home. I'm miserable, I miss my family, and I miss my home. It's not getting any better."

Remaining rational and steady, I knew how I had to respond, but it never got easier. Kayla knew my triggers well. Repeatedly reviving my worst fears and worries, her rants took a lot out of me. Without favorable responses, she went to the extreme, texting, "I want to kill myself."

There was no more frightening statement a mother could hear from her child. I had heard her desperate decree too many times. I had to halt her tantrum. I needed to find balance and peace in my life. I wanted a reprieve. I demanded, "You refuse to hear anything beyond your wish. It doesn't matter where you are. You have to face your demons!"

Kayla continued to threaten suicide and frantically begged to come home. She insisted she would return to her old job where she was loved. She said she would return to county college and that being with her family would make her happy.

I stopped replying. There was no point to offering rational responses to an irrational person.

"I know you don't want me anymore," Kayla insisted, "but I took the last year of my life to get clean and show you I can change and I'm pretty sure I've done that so I'm not spending another month in Florida."

I didn't want to see it, but Kayla's communications were confirming the opposite reality. She was nowhere near ready to come home.

I felt like Prometheus who, punished for eternity, had his liver ripped from his body each day only to regenerate each night. I called upon my strength to heal the pain. I had to accept what I could not change. I stopped myself from asking why I was being punished. I reminded myself I had a choice. I could either grow from the nightmare or let it consume me.

After about a week of silence, I texted, "You have avoided talking to me and refuse to think about anything other than coming home. I would love to help you move through your challenges, and I don't believe the answer is coming back here. You don't like that answer, but it is far from not caring. I always love you and want what's best for you. Your carrying on is exactly what tells me you're not ready to come home."

Receiving no response, I pleaded, "You need help. You are acting like you used to. Learn damn it!"

I accused Kayla of acting like a spoiled brat and urged her to seek support. I suggested she reach out to Camilla or Eden, anyone who might be able to help her stabilize.

Kayla erupted, "I'VE BEEN TRYING TO MAKE A PLAN FOR THE LAST YEAR. YES, I do need your help as my MOTHER... How much longer do you want me to bust my ass for shit pay and go nowhere before you see I'm fucking trying, and I'm miserable and tired of doing this shit?"

There it was again, victimhood. Kayla was still blaming others for her struggles and expecting others to find her solutions. With impenetrable resolve, once again, I tried in vain to speak sense to my daughter.

Continuing to play the guilt card, Kayla demanded, "I need my mother!"

I implored Kayla to take responsibility for her life. I reminded her that her journey was not about me. While I would always be supportive, she had to want success for herself. Until she took full responsibility, I knew her sobriety was at risk.

All of our communication had been via text. Though I called her phone periodically, weeks went by with no answer. I got tired of the self-pitying, angry attacks. Kayla was perpetually hostile. My gut hollered to me; she was slipping.

CHAPTER FORTY-FIVE:
STOLEN

When Kayla was in high school, she suffered her first devastating loss of a friend to overdose. On Tommy's birthday she texted, "The sky is clear and it's sunny, but it's raining." She explained that since Tommy's death four years earlier, it always rained on that day.

Kayla and I had often discussed the unseen forces of nature's messengers and the power of the "other side" to communicate. I invited her to consider the signs and think about what Tommy might be conveying. I encouraged her to "talk to Tommy. Ask him to show you he is okay. Ask for a specific sign. I can help you if you want."

In the wake of losing her dear friend to the scourge, I never understood how Kayla could abuse drugs. In her continued connection with Tommy, I prayed she would receive the message never to go back. I was certain Tommy was there to remind her it was a no-win game.

Mid October, Kayla confided that Connor was not who he had seemed, texting, "I'm honestly starting to think he has multiple personalities. He's narcissistic and entitled. If he doesn't get his way, he throws a fit that doesn't stop. He spends all my money and all of his money on stupid shit and then yells at me that I need to get another job because he can't afford me. I can't do it anymore. He throws tantrums all the time and he's become abusive."

Kayla fretted over how she could get away from Connor. She asked him to leave, but he refused. She didn't want to go back to halfway and couldn't afford an apartment on her own. She was stressed.

I acknowledged Kayla's challenge and encouraged her to proceed with healthy thinking and healthy action. I suggested she work on self-reliance, pointing out how much she enjoyed the freedom Connor's car afforded her. I believed it contributed to keeping her stuck.

Kayla insisted she was not reliant on Connor; rather, she told me, he was reliant on her. Given what she said about his spending habits, I was willing to believe her.

As "Momma Bear," I was eager for Kayla to get away from Connor and live in a safe environment. I urged her to go back to halfway. She pushed the suggestion aside and continued to text furiously about Connor's behavior. For every solution I suggested, Kayla had a reason it wouldn't work.

A perfect storm of challenges seemed to be plaguing Kayla. Besides feeling trapped in a failing relationship with Connor and suffering from the instability in Georgia's house, she claimed she was being treated unfairly at work.

One afternoon she texted that her pocketbook had been stolen. I directed her to file a police report, which she claimed to have done.

As each new struggle demanded Kayla's attention, I worried about her ability to cope. I was afraid one more challenge would push her back to drugs. I knew she had her own path to walk, but the obstacles had become particularly brutal. I reminded myself to trust and let go. If she were going to stay clean, she would manage her challenges. If she was going to relapse, the challenges were irrelevant.

Kayla's food stamp card was amongst the casualties of her stolen purse. Similar to the process for a stolen/lost credit card, once Kayla reported the theft, the card was disabled. It would take a week for a replacement card to arrive. No food card meant no food.

Within days, Kayla was pleading, begging, and bargaining for me to wire food money. She said she had used all her cash to pay rent, leaving her with nothing. She was hungry. She promised to pay me back when she got her next paycheck.

In my life, food equaled love. Kayla having no food was too much for me to ignore. I finally gave in.

"I pray you are telling me the truth," I responded.

"I am, Mom. If I was getting high, you wouldn't be hearing from me at all."

I resolved to help her but would only provide enough money for Kayla to survive the pay period. Given the prohibitive fees, I was unwilling to send a wire. I would find another way to get funds to her.

We had a cousin living about twenty-five minutes from Kayla's location. I reached out to Tanya and asked if she would deliver $25 to Kayla. I told her I would put a reimbursement check in the mail immediately.

With abundant kindness and generosity, Tanya agreed to deliver the cash but refused to give me her address. Not only did she bring Kayla the money the next day, but she also texted me a photo. Kayla's beautiful smile was captivating, but I couldn't help noticing she had gotten very thin and drawn.

I questioned Tanya about Kayla's appearance. She insisted Kayla looked good. I rested uneasily in her opinion.

After Kayla failed to thank me for the food money, I texted, "I thought I'd have heard thank you or something. You got very thin. I hope there's a clean reason."

Kayla replied that she thought she had thanked me. She maintained she wasn't thin; she had "just lost a few pounds that I needed to lose." I fought the impulse to panic.

Clearly, Kayla's misery level was climbing. She texted, "I'm really, really sad...I just feel like everything is wrong with me. I'm at a breaking point, a really, really deep breaking point. I just feel worthless like no one really wants me around."

Intensifying her plea to return home, Kayla insisted my "requirements" were unrealistic. She followed up with additional threats to kill herself. I stood firm and once again implored her to get help.

The cycle of demands began again, "I took the last year of my life to get clean…Maybe I should come home so I can be closer to my family when shit like this (her grandfather's illness) happens…I would rather live on the streets at home than spend another two weeks in Florida. I don't know what you don't understand about me wanting to fucking die."

I acknowledged Kayla's deep pain. Her challenge seemed unbearable, and I hurt for her. I still hadn't acknowledged the definitive signs of relapse. I kept thinking her irrational outbursts were part of the process, a cycling back to sick thinking that would provide the foundation for deep healing.

I demanded, "You need help. You are acting like you used to! This shows me you are not ready."

"How much longer do you want me to bust my ass for shit pay and go nowhere before you see that I'm fucking trying and I'm miserable and I'm tired of doing this shit?"

"As long as it takes to turn your attitude to gratitude," I replied.

I had allowed Kayla's behavior to cause me great suffering. Gratitude was my lifeline. While it was easy to dwell on the awful, to list and recount all the pain and suffering in my life, that was a choice. Survival necessitated a shift in focus. I had much for which to be grateful.

Nonetheless, my patience was running out. I suggested several people to whom Kayla could reach out. I told her to get her shit together and act like an adult instead of an entitled baby. I held a hard line, and I wept inside. The pain was almost intolerable.

"I do need help," Kayla demanded. "I need YOUR help as my MOTHER!"

I couldn't take any more in. I reminded myself I WAS helping. I was doing my best to keep Kayla alive. I knew the alternative. *Did she really want to die?* I had to trust her path. I had to toe the tough love line. I had to find strength again and again. I had to live in my own life, on my own path. I had to choose life.

The texts of despair kept coming. The threats kept coming. The ultimatums kept coming. I stopped reading.

CHAPTER FORTY-SIX:
FIRED

Unfortunately, and not surprisingly, it was glaringly evident that Georgia's house was a cesspool of toxic energy. Excessive drinking and emotional abuse would have been damaging to anyone in or out of recovery. Unquestionably, the longer Kayla stayed, the more her recovery was threatened. It was a miracle she had lasted that long.

When Kayla told me she had moved out of Georgia's house, I was delighted. When she told me she was still with Connor, I was less delighted. Together they had no long-term plan for where they would live. At least, I reasoned, they both had jobs. I prayed they would find a safe, healthy environment in which to reside.

As a short-term solution, Kayla told me she and Connor were spending two weeks in a "hotel-condo thingy" Connor's parents "won in an auction." She claimed his parents were in town visiting and were actively helping them find an apartment to rent.

Though Kayla's story sounded far-fetched, I chose not to get involved. I kept my questions minimal and shallow. At least she had a roof over her head. Her mood had become light and happy. My anxiety was rising rapidly.

Kayla raved about Connor's kind and generous parents. She was jubilant over the attention they lavished on her. She gushed about the easy connection she had with Connor's mom and insisted I would adore her as well.

Every time I questioned the details of Kayla's story, she defensively recommended I speak with Connor's mom. Convinced Connor's mother would subdue my concerns and allay my fears, she repeatedly offered to put us in contact. She never followed through, and I didn't push.

According to Kayla, their apartment search had landed her and Connor an interview. She felt confident they would be approved. If they weren't, she assured me that Connor's parents would help them until they found something. Between work and time spent with Connor and his parents, Kayla's communication with me slowed to a trickle.

I toggled between relief and worry. With Connor's unpredictable behavior, I was uncomfortable about him and Kayla committing to a lease together. *What if he relapsed?* Likely to be appreciably more than what they were paying Georgia, I wondered how they would consistently afford rent. Nonetheless, I rationalized that they were more likely to earn enough money together than apart.

Knowing Connor's parents were involved and actively guiding the kids provided me a modicum of comfort. Though I didn't know them personally, I trusted that they had the kids' best interest at heart. I assumed they would notify me if there were a problem. I assumed Kayla was telling me the truth.

Kayla and Connor were not offered an apartment as a result of their "interview." As their last day in the "condo thingy" came and went, Kayla informed me that with Connor's parents' help, they were staying in a hotel room. I was less than thrilled.

On October 25, 2013, Kayla texted, "I just got fired."

Stunned, I rapidly texted back, "WHAT!" as I dialed the phone. I was eager to hear Kayla's voice, understand what happened, and comfort her. I was certain there had been a mistake.

Kayla didn't pick up. She texted that she was hysterical and couldn't catch her breath long enough to put sentences together. She went on to text that she had overslept, followed by, "I hate my life and want to kill myself."

I asked what happened.

"By the time I woke up I was already a half hour late," she explained, "and I called right away. I've worked there almost a year. I've never ever done that before. I've called out a total of twice the whole time I've worked there and every time I was even going to be two minutes late, I called to let them know. I've seen people get away with MURDER before getting fired there and I feel like this is a little unjust."

I ached for her. I was as indignant as she was, maybe more. Kayla's work ethic was impeccable. I restrained myself from calling her boss on her behalf. I wanted answers and apologies. I pleaded with her to call corporate (company management) and present her case. I told her, "If you're right, they will listen."

Understandably shocked, Kayla also felt frightened, angry, and betrayed. As we texted, she continued to defend herself. She emphatically told me what a good employee she was. She said she tried to get answers and the manager kept telling her, "You need to call your mother."

While my "Momma Bear" was defensive on Kayla's behalf, I was teetering with the awareness that nothing was making sense. My logical mind searched for a way to understand what was happening. "Gather yourself and go talk to Trudy," I insisted. "She should provide clear cause. The only justification would be if you are using. Why would she say 'call your mother'?"

"I have no idea," Kayla texted back, "and even if I was using, it wouldn't be justified. Normal people drink and smoke weed and party and if I was using but still showing up for work and doing what I need to do at work, it's not any of their damn business. I'm not using, but if I was, they can't just fire me because of that."

As Kayla's texts screamed of injustice and personal affront, I urged her to take logical action. I encouraged her to get answers from the manager and/or corporate. *Surely there had been a misunderstanding.*

I trusted truth would triumph over lies. Kayla's story was compelling, and I, too, cursed the unfairness, rallying around my daughter's distress. She had been "friends" with both the manager and assistant manager. I couldn't fathom how they could hurt her that way, without warning or explanation.

Instead of heeding my advice, Kayla balked. "I'd rather just die," she spat.

Re-igniting her rant to come home, Kayla added, "I'm so fucking tired of doing everything by myself Mom. I'm a kid. I belong at home. This isn't fair. I try so hard to make a life for myself and everything just falls to pieces. I can't win. What's the point of living a life that I fucking hate?"

Once again, I found myself bolstering my resolve, reminding myself to stay calm. I tried to speak rationally to my daughter, "You are an adult, Kay. You made bad choices and you are dealing with the result. You will be better for this. Make some calls or start looking for a new job. Do something positive instead of wasting energy feeling sorry for yourself."

"I just want to come home," she pleaded. "I'm not an adult and I don't know how to be an adult. I absolutely despise my life. What would possibly make me feel a need to continue on this way?"

Stuck in an endless loop, Kayla continued to tirade about hating her life and needing to come home. I stopped responding.

I replayed the imaginary phone call in which I was told Kayla's body had been found. I shook the dark thought from my head and yelled at myself for thinking such a thing, again. It played like a bad commercial, over and over.

I wondered if I kept myself in terror as an excuse not to move forward in my life.

I held strong to what I knew: Kayla had to make her own way.

Kayla went silent.

CHAPTER FORTY-SEVEN:

THE BAR

It was easy to obsess, but I had learned to let go what I could not change. I was powerless to change Kayla's choices or their consequences. Practicing tough love gave me the space in which to learn I was not going to fix her condition. Only Kayla could fix Kayla.

For more than a month, Kayla's communication had been inconsistent and volatile. By the end of October, it was impossible to decipher fact from fiction. Though it was my opinion she was making devastatingly bad decisions, I reminded myself she was on her own path. With limited phone calls and texts, she had effectively shut me out.

I was substitute teaching in a middle school science class when the cell phone in my pocket vibrated. A quick peek revealed it was Kayla calling. I was immediately alarmed. Knowing my work schedule, she would only call with urgent need. A room full of active students prohibited me from answering.

Between classes, I listened to Kayla's message, "Mom, I need to talk to you, it's important."

My heart leapt into my throat as I braced for what might come. I had to wade through one more class period before I could call back.

Finally, with students gone to lunch, I was able to call. Without a hello, Kayla began her confession. She caught Connor smoking crack. He used up her food stamps and took $100 from her wallet. She was so angry, in retaliation she took $20 from his wallet, went to a local bar, and got drunk. She knew she had made a bad choice and was checking herself into detox "as a precaution."

"Mom, I'm making a mature choice, you should be glad for me," Kayla encouraged.

Kayla proceeded to tell me someone named "Anthony" was going to take her to the detox facility. She had already arranged her return to halfway after detox, and since she didn't have a job, Camilla agreed to let her pay when she was able.

"I'm surprised you went to the bar and didn't go back to heroin," I observed.

"It was quicker, and besides, I wouldn't even know who to call to get heroin," Kayla responded.

I shook off the inconsistencies in her story and supported her as best I could. I cried hard after I hung up the phone. After almost ten months, Kayla was starting all over. I ached for the setback. It felt like I was starting over too.

At the same time, I was proud of Kayla. The humility in her confession gave me hope. She had made a mistake and was taking the necessary steps to correct course (though it seemed a bit extreme to go to detox after a few drinks). Her decision showed self-awareness and good judgment. I was ecstatic she was going back to halfway. Despite my tears, I felt relief. I took a deep breath and went on with my day.

Shortly after we spoke, Kayla texted, "I'm sorry Mommy. I know you are disappointed in me. I'm just so miserable and I made a bad choice. I guess I do still need to be here as much as it hurts to be away from you. You were right."

While gathering her belongings, Connor had become enraged and violent. Kayla told me she had to call the police to keep him at bay. Once safely in Anthony's car she texted, "I'm on my way to detox now. I feel like I can finally breathe."

Lacking food money and anticipating she would be back to Internal Changes in a week, Kayla asked me to send a care package. Once again I thought, "Food I can do!" Since I had plenty of non-perishables in the house, I didn't even need to go to the store. After work, I stuffed a big box with tuna and pasta, Pop-tarts and popcorn, cereal, teabags, soup, and dried Indian food. I topped it off with Halloween chocolates I had purchased for "trick-or-treaters."

It was the thirtieth of October.

Once at detox, Kayla sent the familiar text, "I'm here. Taking my phone now. I love you."

Barely able to see through my flooded eyes, I responded, "I love you baby. Heal well. Know you are in my heart. XOXO big hugs."

In my journal I wrote, "I'm so sad and also very, very proud of Kayla. As I've thought about it, I'm more and more convinced that she subconsciously saw this as her only choice to get out from under the situation with Connor.

I think she may have been afraid of him, and certainly she was feeling trapped by the car, the computer, the rent. I wish she had talked about it with me. I also think, though, she was embarrassed. She knew she had made big mistakes and didn't want to eat that. Thank God it wasn't heroin."

I told myself to hold onto the positives. That night, I rested more easily.

CHAPTER FORTY-EIGHT:
THE TRUTH

Though I was terribly sad that Kayla was "starting over" again, I felt renewed hope. I held onto the promise that she had learned some big lessons. A new opportunity lay before her. I prayed she would adopt a healthy attitude, do the work, and grow her sense of worth and worthiness.

I held the truth for Kayla. I saw the amazing human who was trapped within her troubles. I wanted her to see that human too. I chose to view our new chapter as a gift and safely tucked my fears away.

Meanwhile, my youngest child continued to struggle with school and life, and my "romantic" relationship remained an obsession, taunting me and leaving me empty. At least one fire was under control for the moment, and for that I was grateful.

Expectations for my life's journey had tangled me up time and time again. Imagining that Kayla's choices, Avery's behavior, and even Leo's attention could fulfill me chronically resulted in disappointment and pain. Staying fully present and accepting what life offered was a continual challenge. I reminded myself I was okay. Life would be what I made it.

Returning home from work on Halloween, I listened to the messages on my answering machine. "Audrey from

Florida Rooms" had called. She was the detox counselor assigned to work with Kayla. She wanted to talk about "Kayla's program."

I was glad Kayla gave permission for my involvement and called back immediately. I got Audrey's voice mailbox. Disappointed and nervous, I left a message. Audrey called back a short while later.

Audrey was a no-nonsense, straight shooting professional. She wasted no time getting down to business. She informed me of Kayla's presence in the room and told me I was on speakerphone.

Expecting to hear the "treat" of my daughter's mature choices and progress, I was assaulted by a cruel "trick." Audrey explained that after detox it was essential for Kayla to continue in their rehab program. "Without rehab," Audrey asserted, "Kayla is guaranteed to fail."

I was confused and argumentative. "After a few drinks?" I mockingly questioned.

Detonating the grenade, Audrey's words exploded in my ears, "Kayla tested positive for every drug EXCEPT alcohol."

Audrey directed her attention to Kayla, insisting she admit the truth to me. After some pushback, sounding like a caged animal, angry and belligerent, Kayla spat out the chilling fact: Right after her brother's September visit, she had begun shooting heroin again. As if that weren't enough for me to absorb, she confessed she had been living on the street when Anthony picked her up and brought her to Florida Rooms.

I was speechless and gasping for breath. As my world blurred, I fought to find equilibrium. Like lightning flashes, the lies I willingly believed emerged in quick succession. I felt humiliated and furious. Nausea rose as I envisioned needles pushing death through my baby's veins.

Why would anyone choose to go back to drugs? Why would anyone want to start over? How could she live that way? All I had was questions.

Audrey calmly explained that Florida Rooms was a highly rated rehabilitation facility. More like "boot camp," their unique methodology made it one of the highest rated drug rehabs in Florida. Audrey emphasized that they pushed their clients hard to uproot and abolish bad thinking.

I was eager to embrace the tough program Audrey described. Clearly, the "softer" approach at Sea Waves didn't work. In light of Kayla's relapse, I was convinced Sea Waves was a failure, and a waste of time and money. Perhaps Kayla needed a no-nonsense, radical program to force her to face and heal her demons.

I couldn't think straight. I was heartbroken, distraught, and sickened. As my anguish rose, I deflected. I wanted to make Kayla feel the pain I was feeling, that she had inflicted on me. I wanted to lash out at her and make her understand the broader impact of her choices.

In truth, I knew Kayla already carried the burden of my pain in addition to her own. She was consumed by self-loathing, guilt, and humiliation. By comparison, my feelings seemed inconsequential. Until she chose to fundamentally confront her issues and shift her ways, whether at Sea Waves, Florida Rooms, or elsewhere, she would not heal. Of that I was certain. She had to want a clean life. If she was going to find peace, Kayla had to learn to love and honor herself.

As Audrey and I discussed her recommendation for Kayla's continued stay, Kayla fiercely and adamantly refused to remain at Florida Rooms. She insisted that being there was an "absolute nightmare." When pressed, she said the staff treated her like a piece of garbage, with no respect or compassion. She asserted that she would not submit to their foul treatment.

In the eyes of the law, Kayla was an adult. I couldn't force her to stay against her will. I didn't know if her objections were based in truth, dope brain, or fear. Regardless, she was threatening to leave even before her detox was complete.

Ending the call with Audrey, I immediately called Camilla for guidance.

It turned out Camilla and her office manager, Daisy, had been in communication with Kayla throughout the relapse. Knowing Kayla's condition, they had encouraged her to seek help the entire time. Camilla told me that prior to becoming homeless, Kayla and Connor were living in a filthy hovel off the highway. Fortunately, when Kayla finally hit bottom, she reached out for help. Camilla and Daisy had arranged her transportation and admittance to Florida Rooms.

In full agreement that Kayla needed rehabilitation beyond detox, Camilla was clear that Kayla would not be allowed back to Internal Changes until she completed a program. That was good news. I could use Camilla's requirement as a bargaining chip to keep Kayla in treatment.

Unfortunately, Internal Changes was not one of Florida Rooms' "preferred halfway houses." Assuming Kayla would continue her rehab at Florida Rooms, Camilla broke the news that Kayla's return to her was not guaranteed.

While concerning, I reminded myself that was the future. Our first challenge was convincing Kayla to stay in treatment. Once in a program, I would do what I could to make sure Kayla went back to Camilla's halfway. In my opinion, Internal Changes was the only choice.

Trying to ease my anxiety, with great compassion, Camilla confirmed she had received Kayla's care package. She assured me she would store it safely. Wherever Kayla landed after treatment, Camilla would make sure she got her box.

I was eternally grateful to Camilla. A radiant angel, she had already exceeded any expectations I had for assistance. She had twice saved my daughter's life, and as I searched for relief, she embraced me too. For the third time, she offered to talk any time, day or night. *How did I get so lucky?*

After my conversation with Camilla, I felt empowered. Not only was moving back to Internal Changes contingent on Kayla completing a program, but if at the end of detox Kayla still objected to staying for rehab, I was going to deliver an ultimatum. Either Kayla stayed at Florida Rooms or I would cut off her phone.

The phone was Kayla's lifeline. I had repeatedly justified the expense, not just for Kayla's benefit but for my own as well. Without it I would have no knowledge of Kayla's whereabouts or status. I couldn't imagine losing contact completely.

I was hopeful my threat would convince her to stay. I didn't want to lose contact. I didn't want to lose my daughter.

During Kayla's days in detox, I ruminated on my pain, and my anger increased. While I understood that Kayla's behavior was not about me, I was exhausted by the phone calls, the worries, and the arrangements. I was frustrated by Kayla's rigid refusal to stay at Florida Rooms and had a hard time believing her reasons. I was convinced she was avoiding the hard, emotional work, and the thought of her relapsing again was more than I could bear.

My inner victim had been activated. *How dare she do this to me again! Why me?*

Because I loved Kayla with all my heart and had remained relatively naïve to the ravages of drug abuse, I was sentenced to repeat the horror I had lived before. I felt guilty for not recognizing the relapse and for not getting her help sooner (as if that were in my power). Fear was the real driver. I was afraid Kayla would die. It felt like we were back at the beginning, and the pain was impossible.

I was not a victim. Guilt was an emotion I consented to.

In my journal I wrote, "While I looked forward to her eventual return, the clock has been set back again. It breaks my heart and further impresses the fact that nothing is promised, always unknown."

Profound sadness settled over me. I worked on acceptance.

After five days, Kayla demanded immediate release from Florida Rooms. She claimed the treatment was unbearable. Contrarily, Audrey portrayed Kayla as an irrational addict who had dope brain and didn't know what was best for her. I chose to believe Audrey and levied my ultimatum.

Seemingly unfazed, Kayla said she would rather be on the street than stay at Florida Rooms. Her absolute refusal leant credibility to the sincerity of her complaints. She willingly offered, however, to return to Sea Waves for rehabilitation.

In the end, Kayla agreed to stay at Florida Rooms for one additional day. Arrangements were made to deliver her to Sea Waves upon her release. While I was doubtful Sea Waves could provide the solution she needed, I had no choice but to acquiesce. At least she would be safe for a while.

As I calmed, I told myself to maintain "I don't know" mind. In curiosity all things were possible. The future was untold, and I didn't need to think about anything but the moment I was in. I tried to return to trust.

Emotional torture lurked around every corner.

Deemed "friendship," my on again off again relationship with Leo provided occasional connection and distraction. Unfortunately, the intense chemistry between us, paired with my sense of vulnerability and need, created a challenging dynamic.

Seeking relief from the agony of Kayla's relapse, I yearned to be held and nurtured. I yearned for a sense of safety, comfort, and support. I sought refuge in Leo's arms.

As if ripping open a gaping wound, the resulting night of intimacy caused my thoughts to swirl and my vision to blur. The rush of intense emotion awakened the truth. Finding safety with Leo was an illusion.

As I processed what had happened, I once again knew I had to sever ties with Leo and heal. I had to stop seeking what I needed from outside. I had to find love and comfort from and for myself. I had to stop willingly stepping on landmines that shattered my well-being.

CHAPTER FORTY-EIGHT: THE TRUTH

While I had concluded similarly before, each repetition brought improved understanding, more resolve, and greater ease. My solutions resided in me, not with any other human. Two steps forward, one step back, I was moving in the right direction.

CHAPTER FORTY-NINE:
REHAB, PART III

I wasn't thrilled that Kayla was back at Sea Waves but found relief in the knowledge that she was off the streets and drug free. My son reminded me it was her choice to make. It was a good reminder.

Securely in rehab, with no need for her phone, I suspended Kayla's phone service to save a few dollars. I wished I had done that the last two times!

Camilla asked me what I wanted to see happen when Kayla was released. I told her I wanted Kayla to return to Internal Changes but that "I will not help her this time. She shot my money into her veins. She has to face her demons."

Camilla agreed. She reiterated that she would take Kayla back and warned that she would be very strict. She validated my anger and urged me to take care of myself, "Find a support group if you don't have one already, and don't beat yourself down. You are doing the best you can with what you have and know."

"One step at a time," I replied. "At least she's off the streets. Hoping for a miracle."

Within days of admittance, Kayla's new counselor, John, called me. While part of me wanted nothing to do with Kayla or her next phase of treatment, I was once again grateful to be included. After he introduced himself, John advised me that Kayla was in the room with him.

A recovered addict himself, John had a gentle, honest, and patient manner. He opened the conversation by telling me how proud he was of Kayla's "achievement." As I listened to him praise Kayla for staying clean nine months, a new level of anger welled up inside me.

Without filter, I expressed my rage and anguish over Kayla's relapse. I asserted my discontent that she decided to return to Sea Waves, certain that their program had failed her, worried that it would fail her again. I bemoaned her fall from grace and openly sought a scapegoat.

Powerfully, yet tenderly, John refuted my view. He was delighted with Kayla's progress, explaining that remaining clean for over nine months was an amazing accomplishment. In his view, Kayla had clearly shown resolve and ability, and he was hopeful.

I couldn't believe what I was hearing. His words were counterintuitive and infuriating. I demanded answers: "If she had resolve and ability to stay clean, why did she relapse?" "How is that a good thing?" "What went wrong?" "What will happen next?" "How can we insure sobriety?" "What is my role supposed to be?" "How am I supposed to keep doing this?" "Why would she choose to be starting over after all that time?" "Now that she has people, places, and things in Fort Lauderdale, how is she supposed to stay clean?"

I felt broken and desperate. I wanted guarantees. I wanted to stop hurting. John calmly responded to each of my questions and encouraged me to trust.

I made known my profound disappointment and disillusionment. I asserted that my ability to trust or hope had been shattered. *How many times could I be knocked down and expected to trust? How many times could I subject myself to the cycle of devastation?* Anger was easier than fear and pain.

John prompted Kayla to join the conversation. She tentatively yet cheerfully greeted me and told me she loved me. It was a far cry from the caged animal I had heard in Audrey's office. My heart melted a tiny bit. It would take every ounce of strength to let down my guard, but I loved Kayla enough to try.

As the week unfolded, I journaled, "Just got off the phone with Kayla and John. I cried. This is so damned hard! One of the things that just came up was that my 'encouragement' is needed but not like 'you're a miracle' or 'I'm so proud of you.' The so-called 'beyond today enthusiasm' is hard for Kayla to hear, and apparently counterproductive. This whole fucking process is counterintuitive and it hurts like crazy. It is just too damned painful. I am hurt and not eager to open the pain door so fast.

"John's responses sounded canned and programmatic, and are hard to hear. He was honest though, explaining that (the process) is a kind of brainwashing. Each day the addict actively tells their brain that if they stay clean today, they've made a great accomplishment.

"What I forgot to ask was what about LIVING that clean accomplishment. How is she supposed to manage holding a job, budgeting, having a social life, and so forth? She's been there a week and great, they are looking at what led to her relapse, what caused it, the particulars she needs to examine. But here's the thing… we only have four weeks in rehab, AND THEN WHAT? So, I will ask that question. I know the psychological work is good, needed, and worthwhile, and still that time bomb is ticking.

"I feel hopeless still. I did not use that word with Kayla, but I did say that I'm wounded and not eager to open myself up again. I will get there. I love my daughter. I suppose my anger is blame. I am angry that she is putting me through this. I truly don't understand. I admit it. It's incomprehensible."

I puffed myself up by blaming Kayla, but really, I was blaming myself. I battled guilt and self-loathing. Kayla and I weren't all that different.

John sent some helpful literature via email. As I read through the information, I was dismayed to realize how little I had actually learned about the scourge that held my daughter hostage.

I emailed back, "I understand that I have more to learn about Kayla's struggle. At the same time, I am not willing to continue to ride the nightmare with her. I love her and know that this is hers to overcome. I will help as I can. I am still hurt and angry. With time I will come to terms."

It felt good to set a boundary.

To my surprise, John fully validated my position, writing, "(The literature) does include such fundamentals like it actually being unhealthy for family members to focus on the sick person. Kayla needs to know it is entirely up to her to make the sacrifices and take the action to overcome addiction, even after her 9-months of successful recovery. Your current stand is valid and I support you. Good news is she enjoys recovery and knows she wants to get it back."

"I guess part of what I am mourning is my ability to help her," I replied. "I know that the best way to help Kayla is to let her do it all herself. It is just painful. I hope she knows that she has forced that hand and will have to forge ahead. There is no current option of coming home.

"Please share with her how much I love her and that I send her light every day with the intention that she find her own light and joy. She is such a special soul, and she is the only one who doesn't know it."

During Kayla's time at Sea Waves, John proved himself to be a wonderful guide and source of support. He helped me process what was impossible to fully comprehend. Having experienced drug addiction himself, his words held some authority. He assured me that Kayla showed promise and encouraged me to be patient.

My logical mind fought for control. It insisted Kayla was oblivious to her wrongs. If she weren't, I reasoned, she would have remained clean. My anger and frustration leaked into every conversation. I found myself pointing out her failures at every juncture. I desperately wanted her to wake up and correct course. I assumed she didn't want to look at the truth, and I feared what would happen if she didn't. Not surprisingly, Kayla pleaded for me to stop. We had been there before, too.

An oozing sore, I was broken and vulnerable. When Kayla called one evening, I confessed that I had no idea how to speak or relate to her. I didn't know how to decipher fact from fiction, clarity from dope brain, sincerity from manipulation. I had nothing positive to say.

Kayla told me she was sorry she called and hung up the phone.

Navigating the waters of my own pain while addressing Kayla's needs was impossible. Parenting had always come relatively easily to me. Sure, there were hurdles, but I was usually able to clear them satisfactorily. With Kayla's addiction and recent relapse, I no longer knew how to be a mom to my child. *How can I be a parent to a child I find repugnant? How do I overcome the pain and fear, and return to love?*

Slowly I came to understand that Kayla's relapse was not unusual. It was my expectations that were out of line. I desperately wanted her healed and had allowed myself to believe, despite indications to the contrary, that she was. I had created a fantasy that allowed me to feel better. I noticed my pattern.

I wanted to believe I was healed as well. I wanted to be complete with the excruciating lessons of that chapter. I wanted to wake feeling whole and happy, fully loving myself and embracing life. I was a work in progress, as was Kayla. Her fall from grace was as much an indictment of my own fall.

I was still in denial and knew it. Denial and expectation guaranteed disappointment, and consequently thrust the sharp pain of betrayal into the mix. In fact, I had betrayed myself over and over. Each time the lesson was presented, the message became clearer. I forgave myself for spiraling back.

As I tried to understand my feelings and my role, I recounted the most recent affronts. Kayla had managed to steal the $300 security deposit I provided for her stay in halfway and then lent her for her move to Georgia's house. She swindled "food money" from me. She billowed forth lies with impunity, leading me to believe she was doing the work of recovery. I had no idea how she would pay for her next stay at halfway, but I was certain I would not assist.

In my journal, I wrote, "I don't hate her. I'm just hurting and want to place that hurt anywhere but on my own shoulders. I will keep feeling what I feel."

One afternoon, as a conference call with Kayla and her counselor proceeded, I came to understand the truth of her pain and the struggle in which she was immersed. As I listened to the words she spoke from John's office, I heard the depth of self-loathing and hatred she felt for what she had done and become. Clearly, she was smothered by the burden of her failures, real and perceived.

The horror of Kayla's bad choices was a noose around her neck. She craved its quick and permanent removal. During that conversation, I became convinced she didn't want to live the life of a drug addict any more than I wanted that life for her. Kayla desperately wanted to be "normal." Ultimately, I heard Kayla surrender. Standing spiritually naked and emotionally raw, wrestling the demon called addiction, I heard my daughter's authentic despair and sincere call for help. I was overwhelmed with compassion.

Something shifted for Kayla and me that day. I was confident we would fight our way out of hell together. Maybe for the first time, I felt real hope.

After living the cyclical devastation of addiction and relapse, hope was a frightening proposition. Hope had previously led me to create a fantasy world in which my daughter was forever cured, setting me up for bone gnawing disappointment. I had to stay rooted in reality while giving Kayla the gift of believing in her.

I put the Universe on notice that anything shy of sobriety was unacceptable. I certainly didn't want to risk growing the monster called addiction by dwelling there. On the other hand, logic and old patterns dictated that preparing for the worst would make disappointment easier to manage if it happened. My emotions argued. I walked a tightrope between hope for the best and preparedness for the worst.

I also chose to focus on my own value. I chose to dwell on thoughts of self-love, kindness, and peace. When triggers incited strong negative emotion, I tried to stop the runaway train of reaction. I would pause to examine the wound screaming to be healed, looking it square in the eye, no matter how ugly or difficult.

Despite the progress I felt I was making; I was still having difficulty relating to Kayla. In our next conversation, I shifted my communication style. Rather than levy an angry complaint as I had done days before, I confided my frustration and sought solution.

In response, Kayla became defensive and angrily demanded I explain my meaning. When I did, she humbled and we talked. We were both learning.

It was a strange landscape we were navigating. I felt numb. I felt angry. I felt frightened for Kayla, and I wondered how she would make it. I caught myself living in the future and reminded myself to stay present.

CHAPTER FIFTY:
BACK TO HALFWAY

Thanksgiving came and went. The angels who owned Sea Waves offered Kayla a scholarship for two additional weeks. She jumped at the opportunity. Kayla spoke with Camilla and they agreed on a payment plan for her deposit and rent. She anticipated getting her old job back. Things seemed to be lining up for her.

I was grappling with loneliness, helplessness, and fear. While Kayla did her work in rehab, I did mine at home.

Besides cycling relentless concerns about Kayla, I was mourning the perception of a lost relationship with Leo. The truth was, it had never been a real relationship. It was predicated on dysfunction. The fantasy I created kept me toggling between yearning and reality, fact and fiction, good and definitively bad. I sifted through, seeking the gift that resided in the struggle.

It had become clear that all of my challenges taught lessons on the same subject. Little by little, I was completing the homework. I was learning to love, honor, and respect myself. I was the only one who could provide the solution to my need. No one else could fill that void.

At 8:26 a.m. on December 17, 2013, Kayla texted, "Back at halfway."

Feeling both excited and weepy, I smiled. Once again Kayla was stepping into possibility. Though I was nervous about her future and feared the challenges she faced, I resolved to have faith that she would stay clean and thrive. *Was there really any other choice?*

Settling back into real life also meant acclimating to roommates and providing for herself. To her credit, with memories of drug use within the walls of her old job, Kayla concluded that returning would be unhealthy and unwise. Already accruing debt at halfway, she would begin her job search immediately.

Despite the substantial challenge before her, I chose to enjoy the moment. Kayla would conquer each hurdle, one at a time. She would manage one day at a time. There was no benefit in worry.

"Welcome back to the real world," I texted. "I love you buckets."

Later that day Kayla texted, "I just got that box of food you sent two months ago... you are out of your damn mind woman! Love it!"

We reveled in the return of free and easy communication. We texted and talked, and I settled into a posture of guarded relief. That evening, when Kayla texted that she was headed to a meeting, I reminded her, "I love you baby!"

She responded, "Thanks for being my mommy! I love you."

In the morning, Kayla headed out on foot to find a job. The process was tiring and the result of her efforts unknown.

With Christmas around the corner, I doubted anyone was going to hire her before the New Year.

Proud of her resolve and determination, I encouraged Kayla to remain optimistic. When idle, she stressed over work and money. As if seeking to torture herself, she added to her burden with thoughts of returning to school. "I'm never going to survive if I don't (go back to school)," she agonized.

Trying to help Kayla halt her rising anxiety, I suggested she stop and take a deep breath. I invited her to consider what made the most sense in that moment and reminded her to take one step at a time. It felt good to confidently share tools that were so pivotal to my own survival.

As if she couldn't hear a word I said, frustrated and rapidly becoming frantic, Kayla continued to spiral. Finding out her food stamp benefit had been reduced, she bemoaned, "I hate Florida. That fifteen bucks of food stamps is gonna hurt."

I recognized the pattern. Kayla's mind (ego) was seeking drama, anguish, and self-abuse. It was seeking to undermine her progress. It was a pattern she needed to break.

I urged Kayla to dwell in gratitude, warning that her feelings of entitlement would land her back in rehab. To my great relief, she agreed, indicating that she understood she had to take responsibility for where she was.

Having great faith, I encouraged, "Listen…you will land on your feet. Stay present. When future fear hits, thank your ego and tell it you don't need to live in fear. You are taking the right steps. Visualize yourself working at your dream job and in a state of ease."

Understandably overwhelmed, without any ideas for a dream job, Kayla worried her decisions would lock her into a future she might not like. That kind of worry was paralyzing.

I emphasized to Kayla that she needed a job to pay bills, not a life commitment. Beyond the requirement that she stay away from drugs, everything else was negotiable. I suggested that identifying attributes of a job she could enjoy might help her attract such a job. At the very least, it would give her a place to start.

We spent time brainstorming Kayla's interests. Like a mantra, I repeated, "This is for now, not forever."

Within days, having blanketed the area with applications, Kayla had three interviews lined up. As she prepared for the first, she texted excitedly, "Asking the Universe to guide my feet in the right direction and to help me be the wonderful, loving, fun person that I know I am."

My heart sang. Kayla had actually been listening, and she was using the tools.

Office Depot offered Kayla a part time job with a start date after Christmas. She was ecstatic and relieved. As an added benefit, knowing she had a job would permit her to relax through the holidays.

Required to purchase a store uniform before she could begin work, once again Kayla was between a rock and a hard place. She had no money. Feeling frustrated and dejected, she timidly reached out for my help.

Despite Kayla's fears, I was not going to let her fall. Together, we considered the options. Without the ability to open a bank account (a consequence of her past), cashing a check was burdensome and costly. Given my own financial constraints, I was unwilling to incur the additional expense of wiring money. I advised Kayla to reach out to the store manager. I was hopeful he would allow me to send a check directly to the store. Compassionately, he agreed.

Kayla was also required to pass a drug test. Fortunately, that was an easy test to pass! Having to rely on public transportation to get to the lab, Kayla texted from the bus terminal, "This place is really scary. I'll probably get raped and murdered."

Not the least bit amused, I was reminded of the considerable hurdles Kayla faced each day. Courageously, one by one, she was confronting and conquering her challenges. I was heartened.

As the New Year approached, I breathed in the promise of Kayla's recovery.

CHAPTER FIFTY-ONE:
NEW JOB

During the winter holidays, I struggled with strong sentimentality and great sadness. It had been that way all my life, but with Kayla so far away and the nightmare always playing in the background, my emotions felt raw.

Reunited with her dear friend Rachel, Kayla spent Christmas Eve "hanging out with Rachel's Jewish family." Throughout the day, the girls sent me "selfies" as they shared laughter and camaraderie. I was thrilled that Rachel was clean again, that she and Kayla were reunited, and that Kayla was in the embrace of a loving family.

On Christmas Day Kayla sent a picture from the beach captioned, "My Christmas." Living in paradise had its perks.

As had been our family tradition for many years, I went to our friends' house to share their holiday. I ached for my daughter's company but took solace in knowing she was clean and moving forward. Gratitude helped soothe my ache.

Returning from the beach that evening, Kayla had a long talk with Daisy, Internal Changes' office manager. Daisy had seen the worst of Kayla's drug induced behaviors and freely shared her observations. Late that night, as Kayla reflected on their conversation she texted, "I can't believe she never gave up on me. That woman saved my life. I'm teary eyed."

"People love you," I responded. "You are a spectacular person."

I desperately wanted Kayla to know how truly spectacular she was. Addiction had a way of undermining the possibility of such thoughts. I continued to hold the truth for her.

Before work began at Office Depot, Burger Place (not the real name) called Kayla to interview for a full-time job. With her experience in a fast-casual restaurant, she was an easy fit. She was hired on the spot and scheduled to begin right away.

Fast paced and diverse, it turned out the restaurant industry was, indeed, a perfect match for Kayla's interests and needs. She felt an immediate connection with the manager who outlined the substantial growth opportunities available in the company. Elated by the prospect before her, she was eager to start. She declined the Office Depot job.

Though she would begin as a cashier, Kayla had visions of working the line as a cook (her favorite part of working at a restaurant) and eventually moving into management. While her previous position promised advancement that never came, Kayla was certain the new promise was sincere.

Kayla was once again walking two-miles each way to work. I found myself worrying about her late-night returns to halfway. I reminded myself she had done it before and was street savvy. I chose to believe she would be ok. *What other choice did I have?*

On New Year's Day, Kayla texted she was "not in good sorts." My anxiety was immediately and profoundly triggered. On a cellular level I feared "bad feelings" would cause relapse. Of course "good" and "bad" emotions were part of life. We all had them. It was imperative that Kayla learn to navigate the best and worst of her feelings. Still, I desperately wanted to prevent temptation.

I encouraged Kayla to find gratitude and told her, "It's also perfectly ok to feel your bad mood." She agreed and acknowledged it would pass. Progress.

Within two days working at Burger Place, Kayla was a superstar. She got along with everyone and required little or no training. She was exceeding all expectations. Quickly recognizing her abilities, management put Kayla on the line. She was thrilled.

I was shoveling snow and dealing with frozen pipes.

Kayla had started over, sounded healthy, and seemed to be doing what she needed in order to stay clean. Nonetheless, failure to execute a promised action or immediately respond to a text sent me reeling in fear. Behaviors I associated with addiction were not-so-subtle reminders that gnawed at my uneasy comfort. I forced myself to stay in the moment, returning to gratitude, trust, and optimism.

There was never a shortage of challenges, however. Kayla contacted me one evening, distressed. She was struggling with her emotions after an interaction she'd had with her father.

I had always encouraged the kids to have a relationship with their father, provided it was healthy for them. I knew healthy relationships required seeing others for who they were, not fantasizing who we wanted them to be. When it hurt too much, I explained there was healing to do.

Kayla said she was willing to think of him differently. Though she was definitively upset, I was glad to hear strength and resolve in her words. She was finally taking a stand toward emotional independence.

Still, the pain of the words spoken to her stung. I tried my best to comfort Kayla, telling her, "Best you can do is prove him wrong about you." I wanted her to know, deep in her soul, that she was in control of her destiny. I encouraged Kayla to recognize she didn't have to be broken because of anyone else's words.

"You have to stop looking to others for some lost piece of yourself," I demanded. "It is in you. You have all you need. You need to move beyond them, not need them, just see them as people with their own challenges."

Once again, I was reminded of two big lessons: First, everything we needed resided within. Others could never truly bring us joy, nor could they take it away. Learning to love ourselves fully and unconditionally freed us from our misguided dependence on others to make us feel good. Being whole meant no one could take our peace, ruin our joy, or push us to illness. Second, respecting the individual journeys of others was transformative. Just like I had no control over Kayla's path, she had no control over her father's. Releasing others to follow their own paths removed a tremendous burden.

I hoped Kayla could internalize the lessons quickly and take responsibility for her own journey.

CHAPTER FIFTY-TWO:
FISH ANTIBIOTICS

Sick as a dog, Kayla called one morning convinced she had developed a sinus infection. When I urged her to see a doctor, she bemoaned the expense. Instead, she told me she would go to the pet store for antibiotics.

"What?" I queried; certain I had misunderstood.

Apparently it was common practice for the girls at half-way to treat their illnesses with fish antibiotics. At the pet store, the sales associate told Kayla, "Yeah, we used to never sell fish antibiotics, but now people without insurance are starting to catch on."

I was horrified. Concerned that her cockamamie solution would cause the bacteria to grow resistant to treatment, and also that when the fish antibiotics didn't work, she would have spent money needlessly, I implored Kayla not to go that route. I encouraged her to drink lots of water, try a natural remedy, and get as much rest as possible.

Wreaking havoc in the background was Kayla's fear of missing work. Losing hours posed a significant financial burden. I could relate!

I asked Kayla what others in her situation did when they got sick. She replied, "People in my situation don't get sick."

Kayla knew I was already carrying too much debt and, to her credit, she wasn't asking for my help. Without telling her, I mentally committed to paying for her doctor visit if needed. Before insisting she go to the doctor, however, I decided to wait a day. History informed me that Kayla could be a bit of a hypochondriac. I prayed she would heal on her own.

Reluctantly, Kayla stayed home from work for one day. As I suspected it might, her "sinus infection" began to clear up. Feeling better and driven by her need to pay bills, she was back to work the next day. Her motivation and commitment were a testament to her forward movement.

I was abundantly proud of Kayla's determination and strong work ethic. During her ten-hour shifts, she was learning as much as she could. She was easily connecting with staff, management, and the public she served. She joyfully shared that she was "killing it!" on the grill.

Meanwhile, Kayla's living situation was changing. Since arriving back at halfway, she had been sharing an apartment with two roommates. By mid-January, one roommate relapsed and was promptly evicted. That same day, the other roommate, whom Kayla liked very much, was given a house mom position and relocated. Suddenly Kayla had her own apartment and was thrilled for the momentary tranquility.

In South Florida the demand for halfway housing was great. Swiftly assigned new roommates, Kayla's sense of peace was shattered. Fresh to recovery, they were angry, messy, and spitting the poisons of victimhood and blame.

For unknown reasons, Daisy, who had been such a strong champion for Kayla's welfare, began singling Kayla out. Being blamed for unfinished chores and other infractions of house rules, Kayla was becoming distraught. She was suffering constant harassment for things she couldn't possibly have known or done.

I advised Kayla to deflect Daisy's absurd accusations and trust that truth would prevail. She had been working so hard to do the right thing; it was heartbreaking to hear her anguish. I urged her to talk to Daisy.

"I'm just so tired of having to stress over everything all the time," Kayla texted.

"I know baby," I responded. "It isn't easy being you. You will move through this to the other side. Remember, you're gonna be doing great (a reminder of Kayla's vision for success). One step at a time."

"Yeah, but WTF am I supposed to do right now?" Kayla questioned. "I'm just hitting this huge wall, and I don't know what to do."

I invited Kayla to look for an action she could take. If there was none, I recommended she do something healthy that soothed her. I suggested yoga, meditation, and music.

At the beginning of February, Kayla missed a required house meeting. Daisy had come to see why and upon seeing Kayla, said she looked horrible. Kayla texted "I think the pork I ate was left in the fridge too long or something."

I held my breath as her "reason" sounded remarkably like the desperate excuse of an addict. I reminded myself that Kayla was regularly drug tested. I would know if she relapsed soon enough.

Later that evening, Kayla texted a picture of the plate of food Daisy brought her because she was "a broke child." Relieved, I let out my breath and smiled. I reminded Kayla how much she was loved.

Ever dynamic, the roller coaster of life brought challenges and forward movement, fear and joy, struggle and triumph. We did our best to hold on.

Out of the blue, Kayla decided to stop smoking cigarettes and switch to smoking a vape. She explained that it was a cheaper, cleaner nicotine delivery system and she needed to save money. She pushed through the challenges and weaned off cigarettes in no time. Once again, Kayla proved her strength and determination.

I didn't know the health ramifications of smoking a vape, but I applauded the change. As days passed, Kayla reported feeling less winded on her long walks to and from work. Little by little she became disgusted by the smell of cigarettes and the lingering stench left on her clothing. While I very much wanted her to quit smoking altogether, it felt like another step in the right direction.

Kayla's food stamp benefit hadn't yet been reinstated, and Burger Place had scheduled her for less than thirty hours two weeks in a row. Stressed about money, she considered finding a second job. That idea stressed her even more.

I encouraged Kayla to breathe and have faith. Balance was important and if she overloaded herself, I feared the pressure would put her at risk of relapse.

While she had been dutifully paying her weekly rent, without extra funds Kayla was unable pay back her debt. As a result, Camilla imposed a strict curfew and restricted her privileges pending repayment. Kayla was frustrated and angry.

With stressors multiplying, I worried Kayla was "off the deep end" and braced for the worst. Instead, I was thrilled to hear maturity in her speech. Though she was extremely upset, when I offered to send her money she replied, "I don't want you to send me any money. I can't even afford to pay you back for what I already owe you. I got myself into this mess and if I have to go without, I will."

We brainstormed solutions. Kayla asked if she should declare bankruptcy. I had no idea what that entailed or how it would help. She bemoaned her inability to get a bank account. I suggested she see if someone in "the rooms," AA/NA meetings, could help her. "Surely," I rationalized, "someone will have experience and expertise."

Kayla agreed.

Jessie, Kayla's drug buddy from home, moved back to Fort Lauderdale.

Kayla's neighbor overdosed. He was revived with Narcan.

Life continued.

I had filed a lawsuit against my ex for an issue unrelated to Kayla. He counter-sued for the child support he had provided while Kayla pretended to be in school.

When I told Kayla about the countersuit, she was livid. She knew the truth better than anyone and offered to come home to testify. I objected, concerned about how such a confrontation might affect her, but she insisted on coming home for the April hearing. I booked her flight.

While preparing for my defense, I made a startling discovery. Unbeknownst to me at the time, there were laws that may have compelled my ex to continue paying support for his "child in need." If deemed incapable of independence, support might have been mandated for Kayla. As an addict, it was likely she would have qualified.

Did I want to counter sue for back support? I weighed the potential gain against the financial and emotional toll such a fight would take on me. I concluded that I had moved forward with grace and was not interested in reliving that past for his money. I was confident we would win his countersuit and chose to let it be.

I continued to seek distraction from my stressful life. As I sought male companionship, I noticed a new pattern emerge in the men I attracted. They all needed a life coach, not a girlfriend. With the illusion of connection, it was easy and natural for me to go into "coach mode." I had given of myself all my life. It was familiar and comfortable to help, but I was learning that without an exchange of energy, it was unfulfilling. I found myself repeatedly disappointed and depleted.

Once again I heard the message. Like Kayla, I had to love myself and find joy within. Until then, I would continue to attract men who didn't love themselves either, men who would take from me and offer little in return, men like Leo.

Kayla's roommate situation was temporarily remedied. She began to make friends and enjoy social outings. Approval finally came for food stamps. She earned a raise at work and then, with a promotion, another. She paid back her debt to Camilla and regained her relative freedom. She navigated the boundaries of friendship and romance with a coworker. She went to meetings.

Someone Kayla knew from rehab overdosed.

Kayla and I spoke regularly. We delighted in easy conversation about our daily activities and worked through our individual challenges together.

Finally and firmly, Kayla concluded it was her responsibility to buy a car, and she was ready to start saving money toward that goal. She asked me to open a bank account into which she could make deposits. Certain her request indicated a turning point; I went directly to the bank and opened an account.

Rain or shine, Kayla walked to work. My heart broke when she arrived soaking wet, but she didn't complain. She loved her job and was climbing the proverbial ladder quickly. She viewed her struggles as part of her recovery and held strong to her determination.

Each day, Kayla inspired me.

I got an official letter in the mail. Court was rescheduled for late October.

Thirsty to see each other, we kept Kayla's April visit intact. We counted down, eager to embrace.

With financial help from my generous parents, I booked Kayla on an October flight. With no more vacation time, it would be a quick, two-day visit, made solely for the purpose of appearing in court. Kayla's fierce support and determination to help me was beyond comforting.

Time moved forward.

CHAPTER FIFTY-THREE:
COURT

With open arms and a swelling heart, I greeted Kayla at the airport on April 11, 2014. As would become our routine, we drove directly to her grandparents' house where bagels and lox awaited consumption. As I sat across the kitchen table listening to Kayla talk, I heard a different young woman than the one I had seen last. She was more confident, more comfortable in her skin, more alive.

During her weeklong stay, Kayla spent two days with her older brother. She visited family and friends, and enjoyed time away from the demands of her job. In a blink, we were saying a tearful goodbye at the airport.

Arriving back at halfway, Kayla effortlessly resumed her routine. Though I already missed her, knowing she was healthy and moving her life forward gave me strength.

One evening, Kayla texted, "I miss my dad." She explained that she had been watching TV, and a commercial featuring a "loving dad" triggered memories.

Familiar worries filled my mind as I breathed in the strength to guide Kayla through her feelings. I questioned whether she missed her dad or an ideal dad she had conjured in her head. She answered with complete honesty, "I don't know."

Fantasy was a set up for disappointment and anguish. Through my own struggles, I had learned that lesson well. I encouraged Kayla to stop torturing herself with wishful thinking. If she was going to heal, she had to face the reality of who her father was and who he was not. If she wanted a relationship with him, she had to accept the connection he was capable of having, not chase the one she idealized or imagined. A healthy relationship demanded she stop seeking what didn't exist.

Knowing life had a way of repeatedly showing us what needed healing, Kayla explored her feelings with maturity and determination. She took responsibility for her thoughts and began to accept the truth: Her father's behaviors and words were not a reflection of her value, nor were they due to her misconduct; he was not the man she wanted him to be. She allowed herself to face down her demons as they showed up, releasing her father, little by little, to his own path.

Quite suddenly Burger Place lost an assistant manager thereby speeding up their need to promote Kayla. Her training intensified, reducing the time she had to think about her father or much else.

On her birthday, Kayla texted, "Thanks for birthing me twenty-two years ago Mommy. You gave me life and then saved my life when I wanted to give up on many occasions. I love you with my whole being, and I wouldn't be here without you."

My heart nearly burst with joy. Inspired and delighted by this young woman I had the privilege of birthing, I felt good about the future. She had turned a big corner; she was actually glad for her life!

The next day, Kayla texted, "Happy Mother's Day to the best mommy I could ever have asked for. You're my rock, my best friend, my mentor, and I am so blessed and thankful to have you. I love you SO much!"

I responded, "You and I fit together perfectly. I love you!"

Indeed, Kayla spoke for us both. Giving birth on Mother's Day so many years past, I was able, once again, to rejoice in the precious gift I had been given. The blessings were countless. Despite what we had been through, or maybe because of it, she was also my rock, my best friend, and my mentor.

By the end of May 2014, Kayla was a salaried, assistant manager at Burger Place. Though expected to work twelve- and thirteen-hour shifts, she was energized by the new responsibility and money. Her financial stress diminished.

My oldest son moved across the country. I was thrilled for him and already missed him beyond words. As he confidently pursued his passions, I reminded myself of my parenting goal to help my children become whole and independent. His was a healthy departure. My heart ached nonetheless.

As summer wore on, Kayla found living at halfway more and more problematic. Roommates' instability and deceitful behavior had Kayla constantly churning. Increasingly she felt she had outgrown halfway. More and more she hated her living environment. Additionally, rumors began to surface that the halfway properties were being sold.

Considering an apartment of her own, Kayla worried about how she would qualify if they ran a credit check. She had no credit, good or bad. She wasn't even sure she could afford her own place but clearly didn't want a roommate. She said the only people she knew were in recovery, and she didn't trust any of them. She procrastinated.

By September, the luxury of consideration became the demand of necessity. Before year-end, Internal Changes would no longer exist. Kayla would have to find a new place to live, and she was certain she didn't want another halfway. She began spreading the word that she needed an apartment.

Within days, her friend from home contacted her with good news. Living in a studio apartment about a mile from Kayla's job, Jessie reported a vacancy in her building. The landlord, Josephine, didn't advertise. All tenants arrived via "word of mouth" and had to pass an "interview." No credit report was required and only cash payments were accepted. Jessie was sure Kayla would be offered an apartment.

Kayla was beyond excited by the possibility. While I found the "cash only" clause cause for concern, I had to admit, Kayla was in a pickle. She had no credit and needed a place to live. She wasn't interested in moving to another halfway house. She contacted the landlord.

As her interview concluded, Josephine offered Kayla a one-bedroom apartment. It was a bit more expensive than Jessie's efficiency, but after running the numbers, Kayla was confident she could manage. Josephine wanted to re-carpet and paint before Kayla moved in. The apartment would be available at the end of October.

My own excitement was tempered by concern. It would be a huge change, and the challenges were mostly unknown. I reminded myself to trust and stay in the moment. Deep down I believed Kayla was ready.

Despite her intentions to save, Kayla didn't have the required $800 security deposit. Though she didn't ask me to help her, my confidence in her recovery compelled me to lend her the money. It didn't take long for her to pay me back in full.

Early October, Kayla flew home to attend court with me. On a bench, awaiting our plenary hearing, Kayla sat between me and her grandparents, skillfully avoiding eye contact with anyone else.

Court convened. As a scheduled witness, Kayla was asked to leave the courtroom until her testimony was required. After she exited, her father's lawyer announced they were dropping their countersuit. That was good news!

Breathing some small relief, I was eager for Kayla to return. Representing myself, my anxiety was through the roof and Kayla's support soothed me. To my great disappointment, the judge barred Kayla from reentering. She stated her opinion: Due to Kayla's history, she should not be subjected to what might be said in this courtroom. It could be damaging.

Receiving the news, Kayla was furious. She wanted to be there to support me. She had flown in from Florida to support me! I shook off the setback and refused to let myself feel defeated. I had to muster my strength. My dad sat behind me in the courtroom, quietly providing me with courage. My mom sat with Kayla in the lobby, waiting.

After the hearing, my parents, Kayla, and I went out for lunch. We toasted to Kayla's good health, seeking comfort in our many blessings. It had been a difficult morning.

The next day Kayla returned to Florida.

We lost the suit.

CHAPTER FIFTY-FOUR

APARTMENT

On October 31, 2014, exactly one year after Kayla quit using drugs for the last time, she packed her clothes and personal items into garbage bags and moved into her very own apartment. She was bursting with excitement. Without a stick of furniture, she rejoiced in the beautiful new carpet and lovely window treatments. She delighted in the spacious quiet that was all hers. She celebrated her accomplishment. Though she would have happily slept on the floor, someone from work was kind enough to lend her an air mattress. She bought a frying pan. Her landlord gave her a lamp. It had been a long journey, and Kayla was finally living on her own!

Between work and the dollar store, Kayla assembled a collection of necessities: a drinking cup, a plate, some plastic utensils, a shower curtain, etc. She made a bookshelf out of a milk crate and bought a small TV. She had what she needed and was willing to work for the rest.

We mused over the very real progress Kayla had made. She worked hard to get to where she was. While I never would have chosen the route she took, my job was to give my children wings, and she had taken a huge step toward flying.

Living in an empty apartment provided the basis for a grand adventure...for a week or so. Sore from sleeping on the air mattress, and tired of sitting and eating on the floor, Kayla's frustration began to rise.

A co-worker offered to sell Kayla his queen size mattress for fifty dollars, but without the means to pick it up, it was only a torment. Her limitations were once again bearing down on her. She felt defeated by her lack of transportation.

Trying to elevate Kayla's mood, I reminded her how far she had come and encouraged her to stay in the moment. I asked her to be patient and suggested she appeal to friends for help.

It was a variation on an old story. My suggestion incited a renewed sense of failure and isolation. Not wanting to risk her sobriety, Kayla had distanced herself from people in halfway and hadn't yet cultivated healthy friendships. Despite her conundrum, she bravely sought help where she could. Unfortunately, promises offered delivered hope, and then one by one came up empty.

The air mattress sprung a leak. Kayla slept on the floor.

My anxiety was rising too. The more despair I heard in Kayla's communications, the more guilt and frustration I felt. Helplessly watching my healthy daughter struggle was intolerable. She had come so far and overcome so much. I wanted SOMETHING to be easy for her.

Tortured by my stymied desire to help Kayla, I considered flying to Florida during winter break. Since the schools would be closed, I would not lose income, but there were other considerations. In her elder years, our dog Lacey had become unreliable with her bathroom behavior. I was reluctant to leave my youngest with the responsibility of cleaning after her.

As Kayla and I shared our mutual frustration, I recounted her monumental achievements. During the nightmare there were times when hope went completely dark and the future seemed unlikely. By comparison, having no furniture was comical! Though understandably upset, Kayla was humbled. We both worked on patience, trusting that all was in perfect order.

Suddenly, just before Thanksgiving, our beloved Lacey tragically died. Kayla was devastated by the news. Within a few days, realizing there was no longer anything holding me back; I decided Avery and I would drive to Fort Lauderdale during winter break. Driving would afford us the opportunity to bring Kayla the makings of a home.

My parents leapt into action, unearthing all kinds of household goods they had tucked away in their basement. We loaded my car with dishes and cookware, blankets and sheets, knickknacks and pictures for the walls. I sorted through my "extras", finding baskets, books, containers, and a lamp. I tucked in an envelope filled with photos of the family, one of Lacey, and some empty picture frames. There was barely room left for Avery and me in my small car.

On the twenty-third of December, right after work, we began the long drive to Florida. Our goal was to arrive for Christmas. Having never driven even half as far, I was managing significant stress, but I knew within two days it would become one more conquered challenge.

With Avery as my copilot, and despite the torrential rain that accompanied us almost the entire twenty-two-hour drive, we navigated our way to Fort Lauderdale. Barefooted, Kayla met us at the corner and directed us the last block to her apartment. We pulled into the parking lot around 11:00 p.m., Christmas Eve. What a glorious arrival it was!

We unloaded box after box, carrying each up the stairs into Kayla's second floor apartment. Once everything was safely inside, we sat on the floor exhausted and mused over the volume of "stuff" fit into my car. Joy permeated the ample apartment.

The day after Christmas, intent on procuring a mattress, Kayla and I went to U-Haul to rent a giant van. Though I had driven a '69 Ford LTD as a teenager (dubbed "The Boat"), the overwhelming size of the van was daunting. Another challenge lay before me.

I'm not sure I breathed on the way to Miami, but somehow we arrived at Kayla's co-worker's apartment building, loaded the mattress into the van, and made it safely back to Fort Lauderdale just after noon. Hoping to acquire a couch also, before returning to Kayla's apartment we drove to Faith Farms. Recycling at its best, Faith Farms was a furniture thrift store where proceeds went to helping addicts. It was a win-win all the way around!

Upon arrival, we found tables, chairs, cabinets, bedroom sets and at least fifteen couches from which to choose. After circling the "showroom" (a mostly outdoor, covered space) several times, we hit the lottery. Yellow with subtle burgundy and olive-green stripes, the couch we settled on was just the right size and in great shape. It even came with matching throw pillows! Kayla happily agreed to pay the sixty dollars requested.

As the purchase was processed, the salesman pointed out that the entire couch reclined! What a bonus! We felt giddy and abundantly blessed as we watched the employees load Kayla's new couch into the van.

We headed back to the apartment to unload our treasures. Avery was waiting for us, ready to help. Getting the couch up the stairs and around the corner was no small feat. After some fancy maneuvering and with Avery's brute strength, we prevailed. We returned the van to U-Haul and went back to Kayla's place to admire her new furniture.

The apartment was beginning to feel like home, but Avery was agitated by the lack of chair or table. Shopping the next day, he bought Kayla an inexpensive, particleboard desk in a box, and I bought her a folding chair. While I made dinner that evening, Kayla and Avery sat on the living room floor and assembled the desk. Life felt right and good.

Though Kayla had to work during our five-day stay, we were able make it a vacation. We celebrated Lacey's life with a special dinner, went to Alligator Alley, and enjoyed the beach. We talked and played as much as possible.

By the time we said our goodbyes, Kayla's apartment felt much more hospitable. With new life breathed into her living space, Kayla was feeling relieved and in turn, so was I. We had a great visit. On the thirtieth of December, Avery and I headed home.

CHAPTER FIFTY-FIVE

BOYS

With the New Year came a new relationship for Kayla. Early January 2015, she began dating Gavin. Thrilled to hear her enthusiasm and joy, I still believed it was too soon for her to be dating. Kayla had been in recovery less than two years, the magical demarcation of "enough time passed." There were risks.

I understood Kayla's desire for companionship, and as a young woman, it was natural for her to want a romantic relationship. Nonetheless, relationship inevitably pushed buttons, and I was abundantly aware of how the last one (with Connor) turned out.

Nonetheless, wanting to support her joy, I maintained cautious optimism. I continued to remind myself Kayla was in control of her life, not me. Gavin seemed to be a kind man, devoted to Kayla's wellbeing. That was a vast improvement.

Periodically, Kayla reflected on how much had changed for her. Early March, looking at the family pictures displayed on her refrigerator, Kayla texted, "Looking at the family I love on my refrigerator, open it and it's packed with food, and I think 'I'm just like my mom.' I look around and think 'I'm in my own (shitty) apartment—the hot water only lasts for five minutes at a time and there's no furniture, but I love it. I have a job I love and a boyfriend who's good to me. I have a great life.'"

It was nourishing to hear Kayla embrace her situation and life. She was far from home, but finally, she was feeling content where she was.

In June, Kayla and Gavin flew home to attend my mother's eightieth birthday party. Meeting Gavin for the first time, I saw firsthand the easy, comfortable interaction between him and Kayla. He was kind and responsive, and he even helped me with a few things around the house.

I liked Gavin very much, though I didn't think he was "the one" for Kayla. By mid-August, Kayla felt similarly. She and Gavin parted ways.

Needing to get away for a few days, Kayla flew home for a brief respite. While visiting, Kayla's grandparents suggested she look at a used car. Sadly, their dear friend Eileen had passed away, and her husband (also a dear friend) was selling her car. Kayla was thrilled by the potential opportunity but wondered how it could be possible.

After a short test drive, Kayla was bursting with desire to purchase the car. Her enthusiasm, however, was tempered by the financial reality. She had not saved any money.

As she fretted over paying the asking price, Kayla's generous grandparents made her an offer she couldn't refuse.

They would lend her the money, interest free. They discussed a monthly payment and agreed on an amount.

Kayla was beside herself with joy. Not only was she about to have a car, but also, her grandparents had enough faith in her recovery to invest the substantial sum! Her life really was turning around.

I agreed to deliver the car to Kayla as soon as possible. Since subbing jobs were scarce early in the school year, I arranged to drive to Florida at the end of September. By then I would have the appropriate paperwork filed, and Kayla could work on a budget. Additionally, I could mentally prepare for the long drive I would take alone.

Kayla returned to Florida with excited anticipation. Getting a car was a dream come true. Her confidence grew exponentially as she realized how far she had come.

I was deeply disturbed when Kayla told me she met a new man, Fred. Having recently ended her relationship with Gavin, experience told me she would need time to mourn, process, and heal. In addition, Kayla's description of Fred provided significant cause for concern. Homeless, underemployed, and physically challenged; Fred had children in another state and was also in recovery.

One of Kayla's most inspiring qualities was her ability to see past someone's outer trappings to their heart. She was also a helper person who often confused relationship with caretaking. In that regard, she wasn't a lot different from her mom! Nonetheless, I had a bad feeling about Fred.

Worrying about Kayla's "bad choices" instigated reflection on my own. I was tired of my relationship history creating pain. I was in no position to judge.

In conversation with a friend I explained, "I believe I know that when something triggers me, it is something within, not without. I can damn (my ex) all I want, but he still holds me hostage if I let him. I don't want to let him."

My friend asked how I would prevent or stop such a reaction. I responded, "Usually, when I have a big reaction, I look at it and say, 'What is triggering me?' Most often it is fear or deep hurt, or sense of failure, or shame, etc. Then I pick that apart. If it's fear, I look it in the eye and ask, 'What is the worst that can happen?' Or I say, 'Is that true?' And I process it through.

"It doesn't go away right away, and sometimes I have to reach out to others who can help me process and find peace. Then I have to look at the hurt; what is under it? Is it shame? Is it disappointment from expectations or hope? Is it mine or someone else's?

"...I'm a work in progress like everyone else"

Like Kayla, I too had come a long way. I was still learning, still healing, but I was seeing my own patterns, and I was willing to change them.

At the end of September 2015, I drove Kayla's new used car to Fort Lauderdale. Tired and hungry, I arrived at her apartment around 7:30 p.m. Fred had graciously cooked dinner for us, and he and Kayla were eager to please me. Still without table or chairs, we sat on the floor and ate.

Making conversation, I shared tales of my long drive. I was fully aware that meeting "the mother" could be intimidating, so I tried in vain to make Fred feel comfortable. In an effort to get to know my daughter's new boyfriend, I asked lots of questions. I became acutely aware of his substantial discomfort and noticed his reluctance to respond to even the simplest of inquiries. My spider sense was twitching.

Like any loving parent, I wanted to protect my child from making painful mistakes. I was well aware that my efforts hadn't worked well in the past, and it was unlikely my opinion would change Kayla's feelings about Fred. Nonetheless, once he left, I offered my impression.

As expected, Kayla pushed back hard. She defended Fred's goodness and her choice to enjoy a relationship with him. I backed off. I knew my fears were magnified because of the nightmare I never wanted to revisit. Kayla was a grown woman who had to make her own decisions.

I made the best of our time together. It was fun to be the passenger in Kayla's car. As she drove around town, I could feel her confidence. Her new freedom created a visible shift in her demeanor.

After a few days, I flew home.

New worries filled my thoughts, but I was learning to let go. I returned to the demands of my own life and my day-to-day schedule. Fred moved into Kayla's apartment. I was not surprised, nor was I happy. I had to accept that it was not mine to choose.

Kayla had been living in her apartment over a year and trouble with the landlord was growing. There had been minor issues before, but Josephine was suddenly making crazy complaints and demands. She accused Kayla of "throwing pennies in the toilet" (in response to plumbing issues) and "leaving scuff marks" on the cement steps she had to climb to her second-floor apartment. She insisted Kayla take her shoes off before walking up the outdoor stairs.

Without warning, claiming it was because Fred had moved in, Josephine raised Kayla's monthly rent. She was harassing Kayla at every turn and Kayla feared eviction. With a month-to-month cash agreement, Kayla would have no recourse.

Very much wanting a new apartment, Kayla was reminded of her unfortunate conundrum. She still had no credit history. Despite her perfect payment record, we were certain Josephine would not provide a positive reference. Kayla felt defeated before she began.

Though Kayla complained vigorously about Josephine, with good reason, she procrastinated looking for a new place to live. She seesawed between terror and complacency for months, until there was no longer another option. Josephine's irrational behavior had become intolerable. Finally, Kayla launched an apartment search.

After a number of disappointments, Kayla called me excitedly to share a "synchronistic" possibility. She had been driving around looking for rental signs when she spotted one in front of her old halfway house. She called the number immediately and, impossible as it seemed, discovered Camilla's husband was the owner! She left a message for him to call her back. She was atwitter with anticipation. As I listened, I knew she had found her next home.

Sam remembered Kayla well. She was a superstar in halfway and had forged strong connections with Camilla and him. Without hesitation he agreed to rent the apartment to her. Rentals, he explained, were processed through a rental company, but he would insist they waive the "credit" requirements. She was in!

Several weeks later, early April 2016, Kayla moved her things to a legitimate apartment. She had a legal contract and no one would be able to hassle her without cause. She would pay rent to a legitimate company and begin to establish credit. In a crazy twist of fate, having never updated the address on her driver's license, her residence once again matched.

We rested comfortably knowing the apartment was meant to be. I was relieved and abundantly grateful. It was as if Kayla had shed one more shackle from her past.

Soothing my own worries, I had convinced myself that Kayla would leave Fred behind when she moved. I was hopeful a new apartment would come with new awareness and the self-confidence to seek better. Sadly, I was wrong. Kayla defended her choice to share her living space. She said she needed Fred's help to meet the increased rent. I was pretty sure she was concocting excuses but reminded myself she was on her own. I had no say.

CHAPTER FIFTY-SIX:

TIME

It was mid-morning on August 5, 2016. Kayla called and directed me to sit down. "I have some bad news," she uttered.

Kayla choked out the words. Her dear friend Rachel had become one of the thousands of overdose statistics. We cried together and cursed the cruelty of that which had stolen such a tender heart. We agreed that a true angel had entered the heavens.

I mourned Rachel and yearned to hold my daughter. *Why did the scourge take Rachel? Why was life so cruel? How was her family going to manage the pain? How did we get so lucky?*

Kayla and I continued to speak as often as our schedules allowed. We eagerly shared our trials and our joys. I remained her steadfast supporter and she mine. We shared our thoughts and stories and avoided conversation about Fred.

Eventually Fred showed his true colors. Kayla told him to move out and then, shockingly, took him back. By November Fred had become an unbearable force. Kayla finally and firmly demanded he leave for good.

Alone in her apartment and feeling alone in her life, Kayla began to explore the possibility of coming home. Her one-year lease would expire April 2017, and if she was going to make a move, that would be the perfect time.

Though my heart screamed "COME HOME," I knew I had to remain neutral in Kayla's decision process. I made it clear that my arms and home were open for her return but that she had to be sure. I carefully avoided any hint of influence, wanting her to make a decision based on truth, not emotional backlash. If Kayla were to be happy back home, she would have to find her own answer.

I encouraged Kayla to list the pros and cons of staying in Florida and of moving home. I insisted she be brutally honest with herself.

Among other frustrations in Florida, Kayla's job had become a huge disappointment. Working up to 70 hours a week, she continued to endure the insult of empty promotion promises. She deserved the general manager position, but they had hired yet another unqualified family friend. For the third time, Kayla was expected to train her boss. She had become understandably disillusioned and angry.

Over the next several months, I received many hysterical phone calls fraught with angst and confusion. One day Kayla was sure she wanted to come home, and the next she was sure she wanted to stay in Florida. As she rode the roller coaster of emotions, I did my best to stay off the ride.

When Kayla sought my counsel, I offered her different ways to think about her decision. I pointed out joys and heartaches she had experienced in Florida, and reminded her that home was not a fairy tale either. I warned her of the pitfalls she might encounter and the reality of living under my roof. All the while, I prayed she would decide to move home.

Finally, toward the end of February, with absolute clarity and confidence, Kayla decided she was done with Florida. She would move home. We began to formulate a plan.

If I was going to help with Kayla's move, it would have to be during spring break, but that was two weeks beyond the end of her lease. We brainstormed alternatives. We discussed, considered, and conjured options. Every idea instigated additional expense. The best scenario involved extending Kayla's lease.

With trepidation, Kayla called Sam to ask if she could stay in the apartment for an additional two weeks. To her delight and great relief, he eagerly agreed saying, "Anything you need, Kayla." He had been another in a line of angels that graced our lives.

I booked a one-way flight to Florida. We determined that between Kayla's car and a minivan, we would have enough space to accommodate her "stuff." I reserved a rental. Kayla began applying for jobs. By the time she returned home, she had three offers. Everything aligned perfectly.

During spring break April 2017, I flew to Florida. We packed the cars, taking her queen-sized mattress but leaving the well-worn yellow couch behind. Kayla said her goodbyes. We drove home, me in the lead, Kayla following. We rejoiced in the adventure.

Kayla had been in recovery for three and a half years and in Florida over five. Her grandmother's simple validation said it all, "It's time."

EPILOGUE

Writing this book forced me to relive the most difficult and devastating moments of my life: the terror, the frustration, the sorrow, and the gut-wrenching pain. There were times I wanted to stop writing and bury my story where it could rest in peace. There were times when I found it difficult to distinguish present from past, and my body shook with despair as if Kayla was still using and still in Florida.

I'm not sure I would have been able to complete the book had Kayla not moved home. Each day her smile and warm hug reminded me the nightmare was past. Each day she urged me to keep writing. We are both aware that publicly sharing the details of that very sensitive time in her life has the potential to cause Kayla discomfort down the road. Despite that possibility, she has been one of my most encouraging forces. Like me, she believes my story can help others.

Waking to the realization that their child is using drugs, every day, parents across the globe are finding themselves in free-fall. As I crawled through the days and months following that same realization, I experienced feelings of isolation, guilt, terror, and sorrow. Those emotions were easy compared to the self-loathing and beratement that oozed from my pores.

To those who ache with the pain of addiction in their midst: It is my hope that my story helps you open your mind and heart to the truths of the disease, and to the realities inherent in loving an addict. I hope you are compelled to learn as much as possible, without judgment. I also hope you embrace the necessity of self-care, self-love, forgiveness, and acceptance. There is help available when you are ready.

We raise our children to the best of our abilities. During their formative years, we forge an unbreakable energetic connection with them. As if by osmosis, values, coping patterns, spirituality, fears, and vulnerabilities are conveyed. At least in part, children begin to understand themselves and their world through our eyes.

As children become teens and young adults, other influences take center stage. We may feel marginalized and stripped of all control. Indeed, in many ways we are. Without doubt, however, our energy continues to affect them. Our attitudes and actions, beliefs and reactions, and interests and behaviors continue to quietly convey messages. Recognizing our subtle power allows us to seize opportunities to help our children heal.

By loving yourself and healing your own emotional wounds, it is my belief you help your addict in ways you can't see or feel, and may never know. You highlight human potential when you focus on improving your own health. As you model strength and determination, so too can your addict find strength and determination. As you model love of self, so too can your addict see the possibility. As you model forgiveness of self, so too can your tortured addict learn to forgive herself. As you heal, so do those around you.

It is my prayer that no matter where this journey takes you, you transform your own life, finding purpose, passion, peace, and love on your path.

In an effort to quantify what went right, I have searched thought and action. Two things I know absolutely: In order to "help" your loved one conquer addiction, you must provide unconditional, unwavering love and support. You must also practice the difficult, inconceivable posture of tough love, cutting off any provision that supports or enables her continued abuse.

You may think these two things are incongruent. Indeed, there were many times they felt impossibly contradictory. In reflection, however, I know they are not. I never, not for one minute, stopped loving and praying for Kayla. I was always, ALL WAYS, there for her to talk, to cry, and to share. But I had to say "no" a lot. I had to ignore her pleas for comfort (my desire for comfort as well) in an effort to keep her alive.

In the throes of your addict's illness, it is easy to momentarily forget how much you love her, to hide behind anger, or to stuff it down so deep inside that you temporarily numb the pain. In my experience, forgetting/hiding/numbing was an illusion. The pain rushed in when least expected time and time again.

Admittedly, the addict before you is not that same person you love. The addict is a selfish alien inhabiting the body of your loved one. Trust that she is in there, trapped. Trust that survival is possible. Trust that you will survive.

I continue to suffer PTSD like symptoms born of the trauma I lived through. Certain triggers are strong. If Kayla doesn't feel well, my mind races to drugs; if she is late coming home, I worry about drugs; every friend is suspect and every comment or action I deem inappropriate can set me off emotionally. Even though Kayla is a healthy, productive member of society, memories of her drug abuse rise up easily.

I have to talk myself off the ledge more often than I want to admit. At times I go to dark places in zero seconds. Fortunately, those moments are decreasing with time. I repeatedly remind myself the past is past. Over and over, I choose to focus on the present. All is well in this moment.

Kayla is good about accepting my process. She calls me out on irrational behavior and thought, and reminds me that she is truly ok. She is!

I don't always agree with or like Kayla's choices. I continue to remind myself she is on her own path, as are we all. I cannot choose for her. I have learned to own my fears, allowing them in so I can escort them out.

The realities of addiction are harsh. The fear is real. The pain is unbearable.

Kayla's experience took her to places I never want to know about. In many ways they have shaped the beautiful woman she has become. Likewise, the nightmare I lived as a result of her addiction contributes to the rich tapestry of my own journey.

Once I moved past my fear and anxiety, soothed my anger and judgment, and wrestled my guilt and self-loathing to the ground, I was able to open to the information available with understanding and compassion. In order to affect real change in the battle against addiction, I believe society must move in this direction as well.

I have learned all I never wanted to know about drug abuse and addiction. It is indelibly tattooed on me and in me. The nightmare pushed me to find my authentic self and fully love me. My toolbox has grown, and having survived the nightmare, I am reminded that I am strong, resilient, and capable of moving forward.

I did not walk this path alone. I was guided, loved, and held by many angels along the way. I have amazing family and friends who continue to contribute to the abundance in my life. I am profoundly blessed and more grateful than words can express.

In my perfect dream, addiction ceases to exist. Rather, people are given the tools, resources, and guidance that enable them to develop healthy, happy lives. We are all imbued with great gifts. I look forward to a time when every individual learns to embrace his/her unique passion, purpose, and potential, thereby living a life filled with meaning and fulfillment.

I continue to practice being present, being grateful, and opening to spiritual guidance. Life offers many challenges and those have not stopped coming. Nothing, however, compares to the emotional devastation brought by loving a drug addict. And for me, nothing has been as transformative.

Kayla's continued success includes a promising career. She is confident and motivated, loved and admired. She is making new friends and discovering what makes her authentically happy. She is now willing to sit with her dark emotions and allow them to depart naturally. She is wise beyond her years and beautiful in every way.

While Kayla's addiction is the thread with which my story is woven, it is MY story of challenge, survival, transformation, and love. Kayla hopes to write her own memoir one day, providing an essential viewpoint to complete the picture of addiction and recovery. We both feel there are valuable insights available from both perspectives.

Kayla is my inspiration, my best friend, and my heart.

My gratitude is immeasurable.

Namasté

Heal yourself, heal your children.

EPILOGUE

EPILOGUE

EPILOGUE

EPILOGUE